The Enlightenment
and religion

The Enlightenment
and religion
The myths of modernity

S. J. BARNETT

Manchester University Press
Manchester and New York

distributed exclusively in the USA by Palgrave

The right of S. J. Barnett to be identified as the author of this work has been
asserted by him in accordance with the Copyright, Designs and Patents Act
1988.

Published by Manchester University Press
Oxford Road, Manchester M13 9NR, UK
and Room 400, 175 Fifth Avenue, New York, NY 10010, USA
www.manchesteruniversitypress.co.uk

Distributed exclusively in the USA by
Palgrave, 175 Fifth Avenue, New York NY 10010, USA

Distributed exclusively in Canada by
UBC Press, University of British Columbia, 2029 West Mall,
Vancouver, BC, Canada V6T 1Z2

British Library Cataloguing-in-Publication Data
A catalogue record for this book is available from the British Library

Library of Congress Cataloging-in-Publication Data
A catalog record for this book is available from the Library of Congress

ISBN 13: 978 0 7190 6741 9

First published 2003 by Manchester University Press
First digital paperback edition published 2008

Printed by Lightning Source

Contents

Contents

Acknowledgements

I am indebted to my colleague John Ibbett for his suggestions on the best way to present my arguments and his close eye on the final copy. Similarly, I am grateful for the patience and scholarly assistance of Yukiko Sumi.

INTRODUCTION

The Enlightenment and modernity

The rationale of this book

In historical studies and indeed most fields of the humanities, the terms modernity and Enlightenment are so frequently linked that either term almost automatically evokes the other. It has become an accepted commonplace, part of the historical canon, that modernity began in the Enlightenment. This begs the obvious but yet problematic question: what was the general character of the intellectual phenomenon we term the Enlightenment?

Since the end of the 1960 and 1970s, Enlightenment studies has, albeit rather slowly and unevenly, moved from a rather narrow preoccupation with a few leading intellectuals, to an acceptance that the Enlightenment was in fact a much broader phenomenon. It is now increasingly recognized that the Enlightenment was as diverse in its protagonists as it was geographically and chronologically disparate. Neither was there unity within the Enlightenment on perhaps the central plank of Enlightenment doctrine, the role of reason in the future of civilization. From the mid eighteenth century we see – especially in France and England in the work of Jean Jacques Rousseau and David Hume – a growing rejection of the simple panacea of reason in favour of the equal recognition of the role of the 'passions' in human conduct. This growing rejection of the rather restrictive notion of reason as the fundamental attribute of the human mind also coincided rather paradoxically with what historians have termed the High Enlightenment, but is more aptly known in literary studies as the Age of Sensibility. It is, therefore, not without difficulty that reliance on reason can be cited as an easy key to investigating the broad intellectual manifestation of the years *c.* 1690–1790 that we have termed the Enlightenment.

1

The Enlightenment and religion

That Enlightenment protagonists were secular in their outlook has also been part of the Enlightenment studies canon. Until the 1970s the characterization of the Enlightenment was most usually that of reason against religion. Since then many academics have preferred the formula reason versus the Church, recognizing that most of the enlightened still retained a belief in God, even if they were hostile to the Church. Belief in an original Creator was part of the deistic view held by some enlightened writers who thought that God had not intervened in worldly affairs since Creation, so rendering the Church's claim to mediation between divinity and humanity fraudulent. For such thinkers, evidence for God and a rational or 'natural religion' lay in the qualities (especially reason and conscience) of an unchanging human nature and the frame of nature itself. The understanding that there was a deist movement (sometimes termed freethinking movement) of some size in Europe has remained the orthodoxy in Enlightenment studies, yet there is no evidence to support this claim. Evidence for the existence of organized deism has not so far been adduced, and evidence for the existence of individual deists indicates the existence of relatively few individuals spread across one hundred years of European history.

It seems, then, that the revision of the character of religion in the Enlightenment was not as thoroughgoing as it might have been, and the traditional linkage of modernity and Enlightenment – in the form of the secularizing deist movement – has continued to be propagated by some and still acknowledged by others. It is not the intention of this book, however, to speculate on the origins of modernity, for, after all, why do the origins of modernity have to be predominantly intellectual? It is equally plausible to suggest other categories of explanation, including that of the broad impact of the Industrial Revolution, which certainly had long-term intellectual consequences when its many powerful protagonists sought to extol its virtues and minimize and justify its less attractive aspects.

Outside of traditional Enlightenment studies there also exists strong support for the Enlightenment-modernity thesis in the form of the so-called postmodernity theory. Apparently (although very few seemed to notice it at the time), modernity gave way to postmodernity in the early 1970s. Without citing any more than the most vague evidence, postmodernists have repeatedly asserted that the secularizing, reason-orientated Enlightenment is the one and only origin of modernity. For postmodernists, modernity is damned because it supposedly placed unfounded reliance on reason as the arbiter of human conduct. Thus reason, Enlightenment and modernity become one. They argue (and here they have a point) that the modern project was a costly failure, bringing not the sweet dreams of reason, but war, famine, disease and ecological disaster. It is true that postmodernism has been responsible for a renewed interest in the philosophy of history, mostly because it asserts that the past is irretrievably gone and our self-interested attempts at reconstructing it are, by their nature, consequently doomed to failure. The great meta-historical narratives (great schemes of history) of modernity were all pie-in-the-sky, the postmodernists argue, and thus postmodernism is typified, they claim, by an incredulity toward meta-narratives (no longer believing in the promises of modernity). The problem, however, is that when postmodern thinkers characterize the nature and origins of modernity, they are still trying to sell a meta-narrative, a grand scheme of history based on their own analysis of modernity and its origins. The pseudo-historical product it wishes to revamp and sell is that older outlook of Enlightenment studies, in which the Enlightenment is seen as a more or less homogenous phenomenon, led by a substantial movement of deistic radicals guided solely by the false prophet of reason.

Of course postmodernists are correct to point out that the writing of history is never neutral and that this fact must be borne in mind by all those interested in historical questions – just as postmodernists themselves have an interest in a certain analysis of the nature, origins and consequences of modernity. While postmodernists wish to condemn both modernity and its supposed Enlightenment origins, modern historians have touted the Enlightenment as a source of modern progressive ideals such as religious toleration, hostility to superstition and a reverence for knowledge. Indeed, modern historians have repeatedly sought for anything in the eighteenth century that resembled the modern secular outlook, and then, in order to ensure that the evolution of progress was incontrovertibly charted, even sought to chart the proto-modern 'precursors' of the Enlightenment. Some rethinking, therefore, is necessary. In essence, the available evidence has not validated the project of linking what has traditionally been understood as the Enlightenment to modernity. Rethinking does not mean freedom from bias – after all, my views are my own – but it does mean that a more frank attitude towards the nature and problems inherent within the historical record is needed and commonplace research assumptions need to be re-examined.

Rarely do the philosophy of history and historical research meet, yet it is only by raising basic but tricky practical and theoretical questions relating to the nature of the historical record that historians can attempt to rethink our understanding of the Enlightenment. It is difficult to overstate the need for a fresh look at the historical record because there is clear evidence to indicate that the protagonists of the Enlightenment also wished to be remembered as 'new thinkers' unsullied with the intellectual baggage of the past. They thus propagandized that which was new or radical in that century, and usually failed to inform us of events, trends and influences from other less radical, traditional sources. There is little evidence that in the achievement of religious toleration – the bedrock of any secularization programme – deistic radicals played any fundamental role. Yet their rhetoric would have us believe just that. On the contrary, there is evidence to indicate that religious toleration began to assert itself as an idea and a practical reality at the grassroots level of eighteenth-century society and that the enlightened responded to public opinion rather than created it. Fundamental social and politico-religious processes have thus been overlooked by historians rather too concerned to relate their present to the past, forging intellectual time-lines and traditions where none really existed.

The following series of discussions represents an attempt to review some of the causes and contexts of religious change in Enlightenment Italy, France and England. Although to a degree different from each other in content and objective, the aim of the case studies is to illustrate how the notion that the Enlightenment founded 'modernity' has led to significant distortions in our understanding of religious and intellectual change. I wish to assert the fundamental role of public opinion in pressure for religious change, but also in the creation of enduring myths such as that of the deist movement. At times, if they did not wish to appear to be lagging behind developments, the philosophes (protagonists of enlightened ideals) were forced to claim broad changes as their own particular victories. If the philosophes cannot be credited with as much as has been traditionally claimed, and other, broader agencies can be credited with more than has been traditionally recognized, then it is perhaps time to broaden the traditional view of Enlightenment studies.

The Enlightenment and modernity

As Munck in his *The Enlightenment* (2000)[1] has illustrated, the dividing line between the enlightened and non-enlightened is at best often vague. Hopefully no historian will wish to argue that determining the practical relationship between the intellectual elite of the Enlightenment and the 'lower orders', or those less intellectually inclined, is of no moment in our understanding of what we refer to as the Enlightenment.

If the philosophes were often motivated to overstate their role and influence, they did not do so unaided. In this respect their greatest allies were often also their greatest enemies: those conservatives who, for their own ends, wished to talk up the deist or freethinker threat to Christianity. The bogeyman of deism was frequently identified by clerics and protagonists of the faith, of both the orthodox and dissenting type, some of whom wished to create reputations for themselves and/or their sect by publicly appearing as stalwart defenders of 'true' Christian orthodoxy. The Church-in-danger cry was, however, also used as a general means of calling the faithful to order. In the process, such ardent Christians played a major role in creating a very public antichristian bogey that did not have any substantial reality. The fact that most European states and kingdoms were still confessional states – that is, with only one permitted state religion – means that religious conflict very often also had a political aspect. Thus the notion of a purely religious conflict is usually problematic, and the term politico-religious is often more appropriate. The content of such conflicts, however, could take quite different forms in response to the varying political and religious circumstances across Europe – as they did in England, France and the Italian peninsular.

In France, more so as the mid eighteenth century approached, the struggle of dissenting Catholics (Jansenists) against the orthodox Catholic Church and state was often conceived as a struggle not only for at least a limited form of religious toleration, but also against perceived Bourbon despotism. In their struggle to achieve greater religious independence from Rome, however, Jansenists in the Italian peninsular favourably contrasted absolutist secular rule with the perceived religious despotism of the Curia and the Papal States. In the case in Britain, which had already developed political parties in the late seventeenth century, it is appropriate to talk also of party-political struggle, in which the condition of the Church was still a very important issue indeed and supposed threats to the

Church were politically exploited in a very public manner. In its various forms, then, an understanding of the broad politicization of religion is central to any understanding of religious outlook and change during the Enlightenment.

If, at first sight rather strangely, defenders of the faith could talk up the threat of deism, many modern historians also seem strangely reluctant (despite compelling evidence) to accept that central to religious change in the Enlightenment was that most modern phenomenon, public opinion. In terms of the traditional philosophy of history, this refusal is, nevertheless, hardly surprising. Enlightenment studies, as is the case in most historical research, has implicitly conceived of intellectual change as a more or less exclusively top-down process. The core of my argument on intellectual change, however, is that it is rarely solely a top-down process and, on the question of religion at least, public opinion is always a major factor. Yet public opinion has usually been regarded as a modern phenomenon, of relatively less importance prior to the French Revolution. I wish to assert, therefore, that religious change in early modern Europe cannot be understood without placing public opinion at centre stage – as the case studies of France and England illustrate – even though it was certainly not always an unsullied force for 'progressive' change.

In summary, my aim has been to begin illustrating the problems inherent in a history of the Enlightenment unduly based on the discourses of the enlightened elite, since in most cases their writings had little impact upon religious change and reform. Instead, historians should concentrate upon a history of the Enlightenment based more upon actual practice, upon a wider, more social-historical conception of the Enlightenment than has traditionally been the case. Above all, I will examine the role of religious opposition in generating events which brought about fundamental change in the religious culture of Western Europe. If this entails less talk about Voltaire *et al.*, and more about other 'lesser' figures and more focus on wider social and religious change, it will certainly not mean undervaluing the philosophes. Rather it will be to understand their lives more comprehensively, to situate them properly and to appreciate the dilemmas and opportunities they confronted. Consequently, this book will offer very little focus on the writings of the philosophes, the deists and their supporters, which have already been widely reproduced, translated, compared and discussed in many publications.[2] It is to these publications that readers unfamiliar with the writings of the philosophes should turn. I claim no particular originality for my theoretical criticisms of modern historians. The problem of the present influencing the past and the creation of false intellectual traditions was raised and discussed some decades ago, before the advent of postmodernism – one only needs to think of Quentin Skinner's 'Meaning and Understanding in the History of Ideas' (1969).[3] What has not so far been attempted is to subject topics such as modernity and religion in the Enlightenment to theoretical analysis alongside a re-evaluation of the available evidence and nature of the historical record. In terms of case studies, where sufficient research data exists (as in the case of France, and partly in the case of England), I offer a new analysis of the data, and I am therefore indebted to a range of other scholars. Where relatively little data exists relevant to my arguments – most significantly in the case of Italy – I supply my own.

The structure of this book

Chapter 1 ('The myth of Enlightenment deism') discusses the reasons why the myth of a deist movement has remained so important to Enlightenment studies, even when the evidence adduced for it has been markedly insufficient. I examine the claims for a deist movement, the actual numbers of verifiable deists, the problem of defining deism and how the desire to identify the roots of and validate modernity has led to long-term distortion of historical evidence and subsequent interpretation. In Chapter 2 ('Historians, religion and the historical record') the historical record and the problems of interpreting it are brought under focus. Here I move from the distortions of historians to the inherently biased and misleading nature of the historical record itself and the role of politico-religious struggle in its creation. Historians must ask which historical reality – as provided by the historical record – they wish to choose, for competing constituencies of interest have bequeathed to us not objective history, but above all their views upon the issues of the period. Thus, the myth of the deist movement is not solely the invention of historians, but was itself first invented in the early Enlightenment with the aid of the powerful tools of politics and public opinion.

The following three chapters are case studies intended to illustrate my main arguments. That they do so in different ways is in part a consequence of the diversity of the Enlightenment experience, which was not intellectually, geographically or chronologically even. The case study of England is the first of the case studies because, as is now well acknowledged, the Enlightenment was at its most precocious in England, decades before the height of the Enlightenment in France or that of the more restricted experience of the Italian peninsula. Discussion on England is also given first place because conditions there relate quite directly to the main arguments of the preceding chapters on the creation of the myth of deism. The subsequent chapter on the French experience focuses much less on the creation of the myth of deism than the supposed role of the philosophes, for it is above all in France that historians have identified the cutting edge of the enlightened campaign against the old regime. The final case study on the experience of the Italian states has yet a different focus, for the relatively limited Enlightenment there suffered under very different politico-religious conditions from elsewhere in Europe, yet nevertheless produced some remarkable although much neglected anticlerical writings.

In Chapter 3 ('The English deist movement: a case study in the construction of a myth') the emphasis is upon the politicization of religion and the reasoning and mechanisms by which the scare figure of deism was manufactured, dealing primarily with the period from the 1690s to the 1730s. I illustrate how sections of the clergy and political class were keen to talk up the existence and threat of a deist movement for their own particular ends. Most importantly, the debate further deepens the discussion on how centrally important was public opinion to the whole process of creating the historical record. The next two case studies on France and Italy, however, contain very little discussion devoted to deism and instead concentrate much more intensely on identifying the broad elements and processes of religious change.

The discussion of the French experience in Chapter 4 ('France: the revolt of democratic Christianity and the rise of public opinion') illustrates that the tiny number of philosophes – few of whom were deists – were more bystanders than activists in the major politico-religious events and developments of the century. In fact, they can hardly be termed consistent fighters for toleration, at least as Enlightenment studies has traditionally understood that term. Again, the discussion focuses on public opinion and broad forces for change, challenging the notion of an all-embracing French absolutism. The *parlements*, Jansenists and broad public opinion achieved what the deists and philosophes never even consistently fought for: the suppression of the Jesuits, the development of a *de facto* toleration prior to the Revolution, and the initiation of the demands for constitutional government.

Chapter 5 ('Italy: Roman tyranny and radical Catholic opposition') is devoted to bringing to light the nature of the polemical challenge that radical Catholics – Jansenists – advanced against Roman theocracy and Church jurisdiction in the independent states of the Italian peninsula. In the practical absence of the voices of deists and philosophes, the 'tyranny' of Rome was opposed by broad Catholic forces in very forceful terms remarkably similar to those of dissenting Protestants. Even in the unusual polycentric conditions of the Italian peninsula, this chapter demonstrates how politics and religion were intertwined, and that the broad politicization of religion is really the key to understanding religious change in the Enlightenment.

The first section of the concluding Chapter 6 ('The "public sphere" and the hidden life of ideas') discusses the significance of 'misreadings'. Eighteenth-century participants and constituencies of interest could – wittingly or unwittingly – 'misread' the publications and events of the period, contributing to the origins of modern myths about the eighteenth century. The main discussion here, however, focuses on the role of public opinion in intellectual change on core Enlightenment topics such as toleration. The dominance of the top-down model of intellectual change has prevented due recognition of the role of the wider public in the formation of the idea of religious toleration. It is also asked whether it is appropriate for modern (or postmodern) historians to place modern definitions of religious toleration upon the shoulders of eighteenth-century thinkers. By doing so historians invite anachronistic comparisons with the twenty-first century. Only by broadening the scope of Enlightenment studies beyond the traditional canon can we hope to grasp and investigate the intellectual dynamic of what we have termed the Enlightenment.

The function of the Appendix is to redress the hitherto frequently misleading impression that, in Enlightenment Britain, the subject of 'natural religion' or the 'religion of nature' was the reserve of deists and other enemies of the Church. For enlightened thinkers, evidence for a rational or natural religion lay in the qualities (especially reason and conscience) of an unchanging human nature and the frame of nature itself. As the Appendix indicates, however, the topic of the positive contribution of natural religion to Christianity was common in Enlightenment England. Of the many English Protestant works touching on this subject, I list just a few examples in order to indicate the tenor and variety of thought upon it.

Notes

1 T. Munck, *The Enlightenment. A Comparative Social History 1721–1794* (London: Arnold, 2000).

2 For general surveys on the philosophes and religion see, for instance, Peter Gay, *The Enlightenment. An Interpretation. Vol. 1: The Rise of Modern Paganism* (London: Norton, 1995; 1st edn 1966); J. Byrne, *Glory, Jest and Riddle. Religious Thought in the Enlightenment* (London: SCM Press, 1996); J. Champion, *The Pillars of Priestcraft Shaken* (Cambridge: Cambridge University Press, 1992); G. R. Cragg, *The Church and the Age of Reason 1648–1789* (London: Penguin, 1962); O. Grell and R. Porter (eds), *Toleration in Enlightenment Europe* (Cambridge: Cambridge University Press, 2000); I. Rivers, *Reason, Grace and Sentiment. Vol. 2: Shaftesbury to Hume* (Cambridge: Cambridge University Press, 2000); F. Venturi, *Settecento Riformatore. Vol. 2: La Chiesa e la Repubblica dento i loro limiti* (Turin: Einaudi, 1976); F. Venturi, *Italy and the Enlightenment*, ed. Stuart Woolf (London: Longman, 1972); B. Young, *Religion and Enlightenment in Eighteenth-Century England. Theological Debate from Locke to Burke* (Oxford: Clarendon Press, 1998).

3 Q. Skinner, 'Meaning and Understanding in the History of Ideas', *History and Theory*, 8 (1969); although I do feel that focus on his notion of illocutionary force will necessarily solve the problems faced by many historians.

1

The myth of
Enlightenment deism

The myth of the deist movement

The first hint of deism in the historical record is to be found in sixteenth-century Lyon. In 1563 Pierre Viret, a close colleague of the Protestant reformer Calvin, wrote the *Instruction Chrétienne*, in which he described various freethinkers who needed to be combated. Amongst them Viret mentioned those 'qui s'appelent déistes, d'un mot tout nouveau' ('who call themselves deists, a completely new word') and his description of them heavily emphasized their lack of religion.[1] It was not, however, until the second half of the seventeenth century that the deism scare really began to take shape.

In 1654 the orthodox Catholic and Bordelais barrister Jean Filleau claimed that the Catholic reformer Jansen, Saint Cyran and five others had met in Bourgfontaine in 1621 in order to plan the destruction of French Catholicism and supplant it with deism.[2] In England, by the late seventeenth and the early eighteenth centuries, many Anglican prelates seemed increasingly convinced – if we are to believe their testimony – of the existence of a deist movement, and similar fears were apparent amongst the orthodox in France, Italy and elsewhere in Europe. The central question is: should we accept the proclaimed fears of eighteenth-century thinkers as a true reflection of reality? If they were real fears, did they necessarily reflect the actual existence of deists or even a movement of them? In short, the answer is negative: on this subject, what we read in the historical record is for the most part the fears and prejudices of writers rather than actual observations. Some of those proclaimed fears were genuine. Some, however, were not entirely so, and were in good part the result of a matrix of personal, economic and politico-religious circumstances and exigencies that prompted some observers to exaggerate threats to Christianity. The results are beyond doubt. The deism scare proved to be one of the great and enduring European propaganda coups, the results of which, in academic terms, are still with us today. Historians, wishing to locate the origins of secular modernity in the Enlightenment, have perpetuated the notion of a secularizing eighteenth-century international 'deist movement', which has been considered 'especially strong in Britain and France'.[3] It has consequently been noted that amongst some historians there has been an 'obsessive iteration of "modernity" as a watchword of Enlightenment'.[4]

In his *Christianity under the Ancien Régime 1648–1789* (1999), Ward has suggested that the number of deist writers was 'immense'.[5] Herrick (*The Radical Rhetoric of the English Deists*, 1997) has claimed that English deists were so numerous that they posed a threat to the social and religious order.[6] In his *Enlightenment Deism* (1999), Daily has even argued that the large Latitudinarian tendency of the Anglican Church consisted of strong advocates of deism.[7] In 1993 Walsh and Taylor too asserted the existence of a deist movement that, in the 1730s, 'became dangerously fashionable in the *haut monde*'.[8] Justin Champion (*The Pillars of Priestcraft Shaken*, 1992), although debating its nature, also accepts the existence of a deist movement.[9] In a recent offering, Margaret Jacob, a consistent advocate of a radical Enlightenment, also contributes to the notion of a deist movement, claiming that deists and freethinkers were 'readily found on the radical fringe' of the Whigs.[10] In her earlier *The Radical Enlightenment* (1981), she argued that the clandestine writings of such thinkers 'fed the flames of … massive conflagration intended to destroy the Christian Churches and their doctrines'.[11] In 1985 J. C. D. Clark informed his readers that '[d]eism was launched as a self-conscious movement in the mid 1690s … and the deist movement found its chief spokesman in John Toland'.[12] Commentators on France too have asserted the unquestionable existence of a deist movement, as does C. J. Betts in his *Early Deism in France* (1984).[13] Rivers, in her *Reason, Grace and Sentiment* (2000), also asserts the existence of a deist (or freethinking) movement.[14] In his *France in the Enlightenment* (1993), Roche argues that 'theism was a public promise that echoed everywhere', and he defines theism as 'a desperate attempt to make sure that religion remained … unattached to any supernatural myth'.[15]

The myth of Enlightenment deism

Two recent works, explicitly focusing on the relationship between the Enlightenment and modernity, make similar claims. In his much-praised *Enlightenment Britain and the Creation of the Modern World* (2000), Roy Porter too has argued that deists were numerous and enjoyed wide support.[16] Perhaps not surprisingly, in his *Radical Enlightenment* (2001), Jonathan Israel alludes to considerable numbers of known and active deists by describing, for example, how 'major segments of British deism evinced close conceptual affinities with Spinozism'.[17]

The forerunners of such claims can be found in much earlier assessments of the numbers of deists and their influence by canonical thinkers such as Ernst Cassirer, Paul Hazard, Frank E. Manuel, G. R. Cragg and Peter Gay. In his *The Philosophy of the Enlightenment* (1932), Ernst Cassirer writes of the 'extraordinary effect' that the English 'deistic movement' had on the Enlightenment, and quotes the late-seventeenth-century Huguenot Pierre Bayle describing his age as 'full of freethinkers and deists'.[18] In his *'Christianity not Mysterious* and the Enlightenment' (1997), McGuinness has asserted that deism was 'very influential in Germany', but his authority is Manuel's *The Eighteenth Century Confronts the Gods* (1959). Using Paul Hazard's *European Thought in the Eighteenth Century* (1946) as his authority, the same writer also asserts that French deism saw the birth of a 'race of men whose sole spiritual nourishment was anti-clericalism'.[19] In his *The Church and the Age of Reason 1648–1789* (1962), G. R. Cragg advanced an analysis that has endured until the present without significant revision, and will thus demand our attention in the following discussions. He argued that, from the last years of the seventeenth century until the mid eighteenth century, deism was a serious threat to organized Christianity.[20] Peter Gay, in his much-lauded *The Rise of Modern Paganism* (1966), asserted that in England 'the dawning deist Enlightenment' produced 'a true school of thought', the deists 'redrew the religious map of Europe' and their teachings became 'commonplace'.[21] The same kind of claims are to be found in Ira Wade's *The Structure and Form of the French Enlightenment* (1977), where it is asserted that the history of French 'religious thought from 1715 to 1750 is dominated by the dynamism of a widespread deism'.[22]

It can be asserted, however, that in any meaningful definition of the term, beyond the virtual reality of history books, the deist movement never existed. The Enlightenment studies canon also holds that Voltaire and the other deistic philosophes constituted the paramount force in the struggle for enlightenment, and initiated the birth of secular modernity. This notion, too, is based more upon supposition than evidence. It is true that the philosophes were opponents (if inconsistently) of the Church, although not necessarily of religion. But it is also true that, rather than leaders and instigators of real change, the philosophes were observers (and not unbiased commentators) of politico-religious struggles and transformations across late-seventeenth- and eighteenth-century Europe.

There have been some voices against the notion of a predominantly secular radical Enlightenment (see below) and a relatively weak Church, amongst whom I wish to place myself. Nevertheless, politico-religious conflicts have still been given insufficient weight in the study of Enlightenment thought. That is to say a profound process of religious change has been relatively neglected because it manifested itself in a traditional early modern politico-religious form, rather than in the 'modernizing' language of the philosophes. That the philosophes have been granted the credit for achievements that were not theirs is not really suprising. They themselves were prone to claim credit for victories of others against the establishment, even if – as in the suppression of the Jesuits in France – these were in fact victories for one wing of Catholicism against another. This circumstance cannot, however, form any general indictment of enlightened thinkers or indeed of the philosophical and scientific achievements of the Enlightenment itself. But it does illustrate how a tiny minority of intellectuals naturally grasped any opportunity to further their own views, claiming favourable winds as universal victories for reason against ignorance and superstition.

We know that d'Alembert, for instance, in his 1765 pamphlet *Sur la destruction des Jésuites en France*, claimed the hitherto unthinkable destruction of that pillar of papal and absolute royal power as a victory for enlightened thought. Yet he knew very well that the dominant force in the battle to disband the Jesuits was other dissident Catholics, Jansenists.[23] Some enlightened readers of Rousseau's *Les Confessions* (finally published in 1782) were also presumably surprised to learn how indebted they were to the author's prompt action in preventing a revolution in 1753. With deft footwork, Rousseau had apparently distracted Paris from acute religious strife with his views on the comparative virtues of Italian and French music.[24] Rousseau's rather amusing megalomania aside,

14

these two anecdotes indicate how the philosophes ought to be seen more often as onlookers in truly tumultuous events which were certainly not 'enlightened' as we have come to understand the term. From this perspective, it is possible to view at least some of the thought of the philosophes as the *result* of a profound politicization of religion especially apparent in France, Italy and England, rather than its cause. Indeed, there is little evidence of religious change brought about by philosophes. At the heart of this book is the understanding that it was the politicization of religion that was central to religious change in eighteenth-century Europe. But the philosophes were rarely central to the process of politicization. For religion to be politicized in reality, rather than in elite theory or sensationalist writings, the politicization process needed to encompass far wider social strata and express significant elements of the political, economic and religious outlook of those strata.

Paradoxically, in England and France the greatest phenomena of the time corresponding to the term movement – something organized and active with a definable intellectual platform – were usually religious in outlook. Major examples were the various sects and tendencies that constituted late-seventeenth- and early-eighteenth-century English Dissent, and in France, Jansenists organized around the very influential journal *Nouvelles ecclésiastiques* and the Camisards (insurrectionary Huguenots). Thus, in agreement with the emerging trend to view the Enlightenment from the perspective of diversity rather than homogeneity, the following discussion will assume that the religious thought of the philosophes was as much a product of their own broad politico-religious experience as of their claimed universalist and classic-inspired thinking.

That historians have been able to refer to deism as a movement, a social force, is a reminder that in important and often vital respects – especially in intellectual history – historians recreate the past based not only upon its more tangible events and achievements, but also upon the hopes and fears of its participants and the historical outlook of the historians themselves. Thus, d'Alembert's claim has been seen as proof of the philosophes' influence. Yet, paradoxically, even though the politico-religious role of Jansenism is in fact difficult to deny, the public face of French Jansenism was always a denial of its own existence: a quite reasonable fear of being condemned and persecuted as schismatics by Rome and Bourbon monarchs. This simple reality has also served to bolster the notion that a 'modern, progressive act', such as the dissolution of the Jesuits, had to have come about on account of the influence of the vocal and progressive philosophes, not at the hands of the fanatically religious and self-effacing Jansenists. Yet the term 'simple reality' is a bold statement, for historical reality is rarely what it might seem at first glance. More precisely, we have to ask *which* historical reality we wish to recover, for we are usually presented with a choice. We know, for instance, that in the opinion of many Jansenists the Jesuits were, in practice, allied with the philosophes, while the Jesuits claimed that the Jansenists were in league with the philosophes.[25] These two claims have rarely been considered as little more than crude propagandizing, yet, as the chapters of this book will argue, there is every reason to consider that at some points and in some respects the claims of the Jesuits, at least, were justified. In sum, if there is any single theme of this book I would wish to stress above others, it is the propensity of the historical record to 'mislead' posterity.

For a variety of reasons, then, the aims, hopes and fears of historical actors represented in and selected from the historical record may not coincide with a more general historical view of the period. Historians have also at times been victims of modern historiography itself, where the deism imposed on the population by a tiny elite – the cult of the Supreme Being imposed during the French Revolution – has often been read backwards into French intellectual history. So, regardless of how ineffective (and even rather ridiculous in aspect) the cult might have been in terms of transforming personal piety, along with the Revolution itself it has often been understood as the logical result of the influential deistic philosophes and their programme of enlightenment. This type of approach helps us understand why the traditional division of labour in eighteenth-century studies – books on the Enlightenment and books on the rest of the eighteenth century – has been so enduring, yet so glaring: one historical story seemed out of place with another. As Dale Van Kley has noted in relationship to France, the problem emanates in good part from the assumption of an active Enlightenment party in contradistinction to a wider inert and passively receptive social context.[26] To view the majority of experience in eighteenth-century Europe through the prism of the deistic philosophes is simply to accept uncritically the world as the philosophes claimed they saw it.

The myth of Enlightenment deism

Deism, diverse in form and thus difficult to define, has generally been accepted as entailing belief in God and even of *post mortem* rewards and punishments. It was, however, a God usually remote from everyday human concerns. Deists thus dismissed the need for any mediation between humanity and divinity in the form of the Church and dismissed the Church's claimed mediation as self-interested fraud. This sort of view was understood as a potential threat not only to Christianity, but also to the established social order, for Christian teachings and the Church were widely acknowledged as the broad foundation for morality and law. Reducing the reliance of society and intellectual endeavour upon religious thought was of course one of the fundamental propositions of the enlightened. By eliminating superstition and clerical influence, which they understood as a key barrier to human progress, the philosophes hoped to renew society. They wished to bring about a new rational, humane and progressive social order, in which the faculty of reason would be free to work for the benefit of all humanity. The problem is, however, only a small minority of even the enlightened were identifiably deist in outlook. That there were fears of the encroachment of such potentially anti-establishment heterodoxy in the seventeenth and eighteenth centuries should not, however, be any surprise. It was a period in which states were still confessional in nature (that is, with only one permitted state religion). Nevertheless, diverse religious divides were common and were of course understood by many of the elite as potentially inimical to the well-being of the state and the social order. Yet, paradoxically, almost all those radical in religion or politics also recognized the vital role of the Church in preserving the status quo. Thus Voltaire, famed as a deist, could crusade against all organized religion, yet he also argued that religious observance was to be tolerated and even supported amongst the masses. It was to be tolerated, however, not because of its value as legitimate divine worship, but as an aid in the maintenance of social stability, including the maintenance of the social and economic status of the philosophes themselves, who, for the most part, were drawn from the moneyed classes. So, even if we accept the simple but controversial proposition that a deist movement did not exist, those deists who certainly did exist held views which might seem at least paradoxical to us and serve to complicate any attempts at a one-dimensional view of eighteenth-century religion.

There can be no doubting that some deists did exist, including – on some counts – Voltaire, Montesquieu, John Toland, Diderot (for a period), Matthew Tindal and Anthony Collins. The problem we face, if we accept the traditional claims for a deist movement, is that the rest of what surely should be a lengthy list of deists is not to be found. There were, it seems, more than those listed above, but not sufficient to validate claims for a European deist movement. The *Dictionary of Eighteenth-Century History* (1996), for example, seems to reflect the relative scarcity of deists quite well. The *Dictionary* lists only seven deists (and even less atheists) – Viscount Bolingbroke, Toland, Tindal, Collins (listed as a freethinker), Erasmus Darwin, Diderot, Thomas Paine and Alberto Radicati – across the whole of Europe in the whole of the century.[27] It hardly needs pointing out that this figure does not, no matter how much we might qualify the term, constitute grounds for the identification of a movement, even an English one consisting of relatively 'small numbers' as Clark has put it in his *English Society 1688–1832* (1985).[28] It is hardly surprising, therefore, that one commentator has ventured that scepticism had less support from the 1690s to the 1740s 'than it had at any time since the Renaissance'.[29] At this point, then, we need to pose two questions: is the *Dictionary* a credible guide to eighteenth-century religious history and what reasons might there be for not recording the names of the rest of the putative deist movement? First, however, let us examine the numbers of deists some other historians have identified in the course of their researches.

A search of Peter Gay's comprehensive *Rise of Modern Paganism* (1966), the first in his two-volume interpretation of the Enlightenment, results in extending our list of deists by only another five or six.[30] Significantly, Cragg's *The Church and the Age of Reason* identifies only three deists with no extension to our list.[31] Byrne, in his *Glory Jest and Riddle* (1996), cites seven, providing one addition to our list.[32] In his *God and Government in an Age of Reason* (1995), D. Nichols discusses only five deists, with one possible addition to our list.[33] Neither does discussion of the deist movement in J. C. D. Clark's *English Society* allow us to augment our list. To our list we can of course add the names of deists less usually discussed, such as the Germans Herman Reimarus, G. Lessing and Moses Mendelssohn. The approximate totals of deist protagonists commonly cited by historians are, therefore, five French, ten English, one Italian and three German. Given that deism is usually given by historians as a movement crossing most of Europe for most of the eighteenth century, these sparse aggregate figures scarcely amount to a movement in any meaningful sense of the term. Equally interesting is the *History of British Deism* (1995), edited by J. V. Price.[34] The eight volumes of reproduced texts which constitute the *History* appear, ostensibly, impressive and a testament to the term 'English deist movement'. In fact, the eight volumes contain (besides three and a half volumes of replies and arguments for Christianity and against deism) the works of only five deists: Charles Blount, Peter Annet, Tindal, Toland and the self-confessed 'Christian deist' Thomas Morgan. Price seems, therefore, to have had some difficulty in coming up with a British deist movement: five writers spanning the period 1693–1761 is hardly the basis for a convincing argument for a deist movement. Indeed, although the work is entitled the *History of British Deism*, Price provides no overall introduction to the work: an introduction to the history of a phenomenon the reality of which palls before its reputation is perhaps not a task many would want to undertake. As Sullivan has commented, 'if Blount, Woolston, Annet, and perhaps Toland were the only deists, then the importance of deism has been consistently exaggerated'. Sullivan also adds the telling remark that even active (usually Anglican) anti-deists 'frequently seemed perplexed about who these men were. Indeed, the Augustans were unable to agree on any single principle as typical of deism.'[35] More recently, whilst he has alluded to great numbers of English deists in his *Radical Enlightenment* (2001), Israel does not allow us to enlarge significantly our list.

As we shall see, compiling a list of deists is not only problematic in numerical terms, for it did not constitute a homogenous set of beliefs and in itself this recognition renders the concept of a deist movement somewhat difficult. No one has yet been able to demonstrate any consensus in deist religious outlook, an identifiable deist programme, or consistent intellectual links based upon it – even if we accept that some, such as Hermann Reimarus for instance, chose to hide their deistic views. Thus, depending on the definition of deism one uses, one or two or more names given above might be struck from the list and one or two added: some might argue Rousseau ought to be added to the list and one name or another omitted (such as the Earl of Shaftesbury or Nicholas Fréret). This does not invalidate the reason for this head-count: to put the received wisdom regarding the existence of a deist movement into tight focus. The figures of deists provided from various sources, then, indicate that, rather than a movement, a tiny group of the European intelligentsia advocated deistic or to some degree similar ideas, at geographically diverse locations and often several generations apart.

The specificities of time and place could, hypothetically, serve to bring our short list closer to the idea of an international movement if the protagonists were at least concentrated within relatively narrow time bands. But this is not the case. In the case of England, it is true that some of the individuals mentioned above may have occasionally used the same coffee houses, but their views differed in various respects and there is no evidence to support any hypothesis of concerted ideological action.[36] The only obvious facts about the chronological and geographical spread of the list above have already become (uncritical) commonplaces in Enlightenment studies: that Enlightenment deism seems to have begun in late-seventeenth- and early-eighteenth-century England and that, by comparison, very large gaps appear elsewhere in Europe for much of the century until 1789. The time has arrived to admit that the hitherto prevailing conception of a deist movement has become more of a hindrance than an aid to the advancement of our knowledge of eighteenth-century intellectual history. It has, in fact, begun to produce very unfortunate distortions. As we shall see, trying to fit the round peg of a deist movement into the square hole of eighteenth-century reality has led to the bolstering of the deist count with individuals for whom the tangible evidence for holding deistic views is extremely thin and unconvincing. It is true, of course, that simple head-counts can be said to prove little, for the question of the influence these individual protagonists exerted is also, in itself, a vital question. Although there is no evidence of religious change brought about by the philosophes, we may say they perhaps contributed to changes in public opinion, but yet even this is not demonstrable. As we shall see, in the hubbub of the great politico-religious events in France, for instance, their voices were most often thin and distant, and the partial exceptions – Voltaire's campaign over the Calas case for example – tend to confirm the point. For now, however, we must resume our consideration of the implications of the rather surprising lack of deists listed in the *Dictionary of Eighteenth-Century History*.

There is certainly no evidence to suggest that the scholarship of the *Dictionary* is in any way suspect and certainly no evidence of religious bias. We should conclude, then, even though its content on the subject of deism seems at odds with much received academic wisdom on the subject, that its 800 pages of offerings in fact constitute a fair balance of the religious outlook of its widely chosen subjects and thus of the Enlightenment itself. We know that deism has become one of the hallowed watchwords of the Enlightenment and that the contributors to the *Dictionary* are specialist and erudite scholars. Thus, we can take for granted that if it were possible for the *Dictionary* to have easily identified a host of other deists, it would have done so. Thus, even allowing for the inevitable minor oversights and naturally extremely tight control on space allocation to subjects, we are still left with a tricky problem: how to equate the findings of the *Dictionary* with the repeated assertions by modern historians of the existence of a deist movement. Yet, it cannot be ignored that the *Dictionary* itself also asserts the existence of a deist movement.[37] For the supporters of the notion of a more radical Enlightenment typified by a vibrant deist movement, this lack of evidence is a little disturbing. In the final instance, the contradiction between claim and evidence has to be overcome if Enlightenment studies is to remain on a balanced footing. To abandon the claim, at least until now, has been unthinkable for most historians, because the existence of a deist movement has been an inherent part of the chain of evidence for charting the roots and evolution of secular modernity. We need only remind ourselves that the term modernity figures large in the title of the latest offerings of respected historians such as Jonathan Israel and Roy Porter.

In its entry for deism, the *Dictionary* notes that 'although it was never a coherent intellectual movement, it reached the peak of its influence in late-seventeenth- and early-eighteenth-century England in the writings of John Toland and Matthew Tindal and in eighteenth-century France in the writings of Rousseau and Voltaire'.[38] What is not apparent from this statement is that (prior to 1789) the *Dictionary* lists only four English deists or freethinkers – Toland, Collins, Darwin and Bolingbroke. Of French thinkers, only Diderot is described as deist – not even Voltaire and Rousseau in the articles devoted to them are termed deists (although there is little doubt that Voltaire and some few others did at least exhibit part of the outlook of what has been termed deism). So, even if deists were a mixed bag, readers are entitled to ask where are they? Unless the *Dictionary*'s deist count can, via head-counts in more specialized works, be multiplied by a relatively large factor, it is difficult to see how 'a peak of influence', which strongly indicates numerous and frequently repeated polemics, can be ascribed to so few writers. In a nutshell, we have the assertion of a historical social force, but we have only ever had the writings of a few disparate figures to suggest its existence. It seems, then, historians have constructed an imposing ideological structure to which all 'moderns' have felt compelled to give assent. The abstract ideas of a few eigthteenth-century thinkers have been reified, imbued by historians with a social force, which has served to construct a wide schema of historical progress upon which Enlightenment studies has been founded. But because of its artificiality, that schema or imputed historical terrain has very often been inhospitable to wider political and social studies of eighteenth-century life. It is important, therefore, to examine some of the factors contributing to the construction of time-lines of intellectual 'progress'.

The deism myth and modern historians

Perhaps one of the oldest practices within historical research has been to identify the sources and authorities present in any given text. This, many young historians have been told, allows one to map the mind of the writer, to identify the influences and sources behind the pen. It is necessary to be very clear on this issue at the outset: finding references to or tracing the use of other writers' works in any given text cannot prove or disprove the existence of influence upon the writer. We can only know for certain that writer A probably read or knew of writer B. In itself this may seem like one bad-tempered historian being pedantic with his colleagues, but the point at issue here merits attention. Historians have repeatedly traced back the ideas found in eighteenth-century texts to their 'source' – anywhere from the classical period to the Renaissance and Reformation period.[39] Yet, in the last two decades, it has become a relative commonplace amongst historians themselves that their own profession and all others have never been nor will ever be without bias or ideology. Why, then, should historians imagine that Enlightenment writers should bequeath a transparent record of their own reality to posterity?

The myth of Enlightenment deism

Tracing back the ideas of deism and the philosophes to the Renaissance, as Peter Gay (and others since) has done so eloquently in his *The Rise of Modern Paganism* (1966), is very often little more than wishful thinking. The 'forging' of such links is a process much related to the desire of modern historians to find the 'modern' in the Enlightenment: the 'modern' in the Enlightenment had to have its own roots, so historians then sought the proto-modern in earlier periods. Historians know very well that the process of writing is most often about justifying their ideas and interpretations: that is to say they most often add 'proofs' in the form of references or allusions to ideas already formulated and not necessarily conceived in direct connection with the authorities they might later cite. This then is the process of 'proving' or bolstering the legitimacy of our work, a post-factum justification, and can be termed the appropriation of ideas. The point here is that the *influence* of ideas is a very different intellectual circumstance from that of the *appropriation* of ideas. This is, of course, not to say that writings of the past never influence the present, nor that the boundaries between appropriation and influence are precise or fixed. Crucially, if this latter point holds true, in textual terms it will often prove difficult if not impossible to separate intellectual development resulting from broad biographical experience from the supposed influence of past writers. Texts are representatives of the past, yet very often represent no more than a simplified (or misleading) version of one layer of a multi-layered but interactive historical reality. As Oakeshott argued some time ago, the contents of the historical record are only 'symbols' of past 'performative utterances' which can never, in themselves, be fully recovered.[40] This admission, however, does not serve to undermine the historian's craft, but only to clarify its very rationale: the aim to reconstruct elements of the past, which means to situate the historical subject in as much or as many layers of its context as we can possibly reconstruct or authoritatively infer.

To cite an example from Dale Van Kley's otherwise informative and rigorous *The Religious Origins of the French Revolution* (1996): when discussing Diderot's article entitled 'Political Authority' which appeared in the first volume of that key Enlightenment publication the *Encyclopédie* in 1751, he notes that '[m]odern scholarship has tracked down the obvious clues concerning this article's intellectual debts' (and he goes on to cite them).[41] I do not want to disagree with the technical scholarship brought to bear on

23

the article, since we must assume it is of impeccable quality. We ought, however, to ask ourselves what is meant by 'intellectual debt'? In this article, it has been discovered, there is evidence that Diderot drew upon several other texts, some from the seventeenth century. But to draw upon or appropriate the work of others does not necessarily or even usually indicate influence. It may well be the case that Diderot had long held those opinions, formed by the experiences of his life, and this is a very different circumstance from influence. So what does 'intellectual debt' signify exactly? Most will agree, I feel, that this term connotes influence. Let us assume, then, that Diderot had long held the ideas expressed in the article, but upon writing the article he exemplified, sharpened and reinforced his arguments via the writings of past thinkers. If his long-held arguments also shifted a little in emphasis because of his appropriation of the ideas of others, this can be legitimately termed influence. But what does it tell us about the major context for the birth of those ideas in the intellect of Diderot? 'Intellectual debt' here can only tell us that he was aware of the writings of others and agreed with them to some extent. Anything more than this, without a good deal of supporting evidence, would be pure supposition. To build intellectual traditions upon sequences of such links is to build ideological edifices where none existed. It is to create social forces from nothing, to reify our own opinions. When an ideological construct becomes dominant, accrues the collective force of a respected and thus powerful layer of professional historians, it can be difficult to dispel. Their shared assumptions form the very window of 'truth' through which they view the past, such that most cannot conceive of another, while a few other sharper spirits may be justifiably nervous about the prospect of abandoning the collective ideological shelter of the community.

So, as in eighteenth-century practice, we present-day historians are anxious to imbue our writings with the appearance of truth. To this end we readily quote and reference in accordance with academic norms and our own discursive needs. We thus supply a trail for later readers to follow. Some historians have felt it possible to follow these trails: the 'origins' of text D traced back via texts B and C finally to its 'source' A. In an occupation always hungry for order and explanation, the cumulative effect of these fancied intellectual time-lines has been to produce a respected body of research, the Enlightenment canon. Once the task of locating the roots of secular modernity in the radicals of the Enlightenment had become a shared imperative, for most it then seemed rather superfluous to study by far and away the greatest bulk of the historical record which is of course less 'radical', thus deemed less relevant. In this manner a created historical reality tends to become self-reinforcing, because there is a tendency for that small, even tiny, part of the historical record to become the preferred object of examination and re-examination for those in that particular field.

The philosophes, then, can become lifted and isolated from the actual context in which they lived – that represented by the rest of the historical record. Thus significant elements of the biographical context of their thought, that is to say their general life experiences, are often relegated to a secondary or even lower status in research. In place of the actual interaction between the subject and context, the subject is made to interact with received intellectual positions on a historical stage created by historians themselves. This, however, is not the full extent of the problem, and to berate only historians on this matter would be unjust. Historical actors themselves have of course rarely wished to portray themselves to their immediate audience and to posterity as products of contexts, rather than as original, 'timeless' or at least gifted thinkers. In this sense, in trying to recover the influences which prompted a writer to this view rather than that, the historian is at the outset often already bedevilled. We can say, at the very least, therefore, that the philosophes themselves did not want to appear mundane, and often simply omitted those facts or generalizations about their intellectual formation which we would today often consider relevant and important. Edward Gibbon, for example, never admits that in his *Decline and Fall of the Roman Empire* (1776–81) the outline of his treatment of the medieval Church is in fact mundane, a rehash of Protestant anticlerical positions dating back to the sixteenth century.[42]

This tendency for writers to 'overlook' their own formative intellectual experiences or milieux can be accompanied by a willingness to ignore and even misrepresent the influences at work in the achievement of their own dearly held goals, as did d'Alembert with the suppression of the Jesuits. Similarly, the philosophes in general portrayed the fideist analysis of the renowned writer Pierre Bayle as religiously sceptical, when (as we shall see later) it is unthinkable that many were not aware of his Huguenot piety.[43] Academic edifices based on influences detected in eighteenth-century texts thus often turn out to have very thin foundations indeed. In many cases it may be reasonable to infer influence, but in perhaps many more it would be more reasonable not to make such assumptions and to look more closely at the life experiences of historical actors. Would it be reasonable to suggest that Edward Gibbon, living for most of his life in Protestant England, had not assimilated the highly critical view of the medieval Church found in the writings of many Protestants? If he wished to write something critical of Church history, it would have been very surprising indeed if he did not consciously or unconsciously draw upon such common-or-garden Protestant critiques.

Gibbon was certainly bitingly anticlerical at times, and as Mark Goldie has put it: 'anticlericalism has long been integral to our idea of the Enlightenment. This used to encourage an heroic mythology of secularisation, in which reason did battle with religion, free-thought with bigotry. Few historians today would endorse so Manichaean a picture.'[44] There is now a growing consensus that the characterization of the Enlightenment as the Age of Reason, in which reason was diametrically opposed to religion, cannot be sustained. It is accepted by many that the Enlightenment represented a challenge to the Church, especially to the established Churches of the day, rather than to belief in God, in whom almost all philosophes and their supporters continued to believe in one form or another. This counter-trend to the more secular-radical Enlightenment thesis had its first beginnings some decades ago. However, although some historians now include Christian belief rather than only scepticism, deism or atheism when researching the Enlightenment, the idea that traditional politico-religious conflict played a major role in the formation and development of key aspects of the Enlightenment is not yet so readily accepted. The idea that the Enlightenment was overwhelmingly formed and driven by radical secularism still retains the allegiance of many historians. Thus part of the intellectual legacy of that earlier more oppositional view of reason versus religion is still with us. Even though many historians came to realize that reason against religion was a misleading formulation, the alternative formulation of reason against the Church continued to assume the existence of a large (if not properly homogenous) European 'party' of deists and fellow travellers. This was because, at root, it was not conceived possible that the project of bringing about secular modernity could have been accomplished by anything less than the concerted efforts of radical thinkers. As we have seen, the myth of the deist movement is not dead, and Goldie was perhaps a little over optimistic in the early 1990s when he declared that 'European thought in the eighteenth century is now seen to have been characterised by an ameliorated Christianity rather than by a militant crusade to overthrow it'.[45]

Nevertheless, amongst the dissident voices in Enlightenment studies – whose work has helped inform my own – the work of Labrousse,[46] Kors, Korshin[47] and Van Kley has been of great importance in establishing Christianity as a legitimate object of study within Enlightenment studies. In particular, Van Kley and O'Brien have contributed to our understanding of how conflict within Catholicism led to the suppression of the Jesuits in France – an order much hated by the philosophes and symbolic of their struggle against superstition and clerical arrogance – and to an increased desire for religious toleration.[48] J. C. D. Clark's *English Society 1688–1832* (1985) also argued for the importance of the Church in understanding the development of the Enlightenment. Similarly the work of Harrison,[49] Fitzpatrick,[50] and especially that of Young has helped to break the undue concentration on the thought of Enlightenment radicals.[51] Champion's work has helped reinsert the importance of the nexus between politics and religion into debate on the origins of the English Enlightenment, as has that of Goldie.[52] In *Religion and Politics in Enlightenment Europe* (2001), edited by James Bradley and Dale Van Kley, the interface between politics and religion across Enlightenment Europe is examined. Also useful in this context has been Nigel Aston's edited collection *Religious Change in Europe 1650–1914* (1997). The research of Haakonssen and Munck (and to a lesser extent Chartier[53]) has helped demonstrate that the traditional clear dividing line between the secular enlightened and the religious non-enlightened does not correspond to eighteenth-century reality.[54] In assessing the context and views of John Toland, I am also indebted to the pioneering content of Sullivan's *John Toland and the Deist Controversy* (1982).

As we have seen, the weakness of the assertion of a deist movement is that there were too few deists to fulfil the role historians have assigned to them. When, by the 1980s, it was accepted by one or two historians that there was insufficient unity amongst so-called deists to continue to use the term deist movement without qualification,[55] the numerical problem remained generally unacknowledged.

As we will see, even those who wanted to rehabilitate religion into Enlightenment studies were still reluctant to accept that there were in fact few deists to be found in the historical record. There was, thus, no discernible shaking of the altar to modernity. In the 1990s, however, some of the strains of the contradiction between claims and evidence began to manifest themselves. As a result of their scarcity in relationship to their perceived historical role, deists were endowed with a collectors' value. Thus, at times, certain thinkers whose writings appeared to be radical have been turned into deists or proto-deists. The supposedly 'lesser figures' of the English deist movement were thereby brought to the fore, so helping to flesh out a very sparse picture indeed. As we shall see, from Clark's *English Society* (1985) to Porter's *Enlightenment Britain and the Creation of the Modern World* (2000), English Dissenters or dissenters (i.e. non-aligned individuals or those who remained nominally Anglican) who were prone to the use of strong critical language, such as Robert Howard or John Trenchard,[56] have been transformed into deists. The question, then, is how, in terms of evidence, could such claims come about? In order to broach this question, we must take into account the broad context in which such radical Protestant thinkers developed their intellectual and religious outlooks.

There is abundant evidence that, amongst Restoration Dissenters, presbyterianism was the preferred form of Church organization. The problem has been a tendency to consider presbyterianism as foremost a form of piety – often identified with Puritanism – rather than as an ecclesiastical polity with broad politico-religious implications. No matter what disagreements might exist amongst historians on the causes or origins of the English Civil War, all admit that Puritanism played a significant ideological role in the momentous conflicts of the 1640s. Virtually all would also agree that the Puritan movement flew apart in those years and could not later be reassembled. The problem is that most historians have also thought that, after the Restoration of 1660, most or all of the key ideas of Puritanism were also dead or in steep decline. As a consequence, a coherent politico-religious challenge to the Anglican Church–state set-up could not be launched. There is evidence, however, to illustrate that, rather than fading away, the presbyterian polity of Puritanism remained a vital component of the Restoration politico-religious context. The heart of Puritanism was the desire for an independent presbyterian grass-roots ecclesiastical polity, modelled upon the simple, non-hierarchical apostolic Church. Presbyterians were thus implacable opponents of Church–state collusion in the denial of religious freedom to good Protestants. An independent non-hierarchical Church was of course anathema to the English political and ecclesiastical status quo, a direct political challenge to the Restoration state and Church settlement, where the Church was seen as a crucial official adjunct of the state in its desire for order and identity.

Those familiar with the history of the Civil War know very well that presbyterian politico-religious thinking could be most radical. Some late Restoration presbyterian polemic was so radical, in fact, that the authors could and have been mistaken for deists. Most notably, this was the case with John Toland, perhaps the most infamous of late-seventeenth-century English religious radicals and eventually certainly a deistical thinker. There is good evidence, however, that when he wrote his most notorious work, *Christianity not Mysterious* (1696), he was a presbyterian of the Unitarian (Socinian) type and commonly known as such. It might seem strange that most modern historians have chosen to ignore this facet of Toland's biography, along with the fact that the label deist was only applied to him in what can only be described as a politico-religious slur campaign. As we shall see, ignoring this evidence is also to ignore how the fabric of the deist movement could begin to be woven by the spin-doctors of the day. The fact that the analysis contained in his radical but reform-orientated *Christianity not Mysterious* does not seem out of place within the deistic canon means, however, that the question of the Restoration transition from Puritanism to a more amorphous or variegated presbyterianism across various tendencies is of some importance. It has been argued by some that presbyterianism – because of its politico-religious past – had become an unattractive alternative to many Whigs, and that presbyterianism stood condemned along with popery and Anglicanism. Such men as Robert Howard and John Trenchard then opted instead for a deistic alternative of 'civil religion'.[57] As we will see, the problem is that the evidence adduced for this decisive abandonment of presbyterianism or a secularizing 'civil religion' is minimal and mostly circumstantial, with potential evidence to the contrary, or at least indicating a different situation, in equal supply.

It was of course natural that, once the fabric of the deist movement had been woven, its demise had, eventually, to be charted.

The Enlightenment and religion

Bishop Butler's *Analogy of Religion* (1736) is more or less unanimously credited with finally defeating deism, that relentlessly dangerous foe of the Anglican Church. But, as we now know, Butler's sharp and learned logic of course only disembowelled a very modern fiction. Or did it? For there is no doubt that the Church and Bishop Butler were indeed understood by some contemporaries to be battling a mighty deist movement. Some modern commentators have even argued that 'the Evangelical movement came as a reaction to the Deists'.[58] Perhaps Anglicanism really was subject to the point of an antichristian bayonet only manfully thrust aside by Butler? Or was it all a scam, a fiction playing on the hearts and minds of the faithful in order to encourage loyalty and bring waverers back to the fold? Eighteenth-century protagonists were just as interested in constructing in the minds of others their own preferred reality for their own ends as many twentieth-century historians have been to construct the history of modernity. The historical record, then, will provide us with some data and vast gaps, but it also provides us with sophisticated projections of how certain eighteenth-century minds perceived their reality according to their own ideological outlook. Thus, for many churchmen, conservative thinkers and others, the deist movement certainly did exist, and self-evidently so. On the other hand, we know that Jansenists and Jansenist supporters undoubtedly existed in some considerable numbers in France (especially in Paris), yet in practice they have to be carefully sought for in the historical record because they habitually denied their own existence.

The myth and the historical record

In setting out to vindicate or conceal their own views, past writers, whether they were conscious of it or not, have often 'falsified' the historical record. That is to say they have simply given *their own* account of their present and past which, in itself, cannot be taken as evidence of historical reality, but rather as one layer of a past reality composed of various interactive layers. If a more general overview is to be sought, historians must contrast one layer against other layers. As if this situation were not difficult enough, what historians are prone to take for granted – the historical record – has also been 'falsified' by historians themselves when they define periods or make characterizations about them. If the Enlightenment marked the beginning of modernity, then the historical record is of course bound to reflect that, and when it does not seem to do so sufficiently, efforts must be redoubled. Those who seem like moderns are brought into the field while vast quantities of 'non-modern' data are left to gather dust.

Fundamental to the now mostly defunct Age of Reason perspective was the view that the eighteenth century saw a large rise in unbelief, eventually producing a sceptical or atheistic tendency or 'party'. Naturally, some historians set out to chart this rise,[59] for, after all, what could be more evidently modern than an atheist movement, and in so doing they constructed a tradition of infidelity going back to the Renaissance or sometimes to the English Civil War. Unfortunately, the death knell for this construct is not yet as strong as it should be. The principal reason is that, whereas the reason-versus-religion view (and the subsequent rationality-versus-the-Church retrenchment) was primarily a review of a generalization, the infidelity tradition prided itself on detailed research relating to individuals, publications and definite ideas. What has thus been regarded by some as a quasi-empirical approach – elucidating a core of self-evident textual truth – has served as a partial shield from the more general shift in perspective. This does not, of course, mean that the tradition of a growth in infidelity is not a construct. We might accept that the texts and individuals were real, although the public 'figure' of the atheist was certainly exploited by interested political and religious tendencies.[60] The connections between real atheists, however, and their relationship to any perceived change in eighteenth-century attitudes to religion amount to little more than the reification of ideas by historians. The problem of reification, in terms of the philosophy of history in general, has not altogether been ignored. Gunnell, amongst others, long ago noted that in principle what has 'been taken to be *the* tradition' of influence or pattern of intellectual development is often rather only 'a piece of academic folklore'.[61] But this lesson or perspective has not so far been sufficiently applied to Enlightenment studies.

There is as yet no substantial evidence to support the notion of any significant rise in unbelief in eighteenth-century Europe. This remains the case despite the fanciful assertion that there was an elite underground atheist 'movement of thought', of which the public mind was unaware. Apparently, via the most subtle of textual devices, this underground subversive movement sought 'to influence the public mind without allowing it to become aware that it was being influenced'.[62] Constructions of tales such as these should be understood as a symptom of a widely shared – almost subconscious – view that one of the primary tasks of twentieth-century early modern studies was to illustrate the history of secular modernity: that is to say, *construct it.* We should hardly be surprised, then, that this underground atheist movement, in terms of hard currency it seems, amounted to very little. In the *Dictionary of Eighteenth-Century History*, for instance, atheists are listed in fewer numbers than even deists. Faced with such little evidence, at least one or two historians have openly questioned the validity of atheistical conspiracy theories of the Enlightenment.[63] As we shall see, a text's notoriety for atheism or atheistic tendencies should not be understood as a necessary indicator of its potential or actual influence, but rather or equally as an indicator of its highly unusual and unrepresentative nature, and as a product of fashionable scandalmongering. There was always a certain audience prepared to be titillated by outrages in print, but whether they themselves held to those ideas is of course a very different question. Thus, what have often been regarded as transparent indicators of radicalism can equally be seen as just the reverse.

So, the problem facing Enlightenment studies is that the revision away from the reason-versus-religion thesis has arguably included insufficient reassessment of the historical record from which historians (at least in part) make their generalizations. Similarly, the ideological position of deism as a factor in early modern Europe has been subject to little specific discussion, rather remaining at the level of often vague generalization or inference from specific cases. One of the aims running through this book, then, is to discuss how one might go about considering such a revision – the central questions, contexts, problems and methodology. In this respect, we are immediately confronted with important methodological and philosophical considerations, the necessarily first of which is whether the 'reality' of eighteenth-century Europe is (as we are told by postmodernists) merely a series of competing tales told by professional historians?

My short answer is no. Indeed, if it were possible in this book, I would like to assert that my aim is to reflect on eighteenth-century *reality*. My deceptively simple aspiration cannot be realized on account of the long-held understanding of some historians that there was not one unified eighteenth-century reality any more than there is any one unified present reality. If we accept that those who lived in the eighteenth century often had disagreements on the nature of their present, why on earth should historians imagine that the writings of a tiny minority of elite but often divided writers can form any straightforward guide to that century? The great scientist Joseph Priestley, for instance, noted that, 'being a Unitarian', he disagreed with the historical interpretations of Trinitarians,[64] even 'when there is no dispute about the facts'.[65] Even if the historical record was not 'falsified' by its participants, how can we expect present-day historians, who cannot agree on the nature of their present, to agree on the nature of the past? Complex societies (and even those less complex) contain, at various levels, moments of consensus and conflict which shift in relation to each other and in relation to their own past, and here we are concerned above all with eighteenth-century urban Europe rather than rural life. This shifting dynamic of change cannot now, or then, be captured in its entirety in any one research snapshot.

Over time, we have seen the development of a variety of approaches (political, social, structural, economic, religious, literary, etc.) to the past. The perennial problem is of course how to generalize from those specialized approaches in order to gain some overall understanding of a period. Making academic distinctions between social, religious, economic and political aspects of history, while helping to deepen our historical gaze in some respects, is in itself an intrinsically problematic procedure, not least so in the early modern period. As we shall see, in order to discuss the early modern Church and religion, it is also necessary to discuss politics, economics, social structure and more. So readers of this book will, in terms of Enlightenment studies rather than eighteenth-century studies, be presented with a less conventional stratum of the reality of eighteenth-century Europe.

On the issue of reassessing the historical record, the obvious point to make is that the early modern historical record is overwhelmingly biased towards the literate and especially the elite – in terms of education, wealth and social standing. On questions of eighteenth-century economic theory, for instance, this consideration is of relatively less relevance. When we are looking at belief systems and the level of adherence to traditional institutional Christianity, however, adopting a frank attitude to the nature of the historical record is crucial: the thought of the vast majority of eighteenth-century minds is unavailable to us because those individuals had the temerity to die without leaving a written record of their own views. We know, however, that the public background to any belief system is of course a gradation of belief to unbelief. This is what, it seems to me, John Bossy in his *Christianity in the West 1400–1700* (1985) has failed to illustrate, that piety and dissent are – thankfully – features of any belief system. Wherever possible we should probe the extent to which public anticlericalism, directed either at the clergy in general or at aspects of it, formed the broad milieu in which the views of elite writers underwent gestation. In early modern France, for example, significant numbers within the lower echelons of society certainly expressed views which dissented to one degree or another from those of the established Church. We can safely assert this much on account, as we shall see, of the level of mass conflict between orthodox and non-orthodox Catholics. Yet relatively few of these lower-order rebellious Catholics left written testimony to their views. Being buried as a good Catholic or leaving a 'Christian' last will and testament is of course no sure guide to the views of the deceased, but more of a guide to established forms of exit from this world and the views of those who continued to live. Thus, in a social echelon more or less unrepresented in the historical record, by definition, anticlericalism and dissent will often go more or less unrecorded.

It is of an entirely different order, however, to assert that religious dissent and anticlericalism were not noticed by contemporaries or did not have influence upon others. Indeed, to have avoided noticing religious controversy and anticlericalism in cities would have been virtually impossible. As we shall see, this is graphically demonstrated by the wide levels of popular and elite politico-religious conflict which finally forced the French monarchy to suppress the Jesuits. This book is primarily about the urban experience, but those who lived and wrote in a more rural setting could not possibly be ignorant of the attitude of the poor to the wealth and corruption of the prelacy. As McManners has noted in his valuable study of the French Church, church tithes had lost their religious content and were viewed as one component of state–Church oppression. Thus, '[t]he history of the guerilla war against tithes waged for so long in law courts is essential evidence in any study of rural anticlericalism in France'.[66] Above all, such considerations

mean that the simple picture of Enlightenment religious development as one of the progressive elite fighting the religiously backward despots of Europe on behalf of the inert masses is rendered
much less secure. It also means that the accompanying traditional
notion of intellectual influence as always proceeding from the top
down becomes less secure in equal measure, for the status of the
Church in eighteenth-century minds formed part of the broad social
mentality in which the philosophes developed their ideas. Hence,
for any researcher interested in the abandonment of the institutional Church and resignation to a non-interventionist God, the
question of the level of forms of non-elite dissent from the Church
in the early modern period cannot be irrelevant. It is surprising –
with the partial exception of England – that such a question is so
infrequently addressed in Enlightenment studies.

Elite opinion is usually portrayed as developing without influence from the lower echelons and, in so far as elite ideas were passed
down the social scale, without any intellectual reciprocity. Yet how
many historians are prepared to assert that hermetic seals or Chinese walls between social orders were possible in early modern
Europe? Voltaire was able to launch his defence of the persecuted
Huguenot Calas family in 1762–63 precisely because of the climate
of opinion against the established clergy which had resulted, much
against the will of King and government, in the suppression of the
Jesuits in 1762. Voltaire joined the struggle against religious intolerance when he, for reasons not yet clear, felt he could no longer effectively ignore religious persecution as he had done for decades. We
know that the leading force in propagating and organizing attacks
upon the Jesuits and their supporters amongst the orthodox clergy
consisted of Jansenists, Catholic dissenters. As Van Kley has noted,
'the Jansenists, in loudly denouncing "despotism", were generally
ahead of the philosophes in the 1760s in disseminating a kind of
political rhetoric that became commonplace in "enlightened" literature on the eve of the Revolution'.[67]

Indeed, as we shall see, there is evidence to demonstrate that
'until less than twenty years before the Revolution the century's
most frontal protest against Bourbon absolutism was organized
largely if not exclusively by Jansenists'. Interestingly, during the
French restoration, the Marquis de Bouillé still blamed the Revolution on the Paris *parlement*'s Jansenist 'party'.[68] As Munck has illustrated in his *The Enlightenment*, the divisions between the

enlightened and non-enlightened in various contexts, times and places were nowhere so stark as we have been too often led to believe.

Instead of being pulled out of space and time and placed on an intellectual but ultimately historically disconnected stage, when the thought of the philosophes is placed alongside the wider battle of politico-religious ideas fought out in great urban centres such as Paris and London, their intellectual stature is certainly not diminished. Their thought does, however, become part of a larger canvas, in which they, as part of a tiny elite and thus relative onlookers, are seen to reflect and express the attitudinal changes which were occurring in front of them. The potential stumbling block for those historians reared on a traditional ideological diet of the hunt for modernity, however, is that these were not always battles which upon first sight might seem to be about secular enlightened ideals, but rather were more about religious rights or class privileges. The essence of the intellectually rich and complex phenomenon we have termed the Enlightenment cannot, however, be captured with such one-dimensional labels as political, religious, philosophical or scientific. The French Jansenist camp naturally included a range of thinkers – from the *advocats* (advocates) of the *Parlement* of Paris, to humble but intensely religious supporters – who opposed what they understood as the despotic nature of the monarch–bishop alliance. The philosophes, it goes without saying, did not want to be associated with such religious zealotry and thus were careful to deny or ignore any religious elements of the struggle against the old regime. Despite the failure of the philosophes to acknowledge it, the struggles of the Jansenists were about the politico-religious issues of the day, equally germane to the philosophes as to the middle and lower echelons of urban society.

It has long been noted how very little the philosophes achieved in terms of enlightened government policy. The implicit assumption, however, has been that they achieved a good deal more in terms of the history of ideas, and were a considerable force in their own right in terms of confining the influence of the Church and promoting a general secularization of thought. We are thus presented with a choice. If the writings of the philosophes themselves, their supporters, and the positive press they have received from historians are considered in isolation, then it may well seem they disposed of very great influence. If, however, evidence for them disposing of influence sufficient to accelerate significantly any general secularization process is actually sought, the case for influence looks decidedly less convincing. On the more narrow issue of curbing the power and influence of the Church, the result is the same (and is not altered by the fact of the brief period of the dechristianization phase of the French Revolution, which was certainly not part of the programme of the philosophes). The gamut of trenchant evidence from the state–Church struggles in France, England and Italy amply illustrates how the most effective opposition to the Church was in fact mounted by dissenting Church factions with various degrees of popular support. Those struggles resulted in a significant deepening of cynicism and anticlericalism towards the Church hierarchy and its political allies. Here lies palpable evidence of what has been termed a general Western European secularization process, the current of which the philosophes (and the supposed deist movement) formed only a tiny part, but with a hugely disproportionate historical visibility.

The myth and the construction of modernity

As a 'modernizing' period, the Enlightenment is said to have had some role in the general process of secularization, and the notion of the secular has almost come to embody the notion of modernity. The term secularization is at times problematic, however, and although the process of secularization does not in itself constitute a focus of this book, a brief comment upon it is perhaps necessary. At least three elements within the secularization process can be usefully isolated in the context of this book. One element is the secularization of government and social norms; another is the secularization of religious attitudes, for example the existence or widespread acceptance of the desirability of religious toleration.[69] Another mode concerns that of levels of piety, belief itself. The now defunct reason-versus-religion view of the Enlightenment held that, on the basis of the evident anticlericalism of the philosophes and a wider recourse to reason in religious thought, levels of belief were declining and piety was becoming increasingly more 'rational'. Most now agree that this view is untenable because study of the Enlightenment presents us with a Europe in which trends and counter-trends were the norm. The greater explicit recourse to reason – or at least the rhetoric of it – was certainly visible, but there is no significant evidence of declining belief. In any case, there were counter-trends to the recourse to reason, as the fideism of Bayle, the considerable growth of Pietism in the Germanic states, Holland, Scandinavia, Switzerland and the United States, the impact of Catholic Pietism (Jansenism) in France and Italy, and the birth of Methodism in England amply demonstrate.

There is no corpus of evidence to suggest that the use of reason constituted the motor of changing attitudes towards the Church. The explicit recourse to reason was visible in religious dispute within Christianity long before the arrival of the supposed deist movement. Thus those who have in effect focused on the secularization of the forms of religious discourse have focused on a certain register of discourse produced in definite circumstances. But language is a means subservient to ends, and reifying language into a force in its own right is very likely to produce distortions in our perception of intellectual change.[70] Of course, it cannot be argued that language has no role in the creation of reality, for that is indisputable. But this is a very different statement from that of according it universal causal primacy in intellectual or practical endeavour. Thus, the language of reason was the product of religious conflict and not vice versa. More accurately, we know that religious conflict was most often politico-religious conflict, and it is to the politicization of religion that we should look for one of the main motors of secularization. As Bradley and Van Kley have succinctly put it, 'religion and religious controversy acted as the chrysalis as well as the casualty of the modern political world, and ... if ideology and ideological conflicts gradually preempted religion's place in a politicized "public sphere" largely of religion's own making, they did not cease in one way or another to bear the marks of various Christian origins'.[71]

Neither can it be argued that deism was an unambiguous, explicit promoter of the secularization process, because there was a very great difference between personal conviction and public reality. One of the important consequences of the deistic outlook is that belief makes no demands upon the Church or indeed upon society. As a deist, one could, in purely spiritual terms, live a life of splendid isolation amongst great religious controversy. So (with the appropriate discretion), deism could form a potential haven for individuals, a personal route of exit from the perceived ills of traditional religion. The question we must ask, however, and one rarely posed, is whether deism was a form of personal piety with the *potential* of becoming a movement? Would the politico-religious culture of early modern Europe have been compatible with relatively large-scale public withdrawal from the pale of the Church (either Protestant or Catholic)? We certainly know that amongst all strata of society there was agreement on one fact: that the Christian ministry might or might not need reforming, but abandonment or abolition of it was unthinkable. Without the ideological tutelage of the Church to reinforce that of the state, most agreed, an acceptable social order was not possible. It was widely believed that without the Church, persons and property were not guaranteed safety. To actively advocate deism and a deist 'movement' was to advocate dissolution of one of the guarantors of property and persons.

The philosophes were clear on this point: that the unrestricted use of reason was not advocated for the lower orders because of the inherent danger posed to social order. For the intellectual elite, usually privileged and wealthy, to advocate deism was, in the final analysis, to play dice with their own social, economic and political circumstances. Clearly, only under exceptional circumstances could a general call to deism be put abroad, as for instance occurred during the French Revolution. The consensus on the need for the Church was a traditional part of the intellectual bedrock of the European intelligentsia, clerics and the wider laity. In seventeenth-century England, as in the Italian peninsula, the vast majority believed there was a benign role for Christianity within the state in terms of social control. Perhaps inevitably, fears for the social order were often expressed by those who had much to lose. Indeed, it was commonly argued that some of the 'complexities' of religious thought should not be made available to the masses in order to avoid the danger of religious 'confusion'. Such fears were acknowledged by the Cambridge Platonists Ralph Cudworth and Henry More, and by later thinkers such as Isaac Newton, Bishop William Warburton and Humphrey Prideaux. In his *A Letter to the Deists* (1696), Prideaux presented what remained in the eighteenth century the standard opinion that the Church 'is so highly necessary and useful, that it is impossible that any Government should subsist without it ... [it alone] makes a Ciment capable of uniting those societies in any manner of Stability'.[72]

English deists and philosophes such as Voltaire also sometimes identified and accepted the need for a 'benign' priestcraft – that is to say the continuation of the established Churches in one form or another for the benefit of society – but both naturally condemned the corruption of religion by crafty priests for their own ends. This public–private dichotomy of radical attitudes to religion must be emphasized if we are to understand the very impossibility of a broad deist movement, for the class outlook of the philosophes precluded it. As Voltaire declared in a letter to Frederick the Great of Prussia, in a sentiment not at all unusual amongst the philosophes, 'Your majesty will do the human race an eternal service in extirpating this infamous superstition [Christianity]. I do not say among the rabble, who are not worthy of being enlightened and who are apt for every yoke; I say among the well-bred, among those who wish to think.'[73] The unspoken logic behind this arrogant tirade was of course based on property and privilege and it would therefore be quite problematical to suggest that deism could have systematically promoted a secularization process. The fear of a social and political order not founded upon Christian precepts and policed by the Church was a consideration which continued to exercise Italian Catholic anti-curial and pro-curial thought in the eighteenth century. It was, for example, a fear sufficient to prompt Sicilian thinkers to draw back from proposing Enlightenment reforms that might have disturbed the delicate but essential symbiosis of Church and state. Thus, as Woolf has noted, in Italy few were ready to follow the likes of Alberto Radicati (Count of Passerano) from religious doubt to deism or atheism.[74] As Champion has argued in his *Pillars of Priestcraft Shaken*, the need for a state Church was also recognized by many English radicals.[75]

In conclusion, the same fear of infidelity, antichristianism and heterodoxy that produced the witchcraft craze of the sixteenth and seventeenth centuries also produced the early origins of the deist scare. In the eighteenth century, deists remained scarce and, aside from a few high-profile moments in France, they never fulfilled the role assigned to them by admirers or detractors. In the twentieth century, deism was resurrected and imbued with new force by historians and made to appear as one of the great contributors towards secular modernity.

Notes

1 C. J. Betts, *Early Deism in France. From the So-Called 'Déistes' of Lyon (1564) to Voltaire's 'Lettres philosophiques' (1734)* (The Hague, Boston and

Lancaster: Martinus Nijhoff Publishers, 1984), p. 6.

2 D. Van Kley, *The Religious Origins of the French Revolution. From Calvin to the Civil Constitution, 1560–1791* (New Haven and London: Yale University Press, 1996), p. 220.

3 D. Outram, *The Enlightenment* (Cambridge: Cambridge University Press, 1995), p. 34.

4 B. Young, *Religion and Enlightenment in Eighteenth-Century England. Theological Debate from Locke to Burke* (Oxford: Clarendon Press, 1998), pp. 4–5.

5 W. Ward, *Christianity under the Ancien Régime 1648–1789* (Cambridge: Cambridge University Press, 1999), p. 162.

6 J. A. Herrick, *The Radical Rhetoric of the English Deists. The Discourse of Skepticism, 1680–1750* (Columbia: University of South Carolina Press, 1997), pp. 6, 10, 12, 205, 211.

7 D. Daily, *Enlightenment Deism. The Foremost Threat to Christianity* (Pennsylvania: Dorrance, 1999), p. 53.

8 J. Walsh and S. Taylor: 'The Church and Anglicanism in the "Long" Eighteenth Century', in C. Haydon, J. Walsh and S. Taylor (eds), *The Church of England c.1689–c.1833* (Cambridge: Cambridge University Press, 1993), p. 21.

9 J. Champion, *The Pillars of Priestcraft Shaken* (Cambridge: Cambridge University Press, 1992), p. 233.

10 M. Jacob, *The Enlightenment. A Brief History with Documents* (Boston, Mass.: St Martin's/Bedford, 2001), p. 12. D. Berman, in his *A History of Atheism in Britain* (New York: Croom Helm, 1988), presents an analysis similar to that of Jacob.

11 M. Jacob, *The Radical Enlightenment. Pantheists, Freemasons and Republicans* (London: George Allen and Unwin, 1981), p. 27.

12 J. C. D. Clark, *English Society 1688–1832. Ideology, Social Structure and Political Practice during the Ancien Régime* (Cambridge: Cambridge University Press, 1985), p. 280.

13 Betts, *Early Deism in France*, pp. 3–4.

14 I. Rivers, *Reason, Grace and Sentiment. Vol. 2: Shaftesbury to Hume* (Cambridge: Cambridge University Press, 2000), p. 15.

15 D. Roche, *France in the Enlightenment* (Cambridge, Mass.: Harvard University Press, 1998; 1st edn 1993), pp. 380, 591.

16 R. Porter, *Enlightenment Britain and the Creation of the Modern World* (London: Penguin, 2000), pp. 112, 115.

17 J. Israel, *Radical Enlightenment. Philosophy and the Making of Modernity 1650–1750* (Oxford: Oxford University Press, 2001), p. 610.

18 E. Cassirer, *The Philosophy of the Enlightenment* (Boston: Beacon Press, 1962; 1st edn in German 1932), pp. 174–5.

19 P. McGuinness, 'Christianity not Mysterious and the Enlightenment', in P. McGuinness, A. Harrison and R. Kearney (eds), *John Toland's Christianity not Mysterious. Texts, Associated Works and Critical Essays* (Dublin: Lilliput Press, 1997), p. 237.

20 G. R. Cragg, *The Church and the Age of Reason 1648–1789* (Harmondsworth: Penguin, 1970), p. 77.

21 P. Gay, *The Enlightenment. An Interpretation. Vol. 1: The Rise of Modern*

Paganism (London: Norton, 1995; 1st edn 1966), pp. 327, 374–5.

22 I. Wade, *The Structure and Form of the French Enlightenment. Vol. 1: Esprit Philosophique* (Princeton, N.J.: Princeton University Press, 1977), p. 178.

23 W. Doyle, *Jansenism. Catholic Resistance to Authority from the Reformation to the French Revolution* (London: Macmillan, 2000), p. 73.

24 Van Kley, *The Religious Origins of the French Revolution*, p. 241.

25 For a discussion on this see, for instance, Van Kley's *The Religious Origins of the French Revolution*.

26 D. Van Kley, *The Jansenists and the Expulsion of the Jesuits from France 1757–1765* (London: Yale University Press, 1975), p. 233.

27 J. Black and R. Porter (eds), *Dictionary of Eighteenth-Century History* (London: Penguin, 1996), pp. 83–4, 151, 166, 187, 198, 538, 627.

28 Clark, *English Society*, p. 289.

29 R. Sullivan, *John Toland and the Deist Controversy* (Cambridge, Mass.: Harvard University Press, 1982), p. 190.

30 Gay, *The Rise of Modern Paganism*, pp. 375–85, Thomas Woolston, Anthony Collins, Thomas Morgan, John Toland, Conyers Middleton, Matthew Tindal, Montesquieu, Diderot, Freret, Boulanvilliers, Voltaire.

31 Cragg, *The Church and the Age of Reason*, p. 159, Tindal; p. 161, Collins and Bolingbroke.

32 J. Byrne, *Glory, Jest and Riddle. Religious Thought in the Enlightenment* (London: SCM Press, 1996), pp. 108–12, Toland, Tindal, Woolston, Collins, Shaftesbury, Paine. On Voltaire see pp. 121–2.

33 D. Nichols, *God and Government in an Age of Reason* (London and New York: Routledge, 1995), ch. 6, Bolingbroke, Blount, Collins, Toland and Tindal.

34 J. V. Price (ed.), *The History of British Deism* (8 vols, London: Routledge, 1995).

35 Sullivan, *John Toland and the Deist Controversy*, pp. 210, 214, 236.

36 Ibid., p. 232.

37 Black and Porter (eds), *Dictionary of Eighteenth-Century History*, p. 191.

38 Ibid., p. 191.

39 See, for example, M. Fitzpatrick, 'Toleration and the Enlightenment Movement', in O. Grell and R. Porter, (eds), *Toleration in Enlightenment Europe* (Cambridge: Cambridge University Press, 2000); I. Wade, *The Intellectual Origins of the French Enlightenment* (Princeton, N.J.: Princeton University Press, 1971); Wade, *The Structure and Form of the French Enlightenment*, p. 177; and Herrick, *The Radical Rhetoric of the English Deists*.

40 M. Oakeshott, *On History and Other Essays* (2nd edn, Oxford: Blackwell, 1985), pp. 38–9.

41 Van Kley, *The Religious Origins of the French Revolution*, pp. 245–6.

42 On Gibbon and Protestant historiography see my *Idol Temples and Crafty Priests. The Origins of Enlightenment Anticlericalism* (London: Macmillan, 1999).

43 In the 1996 edition of his *Reason, Ridicule and Religion. The Age of Enlightenment in England 1660–1750* (London: Thames and Hudson, 1976), p. 35, John Redwood, for instance, still describes Bayle as a sceptic, as does Ward in *Christianity under the Ancien Régime*, p. 165.

44 M. Goldie, 'Priestcraft and the Birth of Whiggism', in N. Phillipson and Q. Skinner (eds), *Political Discourse in Early Modern Britain* (Cambridge:

Cambridge University Press, 1993), p. 209.

45 Ibid.

46 E. Labrousse, *Pierre Bayle* (Oxford and New York: Oxford University Press, 1983; 1st edn 1963).

47 See, for instance, A. C. Kors, *Atheism in France, 1650–1729. Vol. 1: The Orthodox Sources of Disbelief* (Princeton, N.J.: Princeton University Press, 1990); and A. C. Kors and P. J. Korshin (eds), *Anticipations of the Enlightenment in England, France and Germany* (Philadelphia: Philadelphia University Press, 1987).

48 See Van Kley, *The Jansenists and the Expulsion of the Jesuits*; C. H. O'Brien, 'Jansenists on Civil Toleration in Mid-18th-Century France', *Theologischen Zeitschrift*, 37 (1981). On the same subject see also Doyle, *Jansenism*; and G. Adams, *The Huguenots and French Opinion 1685–1787. The Enlightenment Debate on Toleration* (Ontario: Wilfred Laurier University Press, 1991). For its wealth of detail on the French Church see also J. McManners, *Church and Society in Eighteenth-Century France* (2 vols, Oxford: Clarendon Press, 1998).

49 P. Harrison, *'Religion' and the Religions in the English Enlightenment* (Avon: Cambridge University Press, 1990).

50 M. Fitzpatrick, 'Heretical Religion and Radical Political Ideas in Late Eighteenth-Century England', in E. Hellmuth (ed.), *The Transformation of Political Culture. England and Germany in the Late Eighteenth Century* (Oxford: German Historical Institute, 1990).

51 Young, *Religion and Enlightenment in Eighteenth-Century England*.

52 Champion, *The Pillars of Priestcraft Shaken*, see especially pp. 172–3; see also his '"To Govern is to Make Subjects Believe": Anticlericalism, Politics and Power, c. 1680–1717', in *Anticlericalism in Britain c. 1500–1914* (Stroud: Sutton Publishing, 2000). On M. Goldie, see especially his 'Priestcraft and the Birth of Whiggism'. See also J. Bradley, 'The Religious Origins of Radical Politics in England, Scotland and Ireland, 1662–1800', in J. Bradley and D. Van Kley (eds), *Religion and Politics in Enlightenment Europe* (Notre Dame, Ind.: Notre Dame University Press, 2001).

53 R. Chartier, *The Cultural Origins of the French Revolution* (Durham, N.C.: Duke University Press, 1991).

54 K. Haakonssen, *Enlightenment and Religion. Rational Dissent in Eighteenth-Century Britain* (Cambridge: Cambridge University Press, 1996); T. Munck, *The Enlightenment. A Comparative Social History 1721–1794* (London: Arnold, 2000).

55 For discussion of the difficulties in trying to define deism see, for instance, D. Pailin, 'The Confused and Confusing Story of Natural Religion', *Religion*, 24 (1994); Sullivan, *John Toland and the Deist Controversy*; and Harrison, *'Religion' and the Religions*, pp. 61–2.

56 On Howard and Trenchard see also my *Idol Temples and Crafty Priests*.

57 See, for instance, Goldie, 'Priestcraft and the Birth of Whiggism'; J. G. A. Pocock, 'Post-Puritan England and the Problem of the Enlightenment', in P. Zagorin (ed.), *Culture and Politics from Puritanism to the Enlightenment* (Berkeley: University of California Press, 1980); and Champion, *Pillars of Priestcraft Shaken*.

58 J. C. Wand, *A History of the Modern Church* (London: Methuen, 1971; 1st edn 1930), p. 186.

59 On the charting of the 'career' of scepticism and atheism see, for instance, R. H. Popkin and A. Vanderjagt, *Scepticism and Irreligion in the Seventeenth and Eighteenth Centuries* (Leiden and New York: E. J. Brill, 1993); and R. H. Popkin, *The History of Scepticism from Erasmus to Spinoza* (Berkeley: University of California Press, 1979; 1st edn 1960).

60 On the public role of the figure of the atheist see, for instance, M. Hunter, 'The Problem of Atheism in Early Modern England', *Transactions of the Royal Historical Society*, 35 (1985).

61 J. Gunnell, 'The Myth of the Tradition', in P. King (ed.), *The History of Ideas* (New Jersey: Croom Helm, 1983), p. 252; originally published in the *American Political Science Review*, 78: 1 (1978). These sorts of observations were, however, also being made much earlier, as in Quentin Skinner's 'Meaning and Understanding in the History of Ideas', *History and Theory*, 8 (1969).

62 Berman, *A History of Atheism in Britain*, p. 105. For conspiracy theories of the Enlightenment see also Jacob, *The Enlightenment*; Jacob, *The Radical Enlightenment*; Redwood, *Reason, Ridicule and Religion*; and Herrick, *The Radical Rhetoric of the English Deists*.

63 See, for instance, Goldie, 'Priestcraft and the Birth of Whiggism', p. 211.

64 Trinitarianism is the doctrine that God is three persons – Father, Son and Holy Spirit – and one substance, as opposed to the Unitarian (Socinian) view of the unipersonality of God.

65 J. Priestley, *A General History of the Christian Church from the Fall of the Western Empire to the Present Time* (4 vols, Northumberland, USA, 1802–3), vol. 1, preface, p. 12 (This is the continuation of Priestley's *A General History of the Christian Church to the Fall of the Western Empire*, 1790).

66 McManners, *Church and Society in Eighteenth-Century France*, vol. 1, p. 140.

67 Van Kley, *The Jansenists and the Expulsion of the Jesuits*, p. 236.

68 Van Kley, *The Religious Origins of the French Revolution*, pp. 268, 309.

69 On toleration in the Enlightenment see the very useful collection of articles in Grell and Porter (eds), *Toleration in Enlightenment Europe*.

70 This has been a criticism, for instance, of J. G. A. Pocock's view of intellectual change advanced in his *The Ancient Constitution and the Feudal Law. A Study of English Historical Thought in the Seventeenth Century* (Cambridge: Cambridge University Press, 1957). See D. Boucher's *Texts in Context. Revisionist Methods for Studying the History of Ideas* (Lancaster and Dodrecht: Nijhoff, 1985).

71 Bradley and Van Kley (eds), *Religion and Politics in Enlightenment Europe*, pp. 36–7.

72 Humphrey Prideaux, *A Letter to the Deists* (London, 1696), pp. 80–1.

73 Quoted in Daily, *Enlightenment Deism*, p. 44.

74 On the concerns of Sicilian thinkers to preserve the balance of Church and state deemed essential to an acceptable political order see S. Woolf, *History of Italy 1700–1860* (London: Routledge, 1991; 1st edn 1979), pp. 78–9, 139.

75 See, for instance, John Toland, *Tetradymus. Containing ... Clidophorus; or, of the Exoteric and Esoteric Philosophy ... of the Antients* (London, 1720).

2

Historians, religion
and the historical record

The origins of Enlightenment anticlericalism

The politico-religious convulsions across Europe from the Reformation until the eighteenth century were numerous and bloody. The resulting religious divisions were enshrined in confessional states, but, as with the cases of Protestant England and Catholic France, religious minorities remained persecuted and disabled. It would have been truly miraculous if many Christians had not wearied of the constant conflict between and within opposing Churches and begun to question whether war and persecution should really be a feature of religion. Although Christianity certainly underwent change in this period, no antichristian religion or atheist groundswell arose to challenge it. This is, of course, not to say that atheism did not exist, but if it did, it remained a private matter and texts written by atheists quickly gained infamy by the fact of their rarity, and the same can be said of deism. The problem is that the Enlightenment is famous for its challenge to the Church, and the absence of antichristian movements in the immediate period preceding the Enlightenment has been frustrating for many historians. Being convinced that the Enlightenment – as traditionally understood – had to have had radical roots, there was always the danger that wishful thinking might mistake a few swallows for a summer. As Patrick Riley has put it in relation to the search for the origins of Rousseau's theory of the General Will, '[w]hen one is looking for something – influence, for example – one fails to find it only if one is lacking in ingenuity ... [and] that same ingenuity is ingenious enough to construct the object of its search, and to take that construction for a discovery'.[1]

In the absence of proof for the existence of antichristian

movements, however, it has still been possible to induce a number of sceptical or religiously radical texts to 'talk' to each other, producing an often fictitious or suppositious relationship with each other, and so constructing the semblance of a radical tradition or movement. This procedure was adopted, for instance, in Wade's *Intellectual Origins of the French Enlightenment* (1971). Having discussed various 'schools' of thought, but viewing Italy as the originator of the 'movement', Wade sums up by claiming that '[t]hroughout the closing years of the sixteenth century, and during the whole of the seventeenth down to the opening years of the eighteenth, there was always one or other of these groups to carry on the free-thinking tradition'. After informing us that this movement also continued into the eighteenth century, so influencing the major thinkers of the French Enlightenment, Wade then defines its status: 'Freethinking is thus one of the most consistent, coherent, and continuous intellectual movements in Europe we have'.[2]

Yet the story is not quite the same from Betts. In his *Early Deism in France* (1984), he illustrates how the contention that deist thought had a continuous history from the late sixteenth century cannot be proven.[3] So, apparently, deism did not form part of the great tradition affirmed by Wade. He also reveals how relatively few French deist writings there were in the first two decades of the century, and how 'free-thought was either on the retreat or only in mild disagreement with orthodoxy' in the period 1725–41.[4] Usefully, he also reminds the reader that '[t]here may be considerable doubt whether particular writers are Christians tending to deism or deists sympathetic to Christianity', and that 'in about 1715 deism comprised a combination of Christianity and rationalism'. Clearly, then, the historical record and the way it is approached can yield quantitatively and qualitatively different results. Betts, however, still adheres to the idea of a broad deistic or radically religious movement of sorts, for he informs us that '[it] is a matter of history that, roughly at the beginning of the eighteenth century, large numbers of individuals were in the process of detaching themselves from Christian belief and replacing it by a religious attitude in which the belief in God was independent, at least outwardly, of Church or Bible'.[5] Unfortunately, he does not reveal the source for this epoch-making 'matter of history' that, in his account, is formative in the development of the Enlightenment. Perhaps needless to say, however, there is no substantial proof for such an assertion.

46

So far we have been considering what might be termed the dominant trend in Enlightenment studies: the positing of a tradition of radical or extra-Christian Enlightenment roots. We must now, briefly, comment on the claim that Christian texts might, at least in part, be responsible for the development of the enlightened religious outlook. Kors, for instance, has claimed that '[i]t was, above all, within the deeply Christian learned culture of those years [late seventeenth and eighteenth centuries] that there occurred inquiries and debates that generated the components of atheistic thought'.[6] Elsewhere but on the same subject he explains that his thesis 'is precisely that in the late seventeenth and early eighteenth centuries, it was works written from unimpeachable motives, to guarantee the faith, that in fact "cleared the way" for the conceivability of atheistic philosophy'.[7] Given their substantial claims, Kors *et al.*[8] can bewail the fact that, hitherto, '[t]he agency granted to the theological and religious movements of the preceding era had been at most that of an indirect facilitator ... opening a breach exploited by forms of rationalism, naturalism and religious skepticism'.[9] Unfortunately, we are left to guess as to how to interpret the phrase 'cleared the way'. In sum, within elite debate, Kors and others have detected Christian ideas and positions which could, potentially, be turned against Christianity. Indeed, according to Kors, refutations of God (as hypothetical positions in orthodox writings) abounded by the late seventeenth century because of the theological polemic on the issue of the proper philosophical structure for Christian doctrine.[10] We may perhaps understand the term 'abounded' as somewhat of an exaggeration, but even if this were not the case, nowhere do Kors or others present evidence for influence. Hence, although the study of such learned works gives us an insight into the potential contradictions of thought at the time, they cannot be considered, in themselves, as proof of the exertion of influence upon Enlightenment origins.

One traditionally broad avenue of enquiry into the wider origins of the Enlightenment has been to chart the career of reason, the tool the philosophes viewed as central in the struggle for enlightenment. The explicit recourse to the tool of reason in Protestant religious discourse increased in the seventeenth century, so much so that by 1700 the criterion of reason was present in a significant proportion of Protestant writings and was especially visible in England. It has traditionally been argued that, in the late seventeenth century, critics of the Church seized upon the tool of reason and turned it, to significant effect, against the Church. Reason thus became the watchword of the philosophes against the miraculous, the superstitious and backward tradition. As Cragg in his *Reason and Authority in the Eighteenth Century* (1964) put it, religious writers 'conceded the preeminence of reason; they were prepared to test revelation, as well as its evidences in miracle and prophecy, by the standards which reason suggested'.[11] By comparison, in orthodox Catholic writings the use of reason was very much more limited, although more frequently present in dissident writings, including those of Jansenists. One of the key problems with tracing the career of reason as a guide to early modern religious change is that it was above all a polemical tool, and one with no defined content or manner of application. As such, its use was often indiscriminate and *ad hoc*; it could be utilized by anyone in almost any circumstance and cannot be, in itself, termed a sufficient guide to the identification of religious radicalism.

Where links between Christianity and enlightened thinking have been explored, they have most often been based upon precocious elements of elite theological discourse, rather than upon more common-or-garden or overtly sectarian polemics. Precocious movements and tendencies within Anglicanism have often been a focus of attention because of the perceived dynamism of religious change in early modern England, and also because of the recognition by most that developments there marked the earliest phase of the Enlightenment. Thus the Cambridge Platonists (1630s–80s, the most notable element of the Latitudinarian tendency) have been selected for detailed study on the basis of their desire for (relative) tolerance and their conception of reason as the arbiter both of natural and revealed religion. There is, however, little evidence so far adduced that the Cambridge Platonists or other Protestant writers such as Lord Herbert of Cherbury (1583–1648, traditionally known as the 'father' of deism) had any influence upon the development of English deism at all. Indeed, as Pailin has noted, '[a]part from Charles Blount the so-called deists hardly mention Herbert'.[12] So, Herbert may be made to fit neatly into the 'tradition', where Herbert's writings are made to talk to others, but there is no evidence at all of influence. Pailin is certainly correct to point out the lack of references to Herbert, but most importantly – as we shall see below – even if deists had cited Herbert, it would not necessarily constitute what historians very often cite as influence.

Charting the career of reason may, ostensibly, seem a search for the 'modern' amongst the traditional. Yet such a search only tells us substantially what we already know: the impasse of religious disagreement and concomitant polemical stalemate in seventeenth-century Europe resulted in an elevation of the 'objective' tool of reason in religious polemic. In other words, for Enlightenment studies to focus on the career of reason is to focus more upon a symptom than a cause, upon a feature of religious polemic caused by and reflecting wide religious division. If this is the case, some comments on the traditional understanding of those religious divisions are therefore appropriate.

The end of the so-called mid-seventeenth-century European crisis – the widespread wars and revolts of the mid-century and especially the Thirty Years War (1618–48) – has traditionally been considered as a watershed marking the end of the 'last great European conflict in which religion was a vital element'. Most commentators have also been obliged to state the obvious and note that 'the substantial issues which concerned the protagonists were not directly religious', but of course economic and political.[13] This was certainly apparent to many contemporaries and participants in those wars. Thus, in estimating the factors which contributed to the formation of seventeenth-century anticlericalism, it is an inescapable – but frustratingly difficult to measure – fact that the ideological form of those wars undoubtedly caused many to ask whether Jesus had ever intended Christian to fight Christian. The wars ended in 1648 with the Peace of Westphalia, by which time most rulers desired peace in which to recover from the protracted holocaust and reaffirm their rule. Thus historians have felt able to pronounce that the 'Reformation age of astonishing religious development and upheaval, but also of religious darkness, was coming to a close'.[14]

This traditional explanation surrounding the nature and significance of the sixteenth- and seventeenth-century wars and conflicts, however, is based partly upon assumption. It depends upon the assumption that the height of politico-religious crisis was reached around the mid seventeenth century, and that this was also considered to be the case by Enlightenment thinkers. There is certainly sufficient evidence to claim that many Christians before or around the mid-century were disillusioned by divisions within

Christianity and its political use. But what evidence is there to substantiate the claim that late-seventeenth- and eighteenth-century thinkers considered that post-Reformation 'religious darkness was coming to a close'? For those Dissenters struggling against the Anglican Church and state, for Huguenots and Jansenists in France and for other religious minorities across Europe, bitter and at times bloody religious conflict and persecution were still the order of the day. From this point of view, claims about the end of the mid-seventeenth-century crisis bringing a vision of peace to Christendom should not provide legitimation for ignoring or minimizing the importance of politico-religious conflicts yet to occur in the late seventeenth and eighteenth centuries.

So, it is time to return to the historical record and give more weight to the general politico-religious background in which late-seventeenth-century English thinkers lived. To give an example: it has been established that in the two decades after 1605 the pamphlet controversy with Rome alone saw over 500 anti-Catholic publications appear in England.[15] Many of these were pamphlets and short tracts and were relatively popular in style. This is a substantial figure, yet needs to be revised and increased. It needs increasing because not all polemical tracts and pamphlets were anti-Catholic; some were anti-Puritan. It needs revision because some of the publications, notably those of Puritans, were deliberately dual-edged, ostensibly anti-Catholic, but also directed at what was considered the quasi-Catholicism of the Stuart kings. This great polemical effort to delegitimize religious opponents was not unique to England, but formed a central part of the religious competition between Protestants, Catholics and dissident thinkers across Europe.

With this scenario in mind, the term anticlericalism has a much broader application than is usually accorded it in the context of Enlightenment studies. We need to be quite clear on this point. For the century and a half prior to the Enlightenment, for the first time Europeans experienced permanent, institutionalized anticlericalism: Protestants and Catholics were anticlerical with regard to each other, and radical Protestants and Protestant established Churches likewise. As I have illustrated elsewhere, these permanent divisions saw the development of relatively sophisticated anticlerical theories, very often comparative and popular in style,[16] developed and aimed at religious opponents. Those who have searched for the roots of modernity have looked insufficiently at intra-Christian polemical material because of their presupposition that evidence of modernity should take the form of secular or secularizing thought linked to a pronounced development of reason as a critical tool.

Perhaps the most vital battleground of the Christian polemical terrain was history. Protestants, Catholics and their subdivisions sought to demonstrate that the history of their religious opponents was, like that of pagan religions, little more than the history of priestcraft: religious fraud conducted in order to acquire wealth, political power and status, keeping the laity ignorant of true religion. So, part of the ideological heritage of the sixteenth and seventeenth centuries was a deeply ingrained comparative polemico-historical approach which remained in place until at least the end of the eighteenth century, and was not, as many have asserted,[17] the product of the Enlightenment. There is no proof whatever, especially in England, that the proliferation of Christian anticlerical theories in widely available and relatively lowbrow cheap editions were any less influential in politico-religious terms than those of the tiny number of so-called eighteenth-century deists. Anti-Catholics, Dissenters and other religious dissidents were loudly proclaiming the historically demonstrated priestcraft of Catholicism and Anglicanism, and in the process promoting a virulent anticlericalism. In fact, as we shall see, in the life of John Toland it is possible to see the transference of his Dissenter anti-Anglican historical polemic (at some point after 1696 he adopted deistic views) to a new target, that of the Christian ministry in general. However, this is a very different statement from a claim for causal influence upon the formation of the Enlightenment: the anticlerical ideological tool of English dissent was merely that, a tool. In themselves tools cannot exert influence; they must be wielded in definite circumstances.

Emphatically, then, it cannot be said that the dissenting polemical tradition led to the development of the Enlightenment priestcraft theory. But neither should the dismissal of such putative causal links be the occasion to dismiss the general politico-religious background we have identified, for, in conjunction with other events, existing traditions or trends in thought can serve to hamper or aid the development of new trends. England, above all, saw a proliferation of various varieties of vicious anticlerical diatribes, which, as we will see, could seem remarkably like the anti-clericalism of philosophes.

John Toland, Pierre Bayle and the problem of influence

If it cannot be asserted that the sceptical/radical tradition or the Christian priestcraft theory produced Enlightenment anti-christianism, where should we search for the spurs to such developments? After all, we know that scientific developments of the period certainly did not automatically militate against the Church or religion,[18] and science and religion in the lives of leading scientists such as Joseph Priestley often went hand in hand throughout the century. Another element of the matrix usually adduced to explain the rise of anticlerical – even irreligious – thinking and the desire for religious pluralism has been that of geographic discovery. This influence, as it has been usually explained, was the realization that morally just societies could exist outside Christianity, that is to say without the Christian clergy which had claimed its role as indispensable in the formation and maintenance of such societies. The problem with this sort of approach is that the identification of influence is never simple, and the theory can easily (and I think more credibly) be turned on its head. It was rather perhaps that our perception of the new Pacific island discoveries was positively coloured by contemporary negative views on the history and role of the clergy, civilization 'weariness' (famously in the work of Rousseau), and even a desire for toleration itself. Thus, Pacific island culture was elevated to a higher level of esteem than was the case with the discovery of 'exotic' cultures long before the Enlightenment. From this perspective, the island societies were confirmation of what was already felt rather than providing any original spur to the critique of the old regime. Broadly speaking, then, the crux of the matter is to determine the relationship between contemporary events and contemporary thought.

We know that Christian anticlericalism and cynicism grew in the early modern period or at least became more visible, encompassed in thousands of publications. We also know that some of those writings were, if generalized, as devastatingly anticlerical as those contained within elite traditions of sceptical thought. This is to say that, in deciding to move away from dissenting thought to a more freethinking position, Toland and a few other radicals had no immediate need to search scarce atheistic writings for anticlerical theory. In a moment of need, they reached for the handiest suitable tool which seemed sufficient for the immediate task: in their case, common-or-garden anticlerical notions. This, of course, is only a contextual example of the fact that once an idea is committed to paper, the author loses control of it, for such dissident Christian critiques were originally developed as necessary tools for the advancement of Christianity, not its abolition. The fact that English radicals commonly embellished and justified their core anticlerical notions by quoting renowned authors we should understand as mere sensible academic practice rather than evidence of influence.

Traditionally, John Toland's *Christianity not Mysterious* has been understood as a deist work. Yet it can more convincingly be demonstrated that his aim was to show how true Christianity could only be found within the confines of the apostolic – presbyterian – model of the Church. For Toland, shortly after the biological demise of the Apostles and their simple non-hierarchical Church, the clergy had mystified religion in order to gain a monopoly over it and the minds of the people. What is truly startling is not the content of Toland's book, but rather the refusal of modern historians to acknowledge the evidence that, at this time, Toland was known as a Unitarian (Socinian), basing his theological outlook on Unitarian views and supported in his views by, amongst others, a leading Quaker.[19] That he later became what some have termed more deistic (accepting for the moment all the vagaries of that term) in his views is not under contention here. The point is that *Christianity not Mysterious* was a head-on reforming attack on Anglicanism. That it has been considered a deist work is not surprising, for without study of the dissenting polemical tradition, at first sight dissenting works of this period seem to be written by outright enemies of religion. Toland, as other Dissenters, brought reason enthusiastically to his aid, and we should be very surprised if he did not do so. But, as we shall see, there is still nothing at all contained in *Christianity not Mysterious* which is not consistent with dissenting politico-religious polemic of the period. This remains the case even with the fact that, as part of normal dissenting prudence, it fails to attack Anglicanism by name, which has been an integral part of the rationale behind claims that it attacked the Christian ministry in general.

For his intended audience – Dissenters and other religious dissidents – there was simply no need to exempt the presbyterian or apostolic-style Church from his charge of irredeemable priestcraft, because this was one of the polemical givens of the period. But texts, of course, never have only one audience. Other audiences for *Christianity not Mysterious* included staunch and ever-vigilant Anglican clergy, who interpreted the text according to *their* own outlook. Many or most Anglicans knew that Toland never intended to damn dissenting clergy and presbyterianism with his accusation, but for many Anglicans this was of little import. For them, to damn all established or hierarchical Churches since not long after the days of Christ was, in fact, the same thing as condemning the Christian ministry *per se*. Thus Toland was deemed antichristian and a danger to society. In this manner the manufacture of the myth of the deist movement had begun. The fate of Toland was not, however, unique. Others suffered similar 'misreadings', most famously the Huguenot Pierre Bayle.

Bayle's *Dictionnaire historique et critique* (1st edn 1695–97) was written and published in the same period of religious crises and persecution. Bayle not only had to flee religious persecution himself, but lost his older brother Jacob, a Huguenot pastor, who died in a dungeon at the hands of those seeking to bring about his 'conversion'. His *Dictionnaire* quickly acquired recognition for its learned and often daring content. As Toland's *Christianity not Mysterious*, the *Dictionnaire* became the touchstone for deists, sceptics and other religious radicals, yet, during the writing of the *Dictionnaire*, Bayle continued as a genuinely devoted member of the Reformed Church.[20] As a Protestant who had suffered personal tragedy on account of religious intolerance, it is hardly surprising that he advocated toleration. Like *Christianity not Mysterious*, the *Dictionnaire* had, potentially, several audiences. In practice, however, the potential was of a very different order from that in England, in which Dissenters were bitter and disappointed by the limited gains of the Toleration Act (1689), but remained undefeated and full of energy. The Revocation of the Edict of Nantes, the accompanying brutal Dragonnades and the years of persecution which had preceded it, could only be experienced as a decisive defeat for French Protestants. For those historians who wish to chart the career of reason as a symptom of the times rather than a cause, the comparison of Toland and Bayle in 1695–97 is instructive.

Where Toland vaunted reason as the arbiter of right religion and the proof of the iniquity of established Christian ministries, from Bayle's perspective the career of reason looked very different indeed. For Huguenot refugees who had lost family, possessions, livelihoods and property, the seventeenth-century attempt to use reason as a tool for bringing about right religion or at least Christian reconciliation had proven to be a collective catastrophe. For Bayle, at that time, whether it represented majority Huguenot thought or not, it was important to re-evaluate reason. Thus, in his article on reason in the *Dictionnaire* Bayle explains that reason is an extremely powerful critical tool, but as a defence of faith it is fatally flawed, for reason can always find a method to doubt belief, is capable of inventing difficulties, but incapable of finding solutions. Consequently, he explains that the only refuge for sincere Christians is faith, and faith alone. By faith, however, 'Bayle meant belief in the basic Calvinist doctrines, based on the authority of revelation, and the mysteries common to Catholics and Protestants'.[21] For Bayle, the doctrines of the orthodox faith were above reason: they could not be understood by reason and therefore could be neither proved nor disproved by reason. This was, of course, hardly a novel sentiment for a Calvinist, but to sceptics, deists and many Catholics he could appear to be a sly sceptic vaunting the power of reason and the defencelessness of Christianity under its assault. Thus, in France, Bayle was unfortunate enough to find strange bedfellows in sceptics, radicals and other 'infidels'.

It is well known that most or all of the philosophes applauded Bayle as an enemy of the Church and claimed him as one of their own. But the ironic thing is that, as Sandberg has pointed out, when Voltaire and the Encyclopedists repeated Bayle's arguments and comments, they were, in turn, repeating material which Bayle himself had taken from the orthodox Calvinist rationalism of his predecessors and contemporaries and simply repeated and embroidered.[22] By means of the philosophes and many, many others, Bayle's *Dictionnaire* found its way into more private libraries than any other single work in the century. As Rex has noted, 'It was one of the most significant influences upon the *Encyclopédie*, although the fact could seldom be acknowledged'.[23]

It is inconceivable that most of the philosophes, who publicly counted him as one of their own, did not know Bayle was a devoted Christian. Writing in the United Provinces, Bayle had no need of dissimulation for the censor, so his readers knew very well that it could not be claimed he was hiding his radicalism behind a veneer of faith. As Sandberg has written, 'those critics who have placed Bayle outside the religious context [i.e. sceptical context] have had to assume that he was forced by the power of the state or the Church to adopt a veneer of orthodoxy in order to get his books published or in order to avoid a fine or imprisonment ... but Bayle wrote and published all of his works in the Republic of Holland and not in France.' The Dutch authorities accepted the principle of religious toleration, and there existed a freedom of the press that was, for all practical purposes, complete. 'It seems evident, then, that if Bayle had really desired to attack the orthodox faith, he could easily have done so directly.'[24] That Bayle was forthright, even radical in his Calvinist views is in no doubt (his arguments for toleration included Muslims). The condemnation of some elements of his thought by some leading French Protestants further served to make him appear an enemy of the Church, rather than its victim. Modern historians should perhaps marvel at how he managed to keep his faith in such harrowing times, but also note how the historical record can be so potentially misleading. From the English perspective the career of reason might seem to have been the natural direction for progressive Christianity. Clearly Bayle did not agree.

The nature of a writer's opinion at the time of writing is not, then, necessarily the same as the reception of his/her printed opinion. As Labrousse has succinctly put it, the 'history of ideas shows that, once removed from its original socio-historical context, and read as the vehicle of a universal message, a work exerts its greatest influence not through the mechanical repetition of the exact reflection of its ideas, but through the ambiguities, misconceptions and anachronisms which find their way into its interpretation. The posthumous influence of Bayle's ideas provides a particularly striking example of the workings of this law.'[25]

Of course, it might be replied that Bayle was just an individual. We know, however, that fideism was a significant and credible theological position of the period, and one subscribed to by some considerable numbers. More importantly, given the tolerant views of Bayle and others like him, fideism can hardly be written off as necessarily religiously 'backward', as has too often been the case within Enlightenment studies. As we shall see, the Jansenist movement of mid-eighteenth-century France has also traditionally been defined as religiously backward.[26] Like Bayle, many committed Jansensists too had little regard for the role of reason in religion, but in those years they developed a specifically Christian foundation for the toleration of Protestants. We should also remind ourselves that most of those progressive radicals, Dissenters and Latitudinarians in late-seventeenth- and early-eighteenth-century England never advocated the unrestricted toleration of Catholics, a fact which, in the modernity stakes, certainly does not put them ahead of mid-century French Jansenists.

In summary, we can say that intellectual developments – in this case Bayle's response to religious persecution – might not seem, if read on a purely textual level, to be a new intellectual development at all, but rather a resurgence of the supposed sceptical tradition stretching back to Renaissance Italy. Instead, we can see that contemporary thought began to 'catch up' with past sceptical thinkers. That is to say, from a range of fairly common-or-garden possible politico-religious responses to the pressure of events and developments, one happened to be chosen that ostensibly resembled a known option within past intellectual frameworks. We might term this a context-interactive or organic process of intellectual change, which is of course very different from the traditional notion of influence proceeding in some disembodied intellectual form from one text to another. Once Bayle was deemed to have opened the breach for Enlightenment scepticism, leading to what many have considered to be a centrally important feature of the dawn of modernity, the 'career' of scepticism was identified. Turning to England, if, on the other hand (and it seems difficult to refute), Toland and the very few other English Dissenters and religious dissidents who became deists began from the traditional radical Protestant critique of established Churches, we could in one sense claim they were influenced by that Christian tradition. But they were, of course, not guided by that influence to attack Christianity, but rather by events. We can speak of a tradition here only in the sense that it was a polemical tradition of potential use for various politico-religious ends. As a polemical tradition it did not possess social force in itself, but was rather an expression of social forces.

Enlightenment from within or without Christianity?

If elements of traditional Enlightenment studies are open to question, we should perhaps reconsider the very basis for Enlightenment studies: the historical record and the characterizations we extract from it. Patrick Collinson has noted that political history has suffered from a retrospective approach, with the construction of developmental stages which may only be the invention of historians.[27] There are a number of reasons why there may be disagreement on how to characterize and divide up the historical chain into definable periods. Amongst them we can include career interests and specialisms of historians, cultural outlook and ideological factors which may prompt one characterization of a period rather than another. But do these academic disagreements matter? How important is it to address the question of whether, as Peter Gay argued in the 1960s, the Enlightenment came from outside Christianity or was a development from within; or, to cite another example, whether the Enlightenment is to be understood as a clash between reason and religion? If the only issue was the clash between opposing characterizations of the intellectual life of eighteenth-century Europe, with the historical data to provide the ultimate arbiter, then a process of academic conflict and final resolution might be expected. Unfortunately the issue of cutting the chain of history into recognizable chunks is not so one-dimensional. Once a historian has characterized a period, subsequent research agendas (the formation of questions/approaches to historical data) will be generated from inside that general overview. Now, as is accepted by almost all historians, the questions one asks will determine the type of evidence one elicits from the historical record. This is partly because there is too much data for it all to be examined, and, in any case, the same data may be quite legitimately examined from a variety of viewpoints.

One example of particular importance here is the traditional dominance of the characterization of France as a confessional absolutist state. Acceptance of the reality of absolute central rule – rather than viewing it as royal rhetoric – has predisposed historians to preclude or downplay the existence of powerful, broad-based debates on the nature of society's political and religious fundamentals. As a consequence, historians have also viewed the struggles of French *parlements* and church factions as relatively less important in the formation of enlightened thought than might otherwise be the case, for, if debate on the Church was not significant, how could it influence the formation of enlightened thought? In terms of understanding intellectual change and its catalysts, therefore, the question of characterization of historical periods is a very important one. To cite another instance, part of the canon of Enlightenment studies from the 1930s to the 1960s was decisively overturned in the late 1960s by Gay's argument that the Enlightenment was a development external to Christianity, a recovery of nerve of free-thinkers. Carl Becker's influential *The Heavenly City of the Eighteenth-Century Philosophers* (1932) took the view that the philosophes were significantly influenced by Christianity even more than they were consciously aware or prepared to admit. Thus the Enlightenment was at least partly a development from existing Christian thought rather than an imposition from without. From the 1960s, however, the general understanding has been that the Enlightenment was influenced by classical and in part Renaissance thinkers, so tending to eclipse Christian influence. This canon, however, is based on mere assumption, above all on the basis of the authorities cited in the writings of the enlightened.

As we have noted, however, citing authorities is more an indication of standard academic or polemical practice and the need to justify arguments, than any necessary gauge of the influences acting upon any given author. Thus the idea that the promotion of a 'civic religion' by some Enlightenment thinkers was the outcome of reading classical philosophico-political texts is a logical but rather simplistic conception of influence. We know that there were long-standing grievances against state and Church which were more likely to provoke writers to express the desire for a different kind of Church in a different kind of society. Most of the radical writers, along with the clergy, government and monarch, also accepted that the Church was necessary to promote an 'acceptable' social peace: without the public assertion of *post mortem* rewards and punishments, what value would oaths have had? Public and private oaths were still considered to be one of the bedrocks of social order and justice. With all these considerations in mind – and for the moment saving comment upon openly 'atheistic' texts – we must ask ourselves of what use has the outside–inside Christianity distinction been in relation to the origins and development of the Enlightenment? It has, in fact, been a very damaging approach, because at the behest of the modernity thesis it has served to direct research energies disproportionately towards radical texts and 'traditions'. It has also served to conceal somewhat the complexity of social development. As is increasingly recognized, there is no single radical movement or school of thought which can explain the genesis or development of the Enlightenment or at least the enlightened religious outlook. In human activity, whether collective or individual, there is often a world of difference between intentionality and final outcome – that is to say, some who wished to promote Christian piety (such as Bayle) unwittingly helped to undermine the traditional religious forms. As Kors has opined, one must consider how 'a complex culture generated its own antithesis, the possibility of which it always had carried within'.[28]

On subjects which were politically, morally, religiously (or in other ways) 'sensitive', many writers would have naturally wanted to avoid mentioning the influence of living individuals, or indeed for a variety of other reasons may have deemed such admission inappropriate for publication. If influence from a past writer was considered not to be acceptable in public eyes, then identification of the source was also naturally to be avoided. Equally as common was the tendency for writers to think it unnecessary to inform us of influences acting upon them because the context or tradition in question was already widely understood, yet something hardly so clear to posterity. The problem of identifying the influence of Christian thought in enlightened works is also compounded by the frequent 'failure' of the authors to acknowledge Christian influences for other reasons. As Kors has noted, such a lack of attribution was common:

> Because Enlightenment authors themselves sought to contra-distinguish their epoch categorically from the 'orthodox' past, acknowledging as a source of their ideas only, for the most part, what was new in the seventeenth century, scholars often have begun with a similar assumption about influence. What was not part of the 'new philosophy' of the seventeenth century was somehow (however bizarre the assumption appears when stated baldly) without 'positive' influence.[29]

We have said that one of the canons in the study of the enlightened religious outlook has been a teleological approach. To highlight one thinker amongst many, we can note the work of Wade, who traces the intellectual tradition of the philosophes, the 'free-thinking tradition', back to 1384 and the Paduan school.[30] Writers such as Wade have posited schools or movements of thought on the basis of an ostensible similarity of ideas between writers and have presented that 'tradition' as a dynamic within history: as primary causality in the rise of the modern world and modern mind. This type of reification has been very comforting for historians, for it

resulted in the finding that their preferred view of the Enlightenment had 'real, objective' intellectual roots. Lest this discussion be
misunderstood merely as an attack on those who claim the Enlightenment was a phenomenon of extra-Christian origin, we should
note that a similar difficulty is also present in the analyses of theo-
rists such as Kors. The problem has been, he argues, that the sources
of the Enlightenment have been 'sought in those thinkers of prior
generations who most resembled philosophes, Aufklärers and the
"modern" minds of the mid- to late eighteenth century'.[31] As we
have seen, instead he posits that earlier Christian works, 'written
from unimpeachable motives of guaranteeing the faith, in fact
"cleared the way" for the conceivability of atheistic philosophy'.[32]
If 'cleared the way' means influence, however, then this must be
demonstrated or argued for rather than assumed.

Nevertheless, the position of Kors *et al.* was a welcome move
farther away from some of the quasi-conspiracy notions of Enlightenment origins. It was also a step towards a socially broader, more
context-based view of origins and, importantly, recognized the
potentially important consequences of the difference between intentionality and result in Christian polemic. The problem remains,
however, that the question of proof of influence is insufficiently
addressed. Some historians are still insufficiently critical of one-
dimensional accounts of intellectual change, in which intellectual
'traditions' and schemes of thought in themselves possess the power
to bring about large-scale intellectual, religious and social change. If
we too, for the moment, accept the notion that texts in themselves
can possess identifiable social force, we have to ask how we can
account for unintended consequences all too apparent, for example,
in the reception of Bayle's writings. To say 'unintended' is to argue
that, unknown to the author, his work contained more than one
message, and that once the arguments were penned he lost control
of their direction and other latent messages therein made themselves
felt upon the minds of some readers. Put in this way, the argument
seems to be postmodern in orientation: that texts themselves are
history, but the interpretation of them is a matter for the individual
reader and widely divergent readings are all potentially more or less
valid. But I cannot accept that texts are, in themselves, history, for
there is always something beyond texts which the very fact of them
being written, purchased/acquired and read in definite circumstances attests to.

Texts, of course, only represent what the writer saw fit to tell us, which is a very different thing from knowing the writer's thoughts. In themselves, then, texts will not usually enable us to reconstruct reliably the wider social context of their conception and gestation. Historians can also hardly escape that fact that highbrow texts are rarely fully representative of the intellectual outlook of wider society. Selecting the most 'advanced', most 'modern' texts has of course been a preoccupation in Enlightenment studies. In this way, these more 'bold' texts can seem to be continuations of past radical 'traditions', so seemingly demonstrating the inherent intellectual/social force of that 'tradition'. Poor Bayle, we may add, wrote so incisively that he had to be made to fit into such a tradition. As we have seen, it is very difficult to argue that Enlightenment thinkers came to their conclusions entirely without the influence of the Christian society in which they lived. Yet to argue that Christianity exerted decisive or fundamental influence upon characteristic elements of Enlightenment thought by means of certain relatively elite theological texts is just as problematic. Part of any solution to such a potential impasse lies in the direction taken by Munck in his *The Enlightenment* (2000), in which he demonstrates that our understanding of the Enlightenment can be enriched from the vantage point of more ordinary people. In particular, Munck demonstrates how mistaken is the common claim that the Enlightenment, as an intellectual and cultural phenomenon, affected only a very tiny minority, instead illustrating how major elements of its aspirations were shared by the middling sort.[33]

The elite and the written record

Most of the research into Enlightenment thought is based primarily on printed records. The eighteenth-century boom in publishing has meant that we have a rich legacy to mull over, yet, in reality, it represents some of the thoughts of only a tiny fraction of the population. We therefore have massive, even overwhelming gaps in the historical record. In arriving at understandings of the intellectual life of the eighteenth century, however, historians have paid little explicit attention to this problem. The 'rise of irreligion' thesis – the foundation of traditional Enlightenment studies – is thus based on a tiny sample of writers and an assumption about the thought of many more individuals not represented in the historical record.

Consequently, this chapter proceeds from the premise that historians have for long been analysing and reporting on the illusion, the ostensible appearance, of a growth of non-Christian or heretical thinking. To put it another way, historians have allowed themselves to become prisoners of the facts of print culture: assuming relatively greater numbers of heterodox and antichristian (considered 'proto-modern') tracts in print to be a reliable barometer of intellectual change. Yet there is no necessary direct connection between texts in print and thoughts in heads; and various factors can account for changes in print culture.

The fact remains that the number of overtly Christian publications (sermons, tracts, theological treatises, histories, Bibles, etc.) expanded vastly in the eighteenth century and continued to dwarf those of the enlightened type. Is the great statistical difference between the two publication categories of any real significance? What might it tell us about the intellectual tenor of the period? If we were to use the same barometer of intellectual life as those historians who have viewed the relative rise in publications of a heterodox or antichristian type as an indicator of growth of irreligion or heterodoxy, we should conclude that, overall, society remained very heavily, indeed overwhelmingly committed to Christianity and the supposed antichristian threat amounted to little more than the proverbial wasp around the lion's head. Bare print statistics, of course, tell us potentially very little about the centrally important concept of the texts' significance and influence, which depended on the subject at hand, the cost of publication, the condition of public opinion and, crucially, the audience to which it was addressed. Too often the existence of persistently large numbers of Christian publications has been held to be quite irrelevant to research into the Enlightenment. The result has been that run-of-the-mill religious tracts – although perhaps highly critical of the established Church – have for the most part been consigned to the dustbin of historical records because they do not fit the character of 'progressive' enlightened texts.

Of course there are justifiable reasons why the intellectual history of the eighteenth century or of any other period should often be a specialized pursuit, very selective in its delvings into the historical record. Sometimes this is because the historical record is too extensive, and at times because potentially abstruse ideas and debates very often need to be charted with as few complications as possible.

But this should not be justification for concentrating almost exclusively on elite writings and implicitly stating that, in relationship to investigation of the Enlightenment, the rest of the historical record – or indeed the lack of it – is unworthy of examination or consideration. As we have seen, it has by no means yet been established that the formation and transmission of culture is exclusively a one-way top-down process. This has, nevertheless, been a dominant assumption within Enlightenment studies, perhaps even partly a natural outcome of the nature of the subject matter itself. Thus studies of history from below, often seen as challenging the top-down elite-orientated view of history, have been welcomed by many in the broader community of historians who have long felt that intellectual change cannot be properly understood if only elite writings are studied. Yet, in Enlightenment studies, research into the interaction between elite and 'lowbrow' thought still remains marginal, even if studies of elite culture have moved on from the narrow orientation of Peter Gay and his 'family' of philosophes to include a greater spread of thinkers. Thus, beyond set-piece studies of events such as the French Revolution and other revolts where the *de facto* involvement of the masses in political life cannot be denied, the dominance of the top-down model within Enlightenment studies has rarely been questioned.

Although in itself welcome, the problem with the work of Kors, for instance, is that while striving to show how theological debate had unwittingly fed the Enlightenment, he still retained the traditional purview of a top-down process of influence. In searching to illustrate how learned Christian culture generated components of atheistic thought, he focused insufficiently on the vast bulk of less theological or academic publications or the wider, even popular social, religious and political context. Focusing on a few relatively highbrow publications can be misleading in various ways. It has been commonly asserted, for instance, that one of the great tools of the Enlightenment was the practice of comparative religion. Yet, as we have already noted, comparative religion – indeed an elementary sociology of religion – was developed, propagated and imbibed by the vast bulk of Christians many decades before the Enlightenment, and thus forms one of the several broad intellectual and popular currents which eventually came together to form the Enlightenment. It is not true, however, that elite writings do not tell us anything about influence from below. We know, for instance, that the fear of return to the conditions of the English Civil War period or the absolutist strivings of the Stuarts was a vital element of elite and popular consciousness in late-seventeenth- and eighteenth-century England, and consequently cannot be underestimated as a potential factor in the mental matrix which forms the foundation for intellectual development in general. How important those perceptions of the past could be in developing attitudes is illustrated by attempts to claim neutrality for the emerging discipline of science in that period. As Simon Schaffer has noted, the mechanical philosophy was used to create a view of the world beyond the concerns of politics and religion. This attempt to claim neutrality for natural knowledge was of course of great interest to many in post Civil War England, who wished to put a crucial part of intellectual thought potentially beyond the kind of catastrophic divisions of the 1640s and 1650s. But, in practice, an important component of the attempt at neutrality was political. As Schaffer has noted,

> Now, the exclusions which surrounded and defined natural philosophy in seventeenth-century England involved various elements: the construction of a purely mechanical model of nature, the denial of the capacity of natural philosophy to deal with souls in nature; the monopoly of natural philosophers over true natural knowledge; and a means by which natural philosophy could act against radical and against 'grovelling Humanity'. Nature itself was to be described as a machine ('a pregnant Automaton' as Boyle described it).[34]

We also know, strange as it may now sound, that Thomas Sprat, the Royal Society's first historian, commended natural philosophy as a cure for sectarian subversion, 'because it debated issues which touched no-one's interest, because it created a technology for the resolution of disputes which might arise, and because it discredited the false pretensions of individual judgement'.[35]

Any claim to neutrality, then, might be damaged if there arose deep divisions and disputes between natural philosophers. For some natural philosophers who feared damaging disputes, Church history told them 'a great deal about how belief could be propagated and how it could be enforced'. Some made an analogy between the elite concerned with natural science and the elite (priesthood) of the Church. In the context of this analogy, in order to help guard against disputes, Jeremy Taylor 'made the suggestion: "raise not thy mind to inquire into the mysteries of state or the secrets of government or difficulties theological, if thy employment really be, or thy understanding be judged to be, of a lower rank"'.[36] That fear of division and strife, in part prompted by the memory of catastrophic political and religious division in the Civil War period, was of course also fear of the intellectual involvement of the lower orders and the fruit such involvement might bear. In principle, therefore, if we wish to understand the intellectual outlook of eighteenth-century participants, including the philosophes, we can hardly ignore their attitudes to their present as informed by the past. From this point of view, the Enlightenment, or any other broad intellectual phenomenon, is a developmental process which, to be studied effectively, demands that we examine the interaction of various levels and elements of society.

It is probable that many historians themselves are rarely conscious of the decisively important theoretical assumption behind the dominance of the top-down model of intellectual change. The core of that implicit assumption is that for most of the time the masses were intellectually inert or meekly submissive to the ideology of Church, lord and state, passively waiting for intellectual change from above. So, in terms of the history of the process of secularization, the lower orders are often understood to have been for most of the time little more than mirrors in which ruling-class ideology was reflected. Thus the poor unthinkingly went to Church, believed in the tenets of religion as represented to them by the Church prelacy, feared God, respected the monarch and their betters, and trusted in the government of the country, its laws and the administration of them. Again, the paradox is that, although few historians would be prepared to endorse this characterization without some qualification, it is rare to find a modern historian prepared to accept the obvious corollary: if the lower orders were not mere mirrors of elite culture, it is necessary to question the assumption that intellectual influence is a phenomenon only to be exerted top-down. And, most importantly, if the masses have not been mere mirrors, it is unthinkable that those at the top of society, concerned for a social order dominated by a wealthy elite, were not at times cognizant of that fact.

This proposition is exemplified by the character of the critique of Anglicanism developed by those within the broad dissenting camp and some bold Latitudinarians in late-seventeenth-century England. As Sullivan has illustrated, Toland's *Christianity not*

Mysterious was 'an artifact of this culture, and it cannot be understood if it is approached as a freak'.[37] Prelates, lords and monarch understood how potentially influential the anti-Anglican and anti-absolutist dissenting critique could be, and so did their best to stem the tide by means of severe legal restrictions on Dissenter religious activity, pre-publication censorship, blasphemy laws and bars on holding state posts. Similarly, in France Louis XV was well aware of the potential intellectual power of the non-hierarchical polity of the Huguenots to challenge his absolutist goals. Consequently he revoked the Edict of Nantes in 1685 and subjected the Huguenots to severe physical repression, resulting in one of the greatest religious diasporas of the period.

Another of the characteristic elements of Enlightenment culture has been seen as a secular, modern approach to history. Roy Porter, for instance, has commented that 'for Christian history the proper study of mankind was Providence', while the secular history of the *philosophes* took as its proper subject the actions of humanity. Similarly, Peter Gay has stated that the developmental dynamic of history as understood by Christians lay 'in the shadow of the supernatural'.[38] These kinds of formulations, not uncommon, and to an extent useful in order to demonstrate the difference between traditional Christian and Enlightenment historiographical conceptions, are yet potentially most misleading. The uncritical acceptance of such stark divisions has led historians to underestimate the importance and extent of the impact of Christian historical understanding upon the formation of social, political and economic attitudes. Such writers have argued, essentially, that the historiography of the *philosophes* marked a revolution in the potential of historical writing to influence historical and contemporary conceptions of religion and, by obvious implication, of European civilization. Yet the dissenting critiques of Anglicanism and Catholicism in England were often – and evident to all – profound attacks upon the status quo and rooted in highly pejorative historical analyses, albeit in Christian terms. This was only to be expected, for established religion had a political and economic aspect (public appointments in England, France and Italy, for instance, were barred to the non-orthodox). Christian historico-theological polemic, therefore, was hardly solely concerned with the supernatural and thus without potential influence on secular matters.

Scaremongering, public opinion
and the construction of the deism scare

As we shall see in the next chapter, it was precisely the interconnections between Church, state, government and the public sphere which enabled – especially in England – the manufacture of one of the great conservative ideological propaganda weapons of the eighteenth century: the threat of organized deists and atheists to Christian civilization. Deism was, above all, a bogeyman created in political debate and print culture. In late-seventeenth-century England the bogeyman of atheism was frequently identified by Anglicans, some of whom wished to make a name for themselves by publicly appearing as staunch defenders of the faith and thus bringing themselves to the notice of their superiors. The problem was that atheists were hardly to be found at all and thus, as a public scare, atheism was less convincing than desired. It was thus necessary to broaden the scope of the threat in order to make it convincing, and there certainly existed those concerned to do so. As Sullivan has expressed it, '[b]y implicitly making deism in its philosophical sense (a watch-like universe and its detached maker) a form of speculative atheism, Samuel Clarke became the first Boyle lecturer to exploit the tactical potentialities of combating this elusive target'.[39] Another combatant in the fictive war against deism was Humphrey Prideaux, the Dean of Norwich, whose fame rested partly upon his tract against deists entitled *Life of Mahomet* (1697).[40] Modern historians, however, having accepted this creation for the public sphere as reality, have used it as prime evidence of emerging 'modernity'. Yet this was not the only ploy – or 'redefinition' – used by Anglican polemicists. Toland, for instance, was repeatedly charged with being a popish agent. This latter charge has not endured, partly because it is unfounded, but also because it is relatively unattractive to historians of the Enlightenment. The fact that charges of popish skulduggery were repeatedly brought into the public domain is significant, however, and indicates something of great importance about the tactics of Anglican polemicists and the use they hoped to make of public opinion – an important topic discussed below. Indeed, it has been suggested that the linking of papists and deists also helped Anglican polemicists avoid the need to answer the tricky arguments of such men as Toland.

Given that this was a period of conflict and uncertainty in religion, it was only natural – as had been the case with the witchcraft persecution – that scapegoats were found, real or imaginary, on whom to lay the blame for perceived problems facing Christianity. More important, the existence of unbelief or 'dangerous' heterodoxy was of some interest to the Church in helping to enlist the active support of the faithful and maintain the defence of the Church. Furthermore – as we shall see in the next chapter – given that clerics and many politicians were personally interested in preserving and strengthening the status quo, it is not surprising that there was a tendency to overstate the actual size of the threat and exaggerate its iniquitous nature. In an effort to promote their own sects, dissenting propagandists were also inclined to exaggerate rather than minimize threats to Christianity as proof that the Anglican Church–state alliance was leading to iniquity. In an age of widening access to print, therefore, it was only natural that elements of this type of strategy would bequeath significant 'evidence' of deism in the historical record greatly disproportional to actual reality. In this period (and indeed into the next century) heresy and unbelief were often sensationalized and significant print-profit was made: religious infidelity was still represented as a lack of moral fortitude and receptivity to vice, conjuring up potentially scandalous scenarios. We might say, then, that the illusion that was eighteenth-century deism was to some degree a 'media' production.

A few modern writers, however, have realized that a crucial element in understanding the significance of the term deist is the recognition that it was above all a pejorative term, a fairly imprecise insult. It designated, in general, those considered to be in some degree deficient in their faith (and usually outside the recognizable Dissenter parameters). For that very reason, the search for any coherence in the 'movement' has been and will remain fruitless. As Sullivan has put it, 'throughout the eighteenth century, observers placed themselves in the paradoxical position of presuming that deism was a meaningful term, even though they could neither adequately define it nor agree on a list of its advocates'.[41] David Pailin, in 'The Confused and Confusing Story of Natural Religion' (1994), notes that in the seventeenth and eighteenth centuries there were eleven varieties or gradations of what has been termed natural religion, some of which have 'significant sub-divisions'. Consequently, he warns, to ask if a writer was a deist is not a precise or even a fruitful question.[42] Indeed, there is no reason to suppose a term coined as a religious insult should possess precise significance. As he notes elsewhere, the term radical today represents a similar case: its meaning depends on the person who is using it. The term deist 'typically connotes those whom the user considers to be too restricted in what they believe as a result of their understanding of the demands of reason, rather than the adherents of a specifiable set of doctrines'.[43]

Thus there were a number of forms of what has been termed deism and differences between thinkers could be numerous and deep-seated. So, what might seem a profound and useful avenue in the search for Enlightenment origins has, to say the least, dubious value. Perhaps the most contradictory and confusing 'variant' of deism is the so-called 'Christian deism' of such thinkers as Thomas Morgan,[44] Woolston and Tindal. Deists, according to the traditional canon, refuted revelation in favour of reason. If the term deism is to have any such coherence, how can the revelation of Christ be reconciled with the deist denial of revelation? We must be alert, therefore, to the potential for thinkers to hold what to us might seem to be contradictory positions, but for them were resolvable on a personal basis. Thus, without denying the *tabula rasa* theory (*An Essay Concerning Human Understanding*, 1689) of John Locke, Tindal insisted that God 'had implanted in our Natures a Sense of Piety, and a Desire of being belov'd, in order to oblige Mankind to treat one another kindly'. This notion may be broadly reconcilable with a deistic outlook, but still on the subject of the implantation of a sense of piety, Tindal went on to say that God continued 'daily to imprint it'.[45] From the point of view of both deistic views and the censor this further point is unnecessary and strongly indicates his sincerity. Believing in the 'daily imprint' of God's design is hardly writing providence out of daily life, yet deism has traditionally been considered one of the great secularizing forces of the Enlightenment. It is not surprising, then, that the attempt to attribute a characteristic deism to various thinkers has been termed 'a matter of convenience rather than an aid to analysis'.[46] To add to the confusion, historians have tended to identify any thinker who wrote works with the terms 'natural religion' or the 'religion of nature' in their titles as deists, as in the case of Wollaston's *Religion of Nature Delineated* (1724). Yet, as the Appendix at the end of this book indicates, the topic of natural religion (or the religion of nature) and its acceptance within or alongside Christianity was common within

Christian literature of this period, and was certainly not a subject reserved only for the numerous hostile replies to perceived enemies of Christianity.

The Enlightenment period was still in good part one of the confessional state, or significant degrees of it, hence public appearances really did matter to some extent. The potential differences between private and public religious views, therefore, obviously warrant considerable attention. In pre-Revolution France, for instance, it has been noted that some of those who came to Mass came from a sense of religious, social, political and even economic duty, yet were unable to refrain from venting their anticlericalism in various, often disruptive and scandalous manners.[47] This is a tale by no means exclusive to France, and demonstrates how figures for church attendance must be treated with the same extreme caution. As the case of English dissent amply demonstrates, it was of course possible to be quite pious, yet hold profoundly anticlerical views whilst paying public lip-service to Church and state when circumstances absolutely demanded it. In such instances there was no necessary contradiction between the formal recognition of established religious forms and anticlerical thought and behaviour. From the point of view of recovering the past, the private–public problem applies to the social scale at all levels, for, although individuals on the upper levels were more likely to leave some written evidence of their religious views, much of that extant record was for public consumption.

I am advocating, therefore, that it is necessary to construct a model of Europe's religious past that is more dynamic, one in which anticlericalism and piety may often go hand in hand, and one in which the tension between official and private views is acknowledged. To do so, in effect, is to recognize public opinion as a cultural reservoir of forms of anticlericalism and 'infidelity' and the ever-present possibility of it being tapped. The existence of a variety of anticlerical ideas should be assumed as the norm, ever balanced against and in tandem with degrees of piety and submission to the Church. In this circumstance, the necessity of hypothesizing about influence from past anticlerical traditions as the key to the origins of Enlightenment anticlericalism is, if not removed, then significantly attenuated.

Since the publication of Habermas's *The Structural Transformation of the Public Sphere* (1989),[48] it has been generally accepted that the birth of public opinion as a political force came about in the eighteenth century. Habermas argued that in late-seventeenth-century England and late Enlightenment France a secular 'bourgeois' public sphere began to develop that marked the arrival of the undeniably powerful and supposedly modern phenomenon we term public opinion. In the view of Habermas the 'birth' of the public sphere was the outcome of long-term trends, namely the gradual coalescence of nation-states and the beginnings of capitalism.[49] As we shall see in subsequent chapters, whether or not there may be some sense in focusing on those factors in the development of modernity, the notion that traditional 'non-modern' forms of politico-religious struggle were not central in the widening of the public sphere in Enlightenment Europe cannot easily be sustained. In wishing to chart the origins of secular modernity, then, Habermas tended to ignore or downplay the traditional politico-religious content of the emerging public sphere and disproportionately to highlight the 'modern' secular elements.

Happily, John McManners (*Church and Society in Eighteenth-Century France*, 1998), building on the 1980s research of Baker, Echeverria and to some degree Chartier,[50] has sought to recognize politico-religious public opinion as a significant political and social force in Enlightenment France, that is to say constituting a powerful public sphere. Baker and Echeverria argued that the early 1770s – when Louis XV made his final play to cow his rebellious *parlements* by abolishing them (the Maupeou revolution) – was the period when public opinion as a political force was born. Louis's action brought forth a tidal wave of popular and learned literature appealing to the nation against despotism. McManners agrees that this 'brought the empire of "public" opinion to general acceptance, not only by its force and reverberation, but by its direct concentration on the central political issue of power and by its eventual triumph'. But he also notes that '[p]robably, however, [the sway of public opinion] ... should be dated a decade earlier, when the storm of public reprobation swept down upon the Society of Jesus'.[51] That 'storm' was led by Jansenists and its body was composed of vast numbers of Jansenist sympathizers. Yet that 1760s storm was not of a fundamentally different nature from other Jansenist-inspired politico-religious storms that had erupted in France since 1715, and hence the view that the birth of the public sphere in France was a 'secular' late Enlightenment phenomenon is problematic.

Habermas naturally highlights print culture as an important facet of the public sphere. That there was a large increase in the numbers of published works of all types in the eighteenth century, especially in the latter half, and a consequent increase in the print-buying public (although such figures tend to underestimate literacy levels), is now an accepted fact. Even those of quite modest means were able to purchase popular or more learned texts of an increasingly wide variety. This was, of course, an important development in terms of the dissemination of new ideas, and as such had an impact on public opinion. Crucially, we must emphasize, however, that in this context the use of the term public opinion has a different, more passive connotation than McManners's more reactive, politically directed concept of an 'empire of public opinion'. When, on account of the public storm which swept down upon the Jesuits, he suggests that the rise of public opinion should be dated to the 1760s, he is also noting that decisive political battles (the Jesuits were identified with despotic Bourbon rule) can be fought in an ostensibly religious form. Thus the formation or creation of public opinion cannot always be distinguished from the various potential forms of its expression: whether actively in the public domain by printed matter, by physical manifestation, by political manoeuvre, by clandestine activity, by passive non-compliance, etc.

When historians describe the great religious propaganda print battles of the sixteenth and seventeenth centuries, they can only be describing attempts to create and/or express public opinion. Those religious propaganda campaigns were rarely without political content or implications, and their duration for decade after decade indicates that they were regarded as an effective means by which to promote the views of their protagonists. As Tyacke has written, 'it will not do to argue, as some have, that doctrine was of little relevance to ordinary people. We are in fact dealing with some of the intellectual underpinnings of popular religious observance.'[52] Some of the circumstances and statistics of early modern attempts to mould public opinion are significant. Between 1517 and 1520, for example, Martin Luther had published at least thirty major pamphlets in a popular style and plain German language totalling, it is estimated, more than 300,000 copies.[53] Beside these, there were theatre performances demonstrating papal depravity, the propaganda use of the hymn, poetic versions of Luther's doctrine and propagandistic woodcut prints. Apparently, woodcut caricatures of the Pope were selling very well in Nuremburg in 1523. In England, the late sixteenth century saw the popular and notorious Puritan Martin Marprelate tracts, which were hostile to the hierarchy of the Anglican Church and written in probably the most brilliant prose satire of the period.

In the seventeenth century, pamphlets and other popular publications began more than ever to contribute to the formation of public opinion, and reached new heights of influence in England in the tumultuous 1640s and 1650s (Civil War, Republic and Protectorate period), and during the Thirty Years War (1618–48). The Thomason collection for the period 1640–62 totals 30,000 separate titles and editions of books, pamphlets, satires and broadsides. In the Thirty Years War there was a wide proliferation of pamphlets and posters sold in large quantities in shops, so much so that all classes of the population were reached by the polemical output. Early modern rulers, like their forebears, did not ignore the value of propaganda, now enhanced with print technology. The Holy Roman Emperor Maximilian gave patronage at his court for image-building initiatives, and Oliver Cromwell did likewise.[54] From the bottom to the top of early modern society, therefore, it was recognized that public opinion existed and could be cultivated and directed towards certain ends. We know that King Louis XIV of France authorized a propaganda campaign to cultivate support for his government's brutal suppression of the Huguenots. Pamphlets of a popular nature recounting Calvinist 'outrages' were hawked in the streets of towns and villages in order to support the decrees, edicts and declarations against the Huguenots and so justify their cruel reality. Monarchs and rulers clearly thought public opinion was not to be ignored without risk, a point demonstrated in the celebrated 1616 decision of the papacy to condemn the heretical astronomical finding of Copernicus.

There is evidence to suggest that in 1616 Rome had correctly assessed that there was still little broad support for Copernicus's ideas of 1543, and that which existed was not viewed as a significant threat to biblical orthodoxy that the Earth was at the centre of the universe. Rome was forced into the defensive action of 1616 not on account of any broad scientific threat. Rather it was prompted to act in order to combat the growing threat to Roman orthodoxy and biblical doctrine posed by the widespread and far-reaching anti-Rome polemic of Protestants, that is to say European public opinion. The key Protestant charge in this context was that the papacy had tampered with the Bible. As Sella has explained, if the Bible were not to be considered literally true in its account of the universe, 'it might lend credence to Protestant charges that the Catholic Church took liberties with the sacred text. Accordingly, they fell back, defensively, on uncompromising, literalist exegetical standards.'[55] There is reason, therefore, to question the consistency of the traditional story many historians have propagated: that of the self-sacrificing battle of the principled scientist against a backward hierarchy of clerics. At least some of that battle is romantic fiction.

If, however, we wish to identify the role of public opinion in the formation of important elements of Enlightenment context, England in the 1670s and 1680s is an important example. William of Orange of the United Provinces was well informed that English public opinion was increasingly unsympathetic to the 'popery-inspired' absolutist tendencies of the Stuarts, and decided he could exploit it in the interests of the United Provinces, then at war with France and England. As we will see, his propaganda campaign in England, linking the Stuarts to popery and despotism, was highly successful, contributing to the growing political pressure upon King Charles. This and other examples demonstrate the importance of the public arena in late-seventeenth-century England, and it is a crucial factor to be included in any attempt to understand the pace and direction of politico-religious change. With public opinion now more convinced than ever that the King was in conspiracy with popish forces, the pervasive anti-popish hysteria of 1673 did not fully abate in the following years. As a consequence, the wildest tales of conspiracy circulated and gained credence. Throughout the 1670s these crises (as we shall see, in important respects similar in their impact to events in mid-century France) continued, with public opinion a centrally important factor. It has been estimated, for example, that in addition to large numbers of petitions the attempt to prevent the Catholic King James II from inheriting the throne (the Exclusion Crisis, 1679–81) generated between five and ten million pamphlets,[56] as well as the origin of Locke's celebrated *Two Treatises of Government* (1689). So, far from non-existent, or embryonic, early modern public opinion played a crucial role in some of the most dramatic events in English history. It contributed greatly towards the most astounding events leading up to and including those of 1688, when Catholic James II, with wide support, was told he was being replaced by William of Orange. This act saw the final step taken in the irrevocable dominance of Parliament over the God-given monarch and thus the mass *de facto* withdrawal of allegiance from the long-standing theory of the divine right of kings.[57] In essence, it can be said, then, that English late-seventeenth-century public opinion accomplished a definite and relatively rapid step in the secularization of society.

To talk, therefore, of the *gradual secularization* of early modern society, which is the traditional description of the secularization process, can be quite misleading. It was a process that was neither quantitatively nor qualitatively linear. In any case, the term secularization, as commonly used, is also problematic, because it is often intended and understood as denoting how far state institutions, laws and processes are framed and proceed from secular imperatives rather than divine. It hardly needs affirming, surely, that public opinion – or sections of it – may become more secular in its outlook at a different rate from changes in political forms. For observers to measure this change via the various European landmarks of governmental debate, legislation, or scientific advance, is merely to note how two rarefied spheres of thought (government and elite intellectual) have responded to certain broader circumstances and challenges. Their responses, however, may be in harmony, in advance or, as was the case with public support for the recognition of Huguenot marriage in France, just as easily a step behind the process of secularization of social and religious attitudes.

Another traditional means of cultivating public opinion was of course that of the pulpit, and its importance was not underestimated in the eighteenth century. As we shall see in the next chapter, probably the most adroit cultivation of public opinion in Enlightenment England was that achieved by the High Church Henry Sacheverell, who in 1709 wielded the Church-in-danger cry with dramatic effect. From the pulpit of St Paul's, this staunch Anglican managed to conjure up in the public mind a Dissenter threat wildly out of proportion to reality, and in the process decisively rallied the political fortunes of the rigidly Anglican Tory party.[58] During the great public controversy surrounding the so-called Jew Bill of 1753, for example, the Tories again used the pulpit, their traditional medium, mobilizing Anglican clergy to preach against the Bill. Both Whig and Tory, however, utilized the press and mobilized through the traditional channels of coffee-house readership and pamphlets. Newspapers and magazines from London to the midlands carried the debate forward. Sixty pamphlets against the Bill were published in one year alone, some using anti-Semitic arguments. The Tories also used a series of public relations activities and ploys – rallies, dinners, banners – and women wore ribbons or crosses carrying effigies of Jews; 'it thus became a stigma not to wear some anti-Bill identification'.[59] At the more popular end of the propaganda scale, therefore, the distinction between the creation and expression of public opinion can at times seem vague, for the mass expression of public opinion can further reinforce and/or modify its content and scale of impact upon the political and social order. As we will see in the case of mid-century France, at certain moments, what might be termed an organic or collective dynamic of intellectual change can be identified, when the normal processes of politico-religious maturation are accelerated via the concentrated and speeded-up events of public urban discourse and demonstration.

Notes

1 P. Riley, *The General Will Before Rousseau. The Transformation of the Divine into the Civic* (Princeton, N.J.: Princeton University Press, 1986), p. x.
2 I. Wade, *The Intellectual Origins of the French Enlightenment* (Princeton, N.J.: Princeton University Press, 1971), p. 655.
3 C. J. Betts, *Early Deism in France. From the So-Called 'Déistes' of Lyon (1564) to Voltaire's 'Lettres philosophiques' (1734)* (The Hague, Boston and Lancaster: Martinus Nijhoff, 1984), p. 5.
4 Ibid., p. 235.
5 Ibid., pp. 4–5.
6 A. C. Kors, *Atheism in France, 1650–1729. Vol. 1: The Orthodox Sources of Disbelief* (Princeton, N.J.: Princeton University Press, 1990), p. 4.
7 A. C. Kors, '"A First Being, of Whom We Have No Proof". The Preamble of Atheism in Early-Modern France', in A. C. Kors and P. J. Korshin (eds), *Anticipations of the Enlightenment in England, France and Germany* (Philadelphia: Philadelphia University Press, 1987), p. 18.
8 Paul Korshin, Elisabeth Labrousse, Dale Van Kley and Margaret Jacob collaborated on the collection of articles in *Anticipations of the Enlightenment*.
9 D. Van Kley, 'Pierre Nicole, Jansenism, and the Morality of Enlightened Self-Interest', in Kors and Korshin (eds), *Anticipations of the Enlightenment*, p. 69.
10 Kors, '"A First Being, of Whom We Have No Proof"', pp. 17–18.
11 G. R. Cragg, *Reason and Authority in the Eighteenth Century* (Cambridge: Cambridge University Press, 1964), p. 32.
12 D. Pailin, 'Herbert of Cherbury. A Much Neglected and Misunderstood

The Enlightenment and religion

Thinker', in P. Creighton and E. Axel (eds), *God, Values and Empiricism. Issues in Philosophical Theology* (Macon, Ga.: Mercer University Press, 1989), pp. 171–2, 177.

13 For a relatively recent assertion of this tradition see J. Byrne, *Glory, Jest and Riddle. Religious Thought in the Enlightenment* (London: SCM Press, 1996), pp. 28–9.

14 Ibid., p. 29.

15 A. Milton, *Catholic and Reformed. The Roman and Protestant Churches in English Protestant Thought* (Cambridge: Cambridge University Press, 1995), pp. 173–4.

16 On comparative anticlerical theories see my *Idol Temples and Crafty Priests. The Origins of Enlightenment Anticlericalism* (London: Macmillan, 1999).

17 See, for instance, D. Outram, *The Enlightenment* (Cambridge: Cambridge University Press, 1995), p. 40, on the 'new field of study of comparative religion'; and a similar analysis from J. Champion in 'Europe's Enlightenment and National Historiographies: Rethinking Religion and Revolution (1649–1779)', *Europa. European Review of History*, 0 (1993), p. 84.

18 See, for instance, T. Hankins, *Science and the Enlightenment* (Cambridge: Cambridge University Press, 1995), p. 145. On the unprecedented fusion of science and religion in seventeenth-century England see, for instance, A. Funkenstein, *Scientific Imagination from the Middle Ages to the Seventeenth Century* (Princeton, N.J.: Princeton University Press, 1986).

19 R. Sullivan, *John Toland and the Deist Controversy* (Cambridge, Mass.: Harvard University Press, 1982), pp. 9, 23, 110–11, 274.

20 See W. Ward, *Christianity under the Ancien Régime 1648–1789* (Cambridge: Cambridge University Press, 1999), p. 159, on Bayle's active membership of the reformed church while writing the *Dictionnaire*.

21 K. Sandberg, *At the Crossroads of Faith and Reason. An Essay on Pierre Bayle* (Tucson: University of Arizona Press, 1966), p. 2.

22 Ibid., pp. 38–9.

23 W. Rex, *Essays on Pierre Bayle and Religious Controversy* (The Hague: Martinus Nijhoff, 1965), p. x.

24 Sandberg, *At the Crossroads of Faith and Reason*, pp. 99, 103.

25 E. Labrousse, *Pierre Bayle* (Oxford and New York: Oxford University Press, 1983; 1st edn 1963), p. 90. See also E. Labrousse, 'Reading Pierre Bayle in Paris', in Kors and Korshin (eds), *Anticipations of the Enlightenment*, p. 11.

26 This estimation even prevails today; see for instance Ward's *Christianity under the Ancien Régime*, pp. 166–7.

27 P. Collinson, *The Birthpangs of Protestant England. Religions and Cultural Change in the Sixteenth and Seventeenth Centuries* (Basingstoke: Macmillian, 1998), p. 83.

28 Kors, *Atheism in France*, pp. 4, 379.

29 A. C. Kors, 'Introduction', in Kors and Korshin (eds), *Anticipations of the Enlightenment*, p. 2.

30 Wade, *The Intellectual Origins*, p. 655.

31 Kors and Korshin (eds), *Anticipations of the Enlightenment*, p. 2.

32 Kors, '"A First Being, of Whom We Have No Proof"', pp. 17–18.

33 Ward, *Christianity under the Ancien Régime*, to cite a recent example, gives the

percentage of the European population touched by the Enlightenment as 10 per cent.

34 S. Schaffer, 'The Political Theology of Seventeenth-Century Natural Science', *Ideas and Production*, 1 (1983), p. 4. On politics and science see also S. Shapin and S. Schaffer, *Leviathon and the Air-Pump. Hobbes, Boyle, and the Experimental Life* (Princeton, N.J.: Princeton University Press, 1985), especially chs 7–8.

35 Schaffer, 'The Political Theology', p. 5. For a similar analysis see also D. Zaret, *Origins of Democratic Culture. Printing, Petitions and the Public Sphere in Early Modern England* (Princeton, N.J.: Princeton University Press, 2000), pp. 270–5.

36 Schaffer, 'The Political Theology', pp. 5–7, 11.

37 Sullivan, *John Toland and the Deist Controversy*, p. 51.

38 Roy Porter, *The Enlightenment* (Basingstoke: Macmillan, 1990), p. 72; Peter Gay, *The Enlightenment: An Interpretation. Vol. 2: The Science of Freedom* (London: Wildwood House, 1973; 1st edn 1969), p. 386.

39 Sullivan, *John Toland and the Deist Controversy*, pp. 236, 239–40.

40 Prideaux's *A Life of Mahomet* (1697) was preceded by his *A Letter to the Deists* (1696).

41 Sullivan, *John Toland and the Deist Controversy*, p. 212.

42 On the difficulties of defining deism, in addition to the works cited in the previous chapter, see also Pailin, 'Herbert of Cherbury'; J. C. D. Clark, *English Society 1688–1832. Ideology, Social Structure and Political Practice during the Ancien Régime* (Cambridge: Cambridge University Press, 1985), p. 279; and D. Nicholls, *God and Government in an Age of Reason* (London and New York: Routledge, 1995).

43 D. Pailin, 'British Views on Religion and Religions in the Age of William and Mary', *Method and Theory in the Study of Religion*, 6: 4 (1994), p. 354. Rivers makes a similar comment in her *Reason, Grace and Sentiment. Vol. 2: Shaftesbury to Hume* (Cambridge: Cambridge University Press, 2000), p. 5.

44 On the assertion of the Christian deism of, for instance, Thomas Morgan, see Peter Gay, *The Enlightenment. An Interpretation. Vol. 1: The Rise of Modern Paganism* (London: Norton, 1995; 1st edn 1966), p. 375.

45 M. Tindal, *The Rights of the Christian Church* (4th edn, London, 1708), p. 114, and *Christianity as Old as the Creation* (London, 1730), pp. 59–60, quoted in Sullivan, *John Toland and the Deist Controversy*, p. 229. In his *God and Government in an Age of Reason* (pp. 144–5), Nicholls too notes that 'some deists appear to have accepted the notion of divine revelation'.

46 Sullivan, *John Toland and the Deist Controversy*, p. 232.

47 J. McManners, *Church and Society in Eighteenth-Century France* (2 vols, Oxford: Clarendon Press, 1998), vol. 2, pp. 99–100, 103–4.

48 J. Habermas, *The Structural Transformation of the Public Sphere. An Enquiry into a Category of Bourgeois Society*, trans. Thomas Burger (Cambridge, Mass.: MIT Press, 1989; original edition in German 1962). Habermas's ideas only gained a wider hearing after the 1978 French translation.

49 For a useful summary and discussion of Habermas's views see T. Dykstal, *The Luxury of Skepticism. Politics, Philosophy and Dialogue in the English Public*

The Enlightenment and religion

Sphere 1660–1740 (Charlottesville: University Press of Virginia, 2001), pp. 1–15.

50 K. Baker (ed.), *The French Revolution and the Creation of Modern Political Culture. Vol. 1: Political Culture of the Old Regime* (Oxford: Pergamon, 1987); D. Echeverria, *The Maupeou Revolution. A Study in the History of Libertarianism. France 1770–1774* (Baton Rouge: Louisiana State University Press, 1985); R. Chartier, *The Cultural Origins of the French Revolution* (Durham, N.C.: Duke University Press, 1991).

51 McManners, *Church and Society in Eighteenth-Century France*, vol. 2, pp. 534, 672.

52 N. Tyacke, *Aspects of English Protestantism c.1530–1700* (Manchester and New York: Manchester University Press, 2001), p. 13.

53 O. Thomson, *Mass Persuasion in History* (Edinburgh: Paul Harris, 1977), p. 76.

54 Ibid., pp. 77–80.

55 For a discussion on the Tridentine revival and the decision of 1616 see D. Sella, *Italy in the Seventeenth Century* (Harlow: Longman, 1997).

56 M. Knights, *Politics and Opinion in Crisis, 1678–81* (Cambridge: Cambridge University Press, 1994), pp. 168, 227–305.

57 Few dared openly to proclaim their loyalty to James II as the legimate king. The only identifiable (although small) body to do so were the so-called Nonjurors.

58 For a clear account of the Sacheverell affair, see G. Holmes, *The Trial of Doctor Sacheverell* (London: Methuen, 1973).

59 Thomson, *Mass Persuasion*, p. 83.

3

The English deist movement: a case study in the construction of a myth

The essence of this chapter is that it is not possible to understand the development of the myth of the English deist movement without grasping the politico-religious context of late-seventeenth- and early-eighteenth-century England and the growing role of public opinion and opinion-makers within it. Some preliminary remarks on the major elements of the politico-religious configuration of late Tudor and Stuart England are therefore necessary.

Post-Restoration context

It is accepted amongst historians that it is difficult to comprehend the vicissitudes of early modern English religious life without reference to the Puritans (staunch Calvinists). They campaigned against the hierarchical and Erastian nature of Anglicanism, proposing instead an independent presbyterian non-hierarchical Church polity based upon the biblical example of the simple, pure apostolic Church. Regardless of the fact that one of the main aims of the Puritans was to create an independent Church free from the stains of politics and mundanity, in effect their aims were of course highly political: the ending of the state–Church relationship and the monarch as the head of that Church. Tudor and Stuart monarchs naturally viewed the possibility of an alternative Church as a threat to their dominance of such a vital organ of social, political, economic and religious legitimation. Not surprisingly, then, when the Puritans began to set up a rival, underground Church, Queen Elizabeth repressed and destroyed it. She did so because a free, egalitarian Church was not then within the bounds of an acceptable political configuration. Leaving aside the various divisions in the debate over the exact nature of the English Civil Wars, few if any historians doubt that the Puritan apostolic ideal of a presbyterian-style Church significantly informed not only religious debate in the those wars, but also important elements of political debate and action. Indeed deep divisions within the parliamentary camp were not a little to do with presbyterianism and its implicit egalitarian political model.

Most commentators, however, have also asserted that Puritanism was shattered or splintered in the 1640s, and as a consequence it irrevocably lost the power to mount a cohesive challenge to Anglicanism. This statement is technically true. Anyone who has read even a brief summation of the 1640s English experience will know that several radical Protestant groupings emerged, and some of the gentry who might otherwise have been included in the Puritan camp or were sympathetic to it became, under the pressure of political events, more conservative. The problem, therefore, is not that the demise of Puritanism as a cohesive force has been exaggerated or distorted. A difficulty arises, however, with regard to the misleading interpretation or assumptions made by historians about the ensuing decades in relation to one of the most important Puritan ideals, its presbyterian polity.

Few theologians will argue that presbyterianism is a distinctive theological outlook, simply because its grass-roots organizational form can and has been adopted by several Protestant movements or sects before and after the Puritans. Thus, the statement that the Puritan movement became shattered in the Civil Wars does not necessarily tell us a great deal about the fortunes of presbyterianism as an ecclesiastical polity. We know that presbyterianism was alive and well as an ideal at least in most post-Restoration Dissenter thought. Yet historians searching for the roots of the English Enlightenment rarely focus on presbyterianism. Nevertheless, in Restoration Stuart England, it was this implicitly anti-absolutist aspect of Dissenter thought which helped to furnish the dissenting message with polemical force and brought Dissenters into conflict with the state, for instance through their refusal to take the Anglican Oath of Allegiance and Supremacy. Clearly this was not perceived as a phantom menace to the Restoration regime, for the Stuarts brutally persecuted the Scottish presbyterians or Covenanters, and issued a series of punitive acts – the Clarendon Code – against Dissenters in England, resulting in the deaths of some 500 Quakers in prison.[1]

The English deist movement

Against the perceived quasi-popery of Anglicanism, and by association its tendency to aid and abet the absolutist tendencies of the Stuarts, Dissenters continued to advance their ideas of an independent, non-hierarchical and thus uncorrupted clergy. As was the case with the Puritans, Dissenters, although numerous, were of course a minority of the population, but, as in the 1640s and 1650s, minority aspiration could move demographic mountains or at least make them shake. One of the centrally important factors here is that the Dissenters were – as were the Puritans – often relatively prosperous and well educated and naturally had some aspirations of the civic kind. Yet the series of post-Restoration punitive acts included a bar on civic appointments to Dissenters. We have here, therefore, in terms of the origin of the English deist critique of the Church in the politico-religious crisis of the 1680s and 1690s,[2] a confluence of religious, political and economic issues that was of great moment indeed.

It is difficult to over-emphasize the importance of the last decades of the seventeenth century in the development of vital and enduring facets of British history. It may seem strange to newcomers to this field that while it is freely acknowledged that the intense politicization of religion in the Restoration period led to the emergence of the stable two-party political system – claimed as one of the greatest of England's achievements and gifts to world politics – the influence of religion in the development of the Enlightenment has nevertheless been traditionally downplayed. Yet, even a cursory examination of the main events of the period indicates that the same public intensification of the nexus between politics and religion that supposedly gave the world the two-party system also played a fundamental role in producing the broad intellectual climate so conducive to the development of the English Enlightenment. In short, the Stuart Restoration of 1660 was a return to a very different situation from that which Charles I had sought to defend: Parliament had the right to sit every three years and still effectively controlled the supply of funds necessary for any large-scale military or civil undertakings. In effect, England had a limited monarchy. In order to regain the primacy of the monarchy, as it was traditionally perceived and observed in contemporary France, it was necessary to cow the Anglican Parliament, but this was difficult while Parliament controlled essential financial purse strings. Both Charles II and James II looked back upon the claimed prerogatives of Charles

I with some envy and greatly admired those of Louis XIV of France. In essence, the solution seemed simple, even if daunting in prospect: England had to be returned to a more centralized regime similar to that of France, where the monarch's claims were staunchly supported by its very influential Catholic Church. The fact that Stuart admiration for France soon turned to collaboration is denied by few academics today, for the documentary evidence is overwhelming.

Charles II and James II accepted a very substantial pension from King Louis in return for timely suspensions of 'difficult' (i.e. anti-French) parliaments and a series of secret pro-French treaties in defiance of the will of Parliament. These acts are traditionally referred to as the Secret Diplomacy, but can be quite justly understood as treason, in which the Stuarts were selling themselves to France in return for financial independence from Parliament. If the term treason appears to be too strong to apply to a king, then we should ponder the Dover Treaty of 1670, in which Charles demonstrated he was prepared to make use of a foreign army, if needed, in his struggle to re-establish the Roman religion in England. The problem for the Restoration Stuarts was that pro-Catholic sympathies, publicly known to be evident at court and in the King's political outlook, were of course not only heretical, but technically treasonable. England, as most other states of the period, was confessional in nature, and the state religion was the only permitted public religion. Of more importance perhaps was the perceived nature of international popery, of which France – the traditional and much hated foe of England – was the dominant example. In the perception of the public at large, including intellectuals, popery meant absolutist tyranny, the defiling of true religion, the imposition of superstition over reason, and obedience to a foreign despotic power in Rome. The Stuarts, therefore, faced a tricky situation, in which they could only proceed with their project of regaining 'traditional' monarchical prerogatives in secret and with much caution. Although prevented by Parliament, both Charles II and James II made attempts to rehabilitate Catholicism, and their actions contributed to a growing division between the Court and the Country (or pro-court and anti-court) factions, which was soon to provide the basis for the birth of the Tory and Whig parties.

In 1672 England and France jointly declared war against the only other significant European Protestant power, the United Provinces. It was publicly understood that the official reason for war –

threatened trading interests – was in good part an excuse for alliance with expansionist France. William of Orange of the United Provinces, married to Mary the daughter of King James, was well informed of the overwhelming antagonism of English public opinion – especially strong in London – against alliance with France. In 1673, through his agent Moulin, he caused a subversive pamphlet to be widely distributed in England: *England's Appeal from the Private Cabal*. This was propagandistic dynamite, for it portrayed government policy as having been dangerously pro-Catholic for some time, and the Dutch war as part of a popish conspiracy. These accusations contributed to a wave of anti-Catholic hysteria that dominated public thought and parliamentary business of that year. As a consequence, Charles was forced to abandon legislation designed to increase tolerance of Catholicism and, instead, assent to legislation reaffirming restrictions upon them. The emergence of public opinion as a political force and the politicization of religion were thus two sides of the same coin.

With a public now more convinced than ever that the King was in conspiracy with popish forces, the pervasive anti-popish hysteria of 1673 did not fully abate in the following years. As a consequence, the wildest tales of conspiracy circulated and gained credence and Charles was even forced to order all non-householding Catholics to leave the city for the duration of the 1674 parliamentary session. Throughout the 1670s these crises (as we shall see, similar in their impact in some respects to mid-eighteenth-century French politico-religious crises) continued, with public opinion a centrally important factor. In 1677, for example, Andrew Marvell's *Account of the Growth of Popery and Arbitrary Government* burst 'like a bombshell over the country'.[3] Public opinion also played a crucial role in some of the most dramatic events in early modern English history, which were shortly to follow. In the Exclusion Crisis of 1679–81 (the nearly successful attempt to prevent Catholic James II from succeeding Charles II), Parliament, in effect, came close to instituting an elective monarchy. As a result of this deep and enduring politico-religious polarization, Europe's first permanent political parties were born: Whigs and Tories, the former tending to represent Dissenter and parliamentary interests, and the latter favouring High Church Anglicanism and the royal court. These were momentous times, and the culmination of them was certainly the Glorious Revolution of 1688 when the Catholic James II was 'advised' by politicians and prelates to vacate the throne to be replaced by the Protestant William of Orange.

It is important to recognize that these various crises had an international dimension. The vast increase in international contact made possible by massively increased trade – crucially, including printed matter – meant that international news could travel more quickly than ever and inform public opinion. It is of course true that isolated country areas could still remain relatively uninformed, but this discussion is focused upon the centres of cultural production, predominantly the cities. It was to these cities that the news of the bloody continental oppression of Protestants arrived. In France, Louis wanted to finish his project of centralization, and although he had already been persecuting the Huguenots in the decades leading to 1685, in that year he revoked the Edict of Nantes which had given Huguenots some protection in law, and cruelly billeted dragoons upon them. The resultant savagery forced a huge refugee exodus, tens of thousands of whom came to England, and many to London. In 1686 Vittorio Amedeo II, the Duke of Savoy, forcefully expelled the Vaudois – revered by Protestants – from their Piedmontese valleys. Closer to home, the bloody persecution of Scottish presbyterians continued. From the point of view of Protestants, liberal Catholics and other observers, religious toleration had been sacrificed yet again to political expediency. I wish to assert, then, that the 1680s were years of what was publicly understood by many English and Scottish contemporaries as a European crisis of politico-religious freedom.

As I have written elsewhere, in securing a Protestant succession by the ousting of the Catholic James and the invitation of the Protestant William of Orange, expectations of greater tolerance to non-Anglican Protestants had been mightily raised. They were, however, mostly dashed by the very limited scope of the 1689 Toleration Act, which did not remove the severe restrictions and disabilities upon Dissenters and left the Anglican Church's privileged relationship with the state untouched. Perhaps the most anachronistic factor to survive the settlement, one reeking of Church–state collusion, was the continued obligation on all to pay the tithe for the upkeep of the Anglican clergy. So, amongst many of the most well educated yet disadvantaged Dissenters, the failure of the Toleration Act to end discrimination ensured that the 1680s crisis of the Church continued into the 1690s and beyond. In late-seventeenth-century England, presbyterian ideals of Church government were still diffuse amongst the various Nonconformist tendencies. As anti-Catholicism could serve to unite most Protestants, so the presbyterian ideal of a simple non-hierarchical Christian ministry served to unite the numerous and varied army of Dissenters. Presbyterian ideals provided a powerful theological paradigm from within which to launch devastating attacks on all established Church hierarchies and by extension on regimes or Churches perceived to support the tyranny of popery or elements of it. In short, one of the reasons for the endurance of the presbyterian ideal was its ability to express political opposition of the dissenting, well-educated middling sort to the status quo.

For most Dissenters, then, the corruption of 'right religion' was embodied – and so presupposed – in the very concept of an established hierarchical sacerdotal caste. As regards their critiques of the Church and its history, however, the dividing line between Dissenters, other religious dissidents and so-called deists can often seem unclear. Both Dissenters and deists (as traditionally understood), for example, rejected all or most of the history of the Christian priesthood as an example of the corrupting influence of all established hierarchical priesthoods. On the level of polemic, then, the difficulties of distinguishing Dissenter from deist can be significant. In any case, as we have seen in the previous chapter, there is no reason to suppose that a term such as deism, coined as a religious insult, should possess any precise significance.

Deists and Dissent confused

Deists have traditionally been regarded as radicals who rejected revelation as proof for religion and propagandized a rational or natural religion, the evidence for which lay in the qualities (especially reason and conscience) of an unchanging human nature and the frame of nature itself. This outlook also entailed a radical critique of the place of the Church within belief, and usually of the motivation and historical conduct of the priestly caste. Writing about 'natural religion' and evidence for God in the frame of nature (including human nature), however, was not the preserve of deists. To define those who wrote about natural religion as deistic or quasi-deistic serves to exclude perhaps most of those who wrote about natural religion: Christians who were interested in broadening what had hitherto been the accepted range of theological debate. This was precisely the ground of the complaints from many more conservative Christians: that Anglicanism was undergoing change, becoming more latitudinarian (in the lower case sense of the term), that is to say less exclusively focused on traditional theological matters and frames of reference. As Mossner long ago wrote, '[s]o prevalent had the spirit of Latitudinarianism become in England by the close of the seventeenth century that it was not uncommon for divines accepted as orthodox to treat of Natural Religion in the body of a theological work and then to add, as it were, an appendix on Revealed Religion. A writer failing to add this codicil was likely to be denounced as a Deist', even if in polite terms (for an indicative bibliography of Protestant works sympathetic to natural religion see my Appendix below).[4] Writing of Christian sermons of which he disapproved, for instance, in his *Natural Religion Insufficient* (1714), Thomas Halyburton did just that when he argued that often 'heathen morality has been substituted in the room of Gospel holiness. And ethics by some have been preached instead of the Gospels of Christ.'[5] High Church thinkers were particularly concerned to combat the growing trend to discuss evidence for religion in nature alongside more traditional revelatory proofs, and were happy to pin the most pejorative label upon those more liberal in religious outlook. From their criticism and dire warnings of impending catastrophe in the Church, it can seem – quite misleadingly – as if Anglicanism was in danger of disintegrating and that deism was a real threat. As we shall see below, however, this possibility of misapprehension was partly the result of design, for there were those with motives for talking up deism.

The reality, however, is that deists were very few in number and could not possibly have constituted a movement disposing of decisive influence on theological and moral developments in the manner usually attributed to them. Hence Enlightenment studies has always faced a 'shortfall' in the numbers of deists, and historians have compensated for this difficulty by positing underground movements, secret societies, and making vague allusions to those who wrote on natural religion. But we must be clear here: writing on natural religion did not have any necessary connection to deistic belief. Discussion of natural religion was a feature of the political and scientific age, and we ought to be very surprised indeed if the dominant (Christian) culture – quite unexceptionally assimilating and adapting to new philosophical and scientific developments – did not produce a weighty body of thought upon it.

Amidst the vagaries of who exactly were deists, we might profitably focus on a relatively recent claim made by Roy Porter in his *Enlightenment Britain and the Creation of the Modern World* (2000). Porter argues that deists came in many colours. As a consequence, readers are effectively asked not to question his implicit assertion that it is possible to align anyone who wrote on natural religion with the likes of Voltaire. In talking up the numbers of deists, Porter chooses to cite William Wollaston as a deist. Why Wollaston in particular? Perhaps one reason for citing Wollaston is the sales figure for his *Religion of Nature Delineated* (1724), which Porter cites as 'impressive': 10,000 copies.[6] Yet, apart from the fact that he wrote *Religion of Nature Delineated*, in which he builds on the morality theory of the Christian writer and critic of deists Samuel Clarke, no one has ever adduced any significant evidence that William Wollaston was not a more or less orthodox Christian. At this point, Porter's thesis seems strange, for, on the one hand, he argues strongly that the English Enlightenment was conservative in nature, yet he describes how – via the most circumstantial evidence – deism had wide support. It hardly needs stating that anecdotal evidence of anticlerical jokes, 'raillery and even sacrilege' substantiates little, least of all the existence of wide support for deism.[7] Daily's comment that Latitudinarians were the strongest advocates of deism,[8] while at least outlandish if not astounding, is the logical outcome of this tendency.

After Wollaston's initial 1722 private printing of the *Religion of Nature Delineated*, selling 10,000 copies of the 1724 edition was certainly impressive for the period. But more to the point, of what is that figure indicative? If the work and audience were deist, this would be very impressive. But there is no indication that the work was perceived in this manner. It is difficult to deny, however, that the figure indicates both the appetite for the topic and its Christian acceptability amongst the mainstream educated public. If we wish to think of deism on this scale, however, then we are faced with the prospect of identifying massive swathes of respected, learned and even eminent clergy and many, many more pious Protestants as deists, making rather a mockery of the term in its current accepted usage. Instead, we should perhaps be prepared to accept that the Enlightenment was far more Lockean-Latitudinarian or even

Newtonian-Dissenting than it ever was deist. Given the evident confusion over the definition of deism and therefore how deists might be detected, the question of what they shared in common with other religiously non-orthodox thinkers is an important one.

Dissenters, independent religious dissidents and deists could all excoriate established Church hierarchies in a similar manner. So much so, in fact, that their critiques of Christianity could, to the unwary observer, seem quite similar. The result is that some Dissenters and other religious dissidents have been turned into deists.[9] Robert Howard's *History of Religion* (1694) provides an instructive example. In this work the Whig Member of Parliament (MP) Howard (1626–98) illustrates how the Church was corrupted almost from the beginning by priestcraft. But, like other Protestants, he emphasizes how the state adoption of Christianity by Emperor Constantine (early fourth century) was a significant turning point in the hold of priestcraft upon the Church: 'Yet they [Roman Christians] were no sooner freed from those Miseries [of state oppression], but they practis'd upon others all the Mischiefs and Crimes which themselves had suffer'd, and had inveigh'd against'. This was a weighty, if implicit, parallel with the contemporary Anglican state–Church treatment of Dissenters, and naturally struck a very loud chord among his dissenting audience. After discussing the craft of Roman pagan priests, Howard confirms he has endeavoured to show how these pagan practices and powers were retained and even exceeded by the Church of Rome. He contends popes took their 'Pattern from the Heathen Priests' and 'this same Method of Priest-Craft is continu'd in the Church of *Rome*: the Romish Saints and Angels answer to the Demons and Heroes, Deify'd by the Heathen Priests; and their Idol of Bread, Divinity infus'd into crosses Images, *Agnus Dei's* and Relicks, correspond to the Pillars, Statues and Images consecrated by Pagan Priests'.[10]

It has been argued that Howard's work is deist in orientation and that he projects the priestcraft charge against all priesthoods,[11] but what exactly is meant by 'priesthoods'? If the term is used to denote clerical hierarchies typified by the Anglican or Catholic clergy, its usage in relation to Howard's analysis is correct. But this is not the same as abandoning the concept of the Christian ministry. As we know, prevalent in dissenting circles was adherence to, or at least sympathy for, a very different concept of the Christian ministry. Consequently we can safely assert that Howard would certainly have been more sympathetic towards non-hierarchical priesthoods than he was to Anglicanism or Catholicism.

Howard, like many thousands of other Dissenters and religious dissidents, was enraged at what he regarded as the evident popish chicanery and oppression of the Anglican Church and thus wished to jibe implicitly at Anglicanism whenever possible. Consequently, Howard argued that the Christian Church could be considered the heir to the priests of pagan Roman, and even 'among the most Reform'd Christians ... Methods of Priestcraft' are pursued. He was, however, apologetic on behalf of the Church fathers, and left readers in no doubt as to his Protestantism, giving evidence of his piety in excess of ploys necessary to throw any censor off the trail. He also wrote, in typical Protestant fashion, that the Church of Christ is to be found in believers, and cited the Latitudinarian Archbishop of Canterbury John Tillotson (1630–94) as the model of a 'plain and certain way to Salvation'.[12] None of these points suffice to indicate Howard was a sceptic or a deist. On the contrary, there is manifest proof in his work that he was an anti-Trinitarian Dissenter, possibly a Unitarian. Hence it was that Howard wrote his *History of Religion* anonymously, for anti-Trinitarian thought had not been included in the 1689 Toleration Act at all and remained proscribed. For sceptics of the period, Howard's analysis could be construed as a free gift, even a home goal for Christianity. Many High Churchmen and other staunch Anglicans were solicitous to misconstrue and misrepresent the work of Howard and others as a call to deism. In their attempt to stem the reaches of the dissenting tide, how better to discredit dissent than bracket it with the vague catch-all, but ultimately anti-Church, label of deism, which we know was then closely linked to the term atheism? By so doing, Anglicans could credibly be seen to act as defenders of the faith and so bolster or help to maintain the dominant position of Anglicanism in the minds of the faithful.

As we shall see, to tar all opponents with the same brush was not an unusual tactic for an established Church facing growing competition. For some twentieth-century historians the conflation of Dissenters and more radical thinkers has at times meant that the search for what might be termed 'modern attitudes' became a little easier, simply because the hunters were able to identify more heads to pursue. Only in rabidly anti-Catholic and overtly pro-Protestant accounts of priestcraft, such as Henry Care's periodical *A Pacquet of Advice from Rome* (1678–83), was there no possibility of 'confusion' between pro- and anti-Christian critics. The problem of audience – the conceptual and material circumstances and indeed motives of a readership – has rarely been of such pivotal importance as it was in the last decade of the seventeenth and first decades of the eighteenth century. Howard's considerable dissenting audience would have understood his position without difficulty – if not from elsewhere in his book, then from his deliberately unguarded anti-Trinitarian comments.[13]

In *Priestcraft distinguished from Christianity* (1715), written by the critic, playwright and polemicist John Dennis (1675–1734), there is also the possibility of 'misapprehension'.[14] His lengthy pious arguments and language register are clearly those of a dissenting Protestant and, like Howard's, go far beyond any dissimulation or platitudes necessary to placate or mislead a censor. He believes Satan has inflamed the heart of humanity with 'self-love' and destroyed 'the Empire which Heaven had set up in his soul, which was an empire of Reason and Law'. Thus some Christian teachers do 'contaminate the Doctrine of Christ by their own Inventions, and the Doctrines of Devils'. These antichristians have 'opposed [themselves] to the Lord's Anointed, *i.e.* to Christ'. Dennis states his attack is not upon the 'Pious, Learned and Numerous body, who are truly Christian Priests of the Church of England'. However, such encomiums are accompanied by an overview of the Church in some respects more radical than Howard's. Dennis describes how there was more virtue in the times of ancient paganism than since the coming of the Saviour, excepting the first and primitive times of Christianity, 'when the Supreme Magistrate was not as yet Christian [i.e. pre-Emperor Constantine], and the Christian Priests were yet undebauch'd by worldly Power and Greatness'.[15]

Just as Puritans had earlier demonstrated their Calvinist, Presbyterian credentials by publicly appearing the most consistent and implacable opposition to Rome and Anglicanism, so now did Howard, Dennis and other Dissenters display their own brand of piety through the vehicle of their hostility to the corruption of the Christian ministry in general. Times and circumstances had changed, and it was only to be expected that the polemical strategy of dissenting Protestants would reflect those changes. For such thinkers, the enemy of right religion was then more than ever the Anglican Church, and seemingly anti-Catholic critique increasingly became more of a vehicle for conveying anti-Anglicanism rather than an end in itself.

In *The Natural History of Superstition* (1709), written by the Whig MP John Trenchard (1662–1723), is as radical an indictment of the Christian ministry as one is likely to find in early-eighteenth-century England, although one essentially the same as that of Howard or Dennis. The title alone has led some historians to consider it an undoubtedly deist work.[16] This is not the case, for Trenchard's defence of revelation and providence, his condemnation of papists, and other comments – which go far beyond the need to placate any censor – inform us that he was of the dissenting type and not a deist as has been claimed.[17] He relates how the frauds of priests, visions of enthusiasts, impostures of pretended prophets, forgeries of papists, and the follies of 'some who call themselves Protestants ... have so far prevailed over genuine Christianity'.[18] One late-nineteenth-century commentator has, however, argued that Trenchard was certainly not a deist. He was so labelled by his opponents on account of his 'unsparing attacks' on the 'High Church party'.[19] Indeed, given the dissenting orientation of the works of Trenchard, Dennis and Howard, it is difficult to accept that their intention 'was to fragment the narrow Christocentric view of the past'.[20] On the contrary, these men wished to cleanse the Christian priesthood by prompting a return to an original Christocentric and apostolic form of Church government.

In the politico-ecclesiastical tension of late-seventeenth-century England, some Dissenters and fellow travellers, caught in a vice between Catholicism and Anglicanism, were prepared to state the maximum case for the historical corruption of the Christian ministry. What had been the traditional pre-Constantinian point of demarcation for an early Church that was not yet entirely corrupt and so still salvageable, was increasingly abandoned. Little or nothing was thus left of the priesthood's historical legitimacy, only the apostolic Church itself. The product of this deepening critique of the Christian ministry was the illegitimate birth of the Enlightenment view of Church history – illegitimate because, although deists and sceptics came to share a very similar historical analysis with dissenting writers, they did so with diametrically opposed intentions. Peter Gay has noted that rational Anglicanism and deists 'saw the universe as rational ... both despised enthusiasm and mysticism, both were critical of the written tradition ... Yet they were separated by a chasm as impassable as it was narrow.'[21] If liberal Anglicanism is understood to be Latitudinarianism, then Gay's assessment is unsustainable. Yes, they were divided by a chasm, but far from a narrow one: even Latitudinarian Anglicans viewed the Anglican Church as legitimate, while deists and many Dissenters could agree with the analysis of such writers as Trenchard, Dennis and Howard.

John Toland and *Christianity not Mysterious*

At the time of writing *Christianity not Mysterious* (1696), John Toland was a Dissenter. He enjoyed the patronage of London Presbyterians from 1690 to 1696,[22] and eventually came to espouse the outlook of the Unitarians. After 1696, we know Toland went on to dismiss the concept of or at least cease to believe in the reformability of the Christian ministry. Just a few others, including Matthew Tindal and Anthony Collins, also did so. Such a departure was, however, still a potentially risky business. What prompted them to do so? It was clear to Dissenters that the Anglican Church was content to retain much of its privileged position and would continue to defend its relationship with the state. This was no empty fear, for the Occasional Conformity Act of 1711 (repealed 1719) was to restrain Dissenters from qualifying for government posts by receiving the sacrament in the Anglican Church. Church reform increasingly seemed nothing but a utopian project.

The debate as to how practically free or comparatively repressive was the English state–Church regime in the 1680s and 1690s I shall pass over with but brief comment. From their copious writings, we know very many Protestants certainly considered religious tyranny to exist still, and that very pressing religious matters needed resolution. If, by the 1690s, religious persecution and discrimination were less bloody in England, they were still a reality. In any case, as Goldie has noted, 'by the early 1680s the church party, gradually acquiring the new name of Tory, had launched what was, with the possible exception of the 1580s, the most ferocious religious persecution of England's Protestant era',[23] and such measures produced lasting impressions. Hence I cannot entirely agree with Pocock's view that the English Enlightenment was less radical than in France because there was no clerical tyranny to be crushed.[24] The bitterness evoked by Restoration politico-religious reality is evident in John Locke's *Letter Concerning Toleration* (1689), where he wrote that kings and queens of post-Reformation England had been 'of such different minds in points of religion, and enjoined thereupon such different things', that no 'sincere and upright worshipper of God could, with a safe conscience, obey their several decrees'.[25] Bennet has also commented that, after 1688, 'it was clear even to the most detached observer that ... [the] clergy and laity were involved in a radical reappraisal of the whole role of the national Church in English society'.[26] An important factor in the practical reality of that reappraisal was much greater press freedom after 1694, when England's became one of the freest presses of Europe, although there was still a need for some caution. Nevertheless, the relative press freedom enabled Dissenters and other discontents to wage a more public campaign against the established Church. Although greater press freedom was of course welcomed, it did not signify to Dissenters a relaxation of intolerance, but rather the chance to voice publicly deep grievances.

The political and religious turmoil of the 1690s was not of the same scale as that of the 1640s. The political and social disruption was insufficient to generate radical and active popular movements as had existed in the Civil War period. Nevertheless, the strife and bitterness were such that they still provided the essential ingredients for a considerable degree of political and religious alienation. The religious response of the 1690s and the first years of the next century was thus narrower in terms of social class, less politically radical (one searches in vain for Diggers) and dominated by well-educated men. As a result, the polemical expression of political and religious dissatisfaction was less diverse. Yet it was expressed in a polemic that was theoretically and historiographically much more well-founded, and of sufficient intellectual depth to appeal to the frustrated scholar. The response to the 1690s crisis was, therefore, potentially damaging to the legitimacy of the established Church as much amongst the well-off as amongst the poorer but attentive, educated and more liberal Anglicans. For some, the scandal of renewed religious turmoil was the cause of disaffection from Christianity towards deism, or at least accounted for the deism scare. In the work of a writer identified only as D. E., *The Prodigious Appearance of Deism in this Age Modestly Accounted for in a Letter from a Deist to his Friend* (1710), it is explained how the divided nature of British Protestantism is incompatible with Christian truth. He laments how each side justifies its own case by perversion of scripture and 'tricks and subterfuges'. He condemns their self-interest and the prostitution of religion 'to palliate the most enormous pretences'. The 'inveterate Spite and Malice' of religious disputes of the various tendencies, 'openly blazed and published', are to him proof that all Protestant parties are guilty of bringing Christianity into disrepute.[27] It is not possible to determine whether this letter really was written by a deist or by a deeply disaffected Dissenter of the non-Trinitarian type, and it does not help us determine whether, in reality, significant numbers of deists did exist. Its value to us, however, lies in its estimation of the damage done to Protestant piety by politico-religious conflict.

Some years before the letter of D. E. and in the year of the publication of John Toland's *Christianity not Mysterious,* the Whig cleric William Stephens provided a similar explanation for supposed disaffection from Protestantism. In his often-cited *An Account of the Growth of Deism in England,* Stephens opined that having seen 'that *Popery* in all its Branches was only a device of the *Priesthood,* to carry on a particular Interest of their own', some gentlemen 'could not forbear to see that these *Protestant* parties [Anglicans and the 'Presbyterian Kirk'] under the pretence of Religion, were only grasping at *Power'*. As a consequence, he explained, some gentlemen refused to countenance both parties.[28] Such letters are of limited value as evidence of religious reality – and certainly not for the existence of a deist movement or real religious change. After all, we know that clerics were prone to overstating the case for their own ends. Yet this letter has been cited as important evidence of the 'transformation of the Puritan into a whig', that in the transition to Whiggism the religious polity of presbyterianism was abandoned for a secular or civil deistic outlook.[29] It is ironic that both Porter and Goldie argue for a conservative rather than radical Enlightenment, yet both wish to claim that Dissenters such as Howard, Dennis and Trenchard, and Protestants like Wollaston, were deists.[30] There is good evidence for asserting that Howard and Toland for a time were Unitarians or sympathetic to that outlook, but we ought to remind ourselves that very little is known about early Unitarianism in England.[31] We can confidently say, however, that Unitarianism, in principle, entailed a rejection of most or all forms of Trinitarian thought, that is to say rejecting Protestantism and Catholicism – something we know Isaac Newton did in his posthumous *Observations on the Prophecies of Daniel and the*

Apocalypse of St John (1733). We also know that Newton's chronology of priestcraft was very similar to that of such thinkers as Trenchard, Dennis and Howard.[32] Rejection of the traditional Christian ministry, then, is no necessary sign of deism.

It seems that Unitarians grew in number in late-seventeenth-century England, although to say that this 'seriously challenged the Church of England'[33] is to misrepresent the situation. Indeed, considering the very small numbers of Unitarians known to us, Champion's estimation that the presence of varieties of Arianism, Socinianism and Unitarianism was a serious problem is also perhaps to overstate the situation.[34] In addition, we know little, for instance, of the nature of the relationship between Trinitarian and non-Trinitarian Dissenters. Certainly Unitarians (or Socinians as they had often been known), although sometimes persecuted and expelled, had been part of the Protestant Church in continental Europe. There is little or no evidence, therefore, that late-seventeenth-century English Unitarians were hostile to simple Church polities such as presbyterianism. Indeed, in 1773 when John Lindsey seceded from the Anglican Church, an independent presbyterian-style Unitarian Church was initiated. In any case, the targets central to Unitarian polemic were the established clerical hierarchies which were accused of instigating and perpetuating the worst aspects of priestcraft. In short, it cannot be assumed that the accounts of priestcraft in the works of such writers as Trenchard, Dennis, Howard and (at the time of writing *Christianity not Mysterious*) Toland are meant to demonstrate the impossibility of simple, priestcraft-free Church polities. As a consequence, neither can it be assumed that such writers were neccessarily deistical or advocating a classically inspired civil religion.

Toland did go on to espouse deistical views, although the exigencies of politics seem to have bestowed that label upon him rather too early. The son of a Catholic priest, he converted to Protestantism at the age of sixteen and in 1688–89 went to Scotland to study. There he witnessed the 'Bloody Persecution of the Church of Scotland, and must have been an eye witness of many tyrannical and relentless scenes'.[35] Following his relocation to London, espousing the Presbyterian cause, he could not see why 'men who were sound Protestants on both sides, should barbarously cut one another's throats'.[36] Nevertheless, like most dissenting Protestants, he was not about to offer toleration to all and sundry – certainly not to atheists and Catholics. In his anti-Catholicism, Toland was in very good liberal company. As a typical reforming Protestant, John Locke (who championed toleration as a natural right) also excluded Catholics and atheists from his pleas for toleration, as did a whole range of eminent men from poets to bishops. In politics, Catholicism was inseparable from the threat of Catholic absolutism, the sort it had been feared James II wanted to introduce and which was then perceived to exist in the France of Louis XIV. Catholicism could only be tolerated in private. Toland's anti-Catholic views, like those of most other Protestants, were based upon a mixture of religious conviction and a widely shared understanding of the – real or received – Catholic threat to life and liberty. Catholic rulers were either subject to the priestcraft of the Catholic Church, or as in France were perceived to be in cahoots with popery. This politico-religious stance was also promoted for nationalistic ends, something hardly surprising, given that King Louis declared war on England in 1689, which endured until 1697. This was the bleak and often fearful outlook which enabled Protestants to detect no contradiction between the suppression of Catholicism on the one hand and earnest pleas for religious toleration on the other.

Toland was Whig in outlook for much of his life. He was, therefore, in favour of a limited monarchy, that is to say a monarch whose actions were limited by Parliament. Yet Toland has been described by some historians as a radical republican. For much of his active intellectual career, however, he was patently not a republican in the usual twentieth-century sense of the word, which pits monarchism diametrically against republicanism. In 1697, one year after the publication of his *Christianity not Mysterious*, Toland broke publicly with the cause of Dissent. That shift did not, however, indicate a political transition towards republicanism in the modern sense of the word. It is difficult to see how a radical republican could write a such a work as *The Memorial of the State of England, in Vindication of the Queen, the Church, and the Administration* (1705).[37] If Toland ever became a radical republican in the modern sense, it seems it was after 1705.[38]

Like many other Dissenters and radicals, throughout his life Toland was concerned to promote and ensure the Protestant succession in England as a counter to the threat of European Catholic hegemony. The heart of the Whig historical view, at that time synonymous with the general Protestant scheme, depicted Europe's fall from the glory of ancient Rome to the superstition and tyranny of the medieval Catholic Church.[39] In this scheme, the Reformation had partly broken the Church's stranglehold on European culture and political life. But Catholicism was not yet fully defeated, and had to some extent revived in the Counter-Reformation. Thus, for most Protestants, the future for religious toleration and political freedom for the whole of Europe was manifestly not yet assured. Despite Dissenter hostility to the Anglican Church and its relationship with the state, the principle of advocating a Protestant succession – free Christian Europe against antichristian tyranny, light against darkness – was a principle then almost inviolable. Six years after his break with Dissent, Toland left his readers in no doubt as to his Protestant, anti-Catholic orientation. In his *Vindicius liberius* (1702), he replied to accusations of heterodoxy by stating that he considered himself a member of the 'establisht Religion', and, although it is not perfect, it is the best religion in the world. He does not adhere to any particular 'society', but has joined with all Protestants against the superstition, idolatry and tyranny of 'Popery'. He is a 'true Christian' and as such cites his 'conformity to the public Worship', which proves him a 'good Church man'.[40] No longer tied to the dissenting cause, without embarrassment he could now afford to be seen paying at least public lip-service to the 'establisht Religion'. Yet that affirmation was, if not altogether true or honestly pious, not just lip-service, for Toland, as most freethinking radicals, was still committed to the maintenance of some form of national Church for the good of public order.

All this, however, was yet to come, for now we must now ask if the content of his *Christianity not Mysterious* supports the traditional view that it was the work of a deist. Several scholars, including myself, consider *Christianity not Mysterious* to be a reforming Dissenter work,[41] and as a consequence one should expect to find an unmitigating hostility to the history of the Christian hierarchy central to its contents. In the preface, Toland wrote that he was raised in the 'grossest superstition and idolatry'. Contrary to the often repeated claim (or sometimes assumption) that *Christianity not Mysterious* categorically rejected revelation, Toland also explained how the instructions of Jesus Christ were clear and convincing, contrasting Jesus's simple clarity with the intricate and ineffectual declamations of the scribes or priests. Whilst this statement may be insufficient to indicate a Trinitarian outlook, it is at least broadly consonant with that of a Unitarian. As a Unitarian, he could of course praise the moral and spiritual humanity of Jesus, without necessarily accepting the revelation of Jesus or indeed His miracles and those of others. Like Trenchard, Howard and Dennis, Toland's aim was to show how '*Christianity became mysterious*, and how so divine an Institution did, through the Craft and Ambition of the *Priests* and *Philosophers*, degenerate into mere paganism'. It was the '*Contradictions* and *Mysteries*' charged to Christianity which caused so many Christians to become deists and atheists. Then, wishing to emphatically underline his reformist stance, he observed he was only doing that which the Reformation had set out to achieve, namely laying bare priestcraft.[42]

As in the works of Trenchard, Dennis and Howard, in Toland's work there is little or no analysis specifically targeted at the papacy and the Catholic Church. This should be no surprise. Indeed, this phenomenon has been one of the factors that has led some historians to consider *Christianity not Mysterious* a work of deist inspiration, that is to say attacking the very concept of the Christian ministry. Dissenters such as Toland felt no need to reiterate the common-or-garden critique of the medieval or contemporary Catholic Church. It was the one facet of English Protestant thought which was not accompanied by widespread and damaging controversy. Catholic priestcraft was an uncontentious subject, a given, something safely relegated to the conceptual anti-Catholic evidence supplied by the Protestant readership. When polemicists such as Toland had other, more pressing concerns, why devote valuable space to an argument that had already, long ago, achieved hegemony. Thus, when the frauds of pagan priests are described, the comparison with the medieval Church, Catholicism *and Anglicanism* was usually understood. Dissenting writers usually failed to exempt the Anglican Church from the devastation of their priestcraft allegations, or gave only a polite nod to the difference between Catholicism and Anglicanism. The less the explicit exemption of Anglicanism, the more the worst horrors of priestcraft – without loss of critical efficacy – could be tacitly attributed to Anglicanism. This tactic of guilt by implicit association had been exploited earlier in the seventeenth century by many writers, including Henry Ainsworth and Herbert of Cherbury,[43] and was a tactic too efficacious in the battle for right religion to be easily abandoned. Unsurprisingly, then, Toland did not exempt Anglicanism from the blistering invective of his *Christi-*

anity not Mysterious, allowing its scourge to be applied implicitly in full measure to the Anglican Church. Convocation (the government of the Anglican Church) was, therefore, absolutely correct when it noted in 1711 that 'Priests without Distinction ... [had been] traduc'd, as Imposers on the Credulity of Mankind'.[44] The bonus of this tacit comparative technique was that the burden of contemporary proof (including space) for charges against Anglicanism was avoided. In addition, and certainly most importantly, the possibility of arousing the public ire of Church and state was reduced. Even when it was aroused, specific and official charges were made more difficult to formulate and prosecute if the indictment of Anglicanism was understood rather than made explicit.

In *Christianity not Mysterious*, therefore, the indictment Toland formulated against the primitive Church was meant to be fully applied by his readers to the Anglican Church, yet elements of piety beyond the need to mislead any censor are also apparent in his thought. In historical summary, Toland argued it was the motive of 'their own Advantage ... that put the Primitive *Clergy* upon reviving *Mysteries* [and] they quickly erected themselves into a separate Body'. Utilizing the language of piety appropriate to his religious outlook, he then relates how soon distinctions of rank and orders in the clergy and other usurpations made their way 'under pretence of *Labourers in the Lord's Vineyard*'. These priests ornamented ceremony and rite with 'Extravagancies of Heathen Original'. Thus, the Eucharist was 'absolutely perverted and destroyed' and is 'not yet fully restor'd by the purest Reformations in *Christendom*'. Matters became worse, almost incurable, when Emperor Constantine endorsed Christianity. As a result the multitudes flocked to Christianity from 'politick considerations', and the Christian priesthood was enriched with the endowments and benefices of the pagan priests, flamens and augurs. When philosophers became Christians, a further degeneration was set in train, because the erroneous opinions of philosophers entered Christianity, and the simple precepts of Christ became intelligible only to the learned. He explained how

> Decrees or Constitutions concerning *Ceremonies* and *Discipline*, to increase the Splendor of [the clergy] ... did strangely affect or stupify the Minds of the ignorant People; and made them believe they were in good earnest Mediators between God and Men, that could fix Sanctity to certain Times, Places, Persons or Actions. By

this means the *Clergy* were able to do anything; they engross'd at length the sole Right of interpreting *Scripture,* and with it claim'd *Infallibility,* to their Body.[45]

In the years after 1697 Toland drew away from his reforming stance. Even after abandoning his dissenting ideals, Toland of course had no need to retract or regret almost anything contained in his reforming work *Christianity not Mysterious.* His Dissenter historiography continued to serve his more radical aims very well indeed, and is something that has helped to produce or reinforce the impression that Toland was a deist in 1696. Later deistical writers such as Tindal and Collins used the critique of Toland, Dennis, Howard and others as the historical and sociological foundation for their own various politico-religious attacks upon the Church. To the frustration of many staunch Anglicans, public opinion also doggedly refused to assent to stricter controls on dissenting publications that were so potentially damaging to Anglicanism. The Printing Act had not been renewed in 1694 for various reasons, but primarily simply because public opinion was against it, and neither Whig nor Tory trusted each other with its partisan implementation. Between 1695 and 1698 four modified versions of the Act were presented, but Parliament could come to no agreement. Attempts to revive it continued and anxious messages were sent from the throne, but none were successful.[46]

Early modern politico-religious propagandists and modern historians

According to some modern writers, however, the situation was far, far more grave: '[b]y 1680, the virulent skeptical movement known as Deism asserted itself in British cities and universities ... a popular religious and rhetorical movement'. Apparently – and this claim is not unusual – 'by 1720 Deism was widespread in British cities, posing a serious threat to social and religious stability ... [it was a] war waged for the religious mind of Britain and eventually of Europe and the Colonies ... A rising tide of skepticism, heresy, blasphemy, and atheism swept the realm as the foundational presuppositions of Christianity were assaulted.'[47] Even more sober commentators have been seduced by the fog of myth and confusion on the question of deism, one even venturing to assert that on the 'deist side the number of petty scribblers was immense'.[48] To some of those looking closely at the evidence, these claims may seem to have a touch of rhetoric about them. It is ironic, therefore, that the term rhetoric features so prominently in the title of Herrick's work. As Herrick has been forced to admit – despite the efforts of Margaret Jacob[49] – the occasional speculation that the size of the deist movement has been hidden from posterity by its exploitation of secret societies such as the Masons cannot be proven.[50] Indeed, apart from the most scanty, even circumstantial evidence for such a situation is mostly lacking, and his proposition – via Berman – that radical publicists such as Charles Blount should be seen as 'vehicles of a subversive, threatening social unconsciousness' is unfounded.[51]

We must assume, for it is not explicitly stated, that for Herrick the date 1680 is significant because of the work of Charles Blount.[52] Yet an analysis of the post-1680 figures of this supposed virulent deist movement cited by Herrick amount only to twelve over a period of about seventy years.[53] It is unfair, of course, to single out one particular historian on this subject, for, as we have seen in previous chapters, many modern historians face the same dilemma: placing the square peg of the supposed deist movement into the round hole of the actual evidence. How can we explain the consistent claims for the existence of a deist movement when the paucity of evidence for its existence is clear? The answer is that historians have been hampered by their own research agendas and have adopted an insufficiently critical attitude towards the historical record.

Although not denying the existence of an Enlightenment deist movement, Popkin has, however, commented on the tiny number of active deists in Europe in the years immediately preceding the Enlightenment. He has noted that 'in fact, it is unclear whether there was more than a handful of Deists in England, France, or the Netherlands in 1688'. This fact – and it can hardly be disputed – is nevertheless of no real importance for Popkin, for he continues: '[h]owever, the views attributed to them ... played a most important role in providing a basis for religious and political toleration in England, in the British American Colonies, and later in Revolutionary France'.[54] So, uncomfortable as Popkin's assertion might seem to be for some historians, it can still be considered by some as not necessarily as damaging as it might be. This is because, in effect, Popkin's claim is that several tiny deist cogs managed, by degrees, to turn the comparatively vast wheel of the early European and English colonial Enlightenment by the force of their argument. It might well be the case that it is possible to detect general similarities between some of the arguments for political and religious pluralism in Enlightenment England, America and France, and those expressed by some supposedly early deists. This does not *per se*, however, prove influence at all; it merely means that some similarities have been detected and does not of necessity settle the question as to why similarities might exist. Much earlier, in his *The Church and the Age of Reason* (1960), Cragg helped provide the basis for the views of later thinkers by arguing that deists disposed of undoubted influence. It is true that Cragg admitted that 'the Deists were not a large group, and never formed a party in any formal sense'. Nevertheless, for him, 'it was clear that they appealed to an extensive reading public. Hence their works elicited a large number of replies. One of Collins' pamphlets inspired thirty-five answers, Tindal's *Christianity as Old as the Creation* at least one hundred and fifty. For a couple of decades (1720–40) the interest in the debate was intense. Then it suddenly waned.'[55]

Locating a research tool to measure influence is the historiographical equivalent of the search for the Holy Grail. Popkin's and Cragg's forthright statement of historical influence is, of course, merely their opinion. It is based on a particular, yet common perspective in which deists and their views had a major public and private impact on the intellectual life of eighteenth-century Europe, and by the force of their thought brought about toleration and thus modern religious pluralism. It is this reading of the past that I wish to challenge in this and subsequent chapters on France and Italy.

Cragg himself never mentions by name any more deists than those few we have already identified. Confusingly, he does, however, implicitly talk of deism as a movement or something like it, as for instance when he notes that 'Deism, though worsted in the controversy, really collapsed through its own inherent weakness'.[56] If there were just a few writers across several decades, what was there to collapse? If, on the other hand, he is referring to the influence of the deists, evidence of such influence must be brought forward and critically examined. His evidence concerning the scale of the public debate can more convincingly be construed as evidence to the contrary: evidence of isolation in the face of general animosity. What he and other writers do not make sufficiently clear, or at least properly assimilate into their overall assessment of the available evidence, is that these replies/answers were of course trenchantly hostile. Most copies of deist works were undoubtedly purchased by enemies of deism and those interested in public scandal rather than supporters. It is difficult to escape the conclusion, therefore, that large print runs or sales figures of texts do not necessarily indicate support for the authors' views. It goes without saying that, in order to mount a hostile reply, one must at least read the offending text. If deists could, with some caution, publish their views, so could supporters cautiously publish their support; consequently we must ask where are the pro-deist publications demonstrating the existence of a deist movement and/or influence? The point is this: in an age still unused to the questioning in public of the central tenets of its official faith, those who saw themselves as public defenders of the faith and/or fighting for recognition in the ecclesiastical world could hardly be expected to ignore the publication of 'blasphemous' texts.

In pursuit of an answer to the question of how the bogey of a deist movement was manufactured in the late seventeenth and early eighteenth centuries, we can profitably pose the question of how and why John Toland – at the time of the publication of his *Christianity not Mysterious* – was publicly transformed from a Unitarian into a deist. As we have already noted, in 1696 Toland was known as a Unitarian and was supported by a Quaker leader. In 1697 the Latitudinarian John Locke was unhappy that his friend Toland did not bid him farewell and obtain proper introductions before he departed for Dublin in order to serve as secretary to the new Chancellor of Ireland, John Methuen. But it would not be long before politico-religious pressure forced Locke to effectively repudiate Toland as a deist. Prior to Toland's departure for Dublin his *Christianity not Mysterious* was condemned in England as injurious to orthodox Christianity. It is true that Toland's reputation had preceded him to Ireland and hostility to him had been aroused in some quarters. *Christianity not Mysterious* inevitably seemed more outrageous in a provincial capital than in London. As Sullivan has illustrated, 'commonly, Irishmen took it [*Christianity not Mysterious*] as a Socinian production ... which prompted the archbishop of Dublin to inspire a pamphlet which called on the civil arm to "suppress his Insolence"'. It cannot be said, however, that this was the cause of Toland's prosecution and hurried flight from Ireland. The key – but usually overlooked – factor was political in nature. Just as Methuen was appointed, there arose in Ireland a bitter political polemic against England, or specifically against the Whigs who had dominated the administration since 1695. 'When, at the end of summer, the chancellor's enemies considered a means of striking at him, his visible and controversial dependent [Toland] seemed a convenient stick.'[57] Consequently, the Irish Commons condemned Toland's work as heretical, ordered it burnt by the hangman and Toland to be arrested and prosecuted.

As the (failed) prosecution was primarily political in intent, it is not surprising that in his account of that parliamentary session the Bishop of Derry, William King, takes note of only three religious actions – all penal measures against Catholics – and does not mention Toland at all. As he later wrote to the Archbishop of Canterbury, 'Toland's prosecutors' real "design was against some greater persons, that supported him"'. Now, in good part thanks to politics, Toland had notoriety (and thus a potentially greater audience for his works), but he also

> became a pawn in the political struggle between the ascendant Latitudinarians and the emerging High-Church party for control of the Church of England. The [High-Church] insurgents, appointing themselves the church's defenders against both external and internal enemies, found in Toland a notorious figure whom they could identify with the most threatening of these foes.... he was ... made a Socinian cat's-paw with which the High-Church majority of the lower house of convocation of 1698 could strike at the Whiggish and Latitudinarian upper house.[58]

In their efforts to further their own partisan interests, the furore High Churchmen could raise against 'heretics', even if contrived, could be effective in forcing Latitudinarians and other theological liberals into retreat in order to preserve their political well-being. In this type of political climate, it is no wonder Locke began to feel the need to distance himself from his one-time friend and his now seemingly so dangerous opinions. In an attempt to discredit Socinianism (Unitarianism), some Anglicans had linked it with deism, for deism was understood to be virtually atheism, the worst enemy of Christendom. While Locke did not actually denominate Toland a deist, 'he tried to nudge his readers into including the Irishman among these notorious, if obscure, heretics'.[59] Locke and other determined assailants were certainly successful. From the 1690s a public image of an organized deist/atheist threat became part of the politico-religious landscape in both intellectual and more popular circles.

The English deist movement

Aside from the fear of France, deism was the public bogey of the day and continued to be so into the 1730s.

The dominant explanation for the decline of English deism amongst historians today remains more or less that of Cragg: 'Bishop Butler's monumental work, *The Analogy of Religion, Natural and Revealed, to the Constitution and Course of Nature* [1736], was the most formidable and the most decisive work that the deist controversy called forth. On essential matters it virtually ended the debate; skirmishing continued for some years, but it was clear that the fundamental issues had been settled.'[60] Amongst the few recent historians who significantly diverge from the Butler-triumphant explanation is Roy Porter and his 'laicization' thesis. We have seen already that Porter argues for a conservative English Enlightenment, yet one populated with numerous radical deists who were 'novel, incisive and influential'. On the decline of deism, he argues that the deists were less read later in the century because they had already achieved their aims and that 'threats to a gentleman's privilege of being religious on his own terms' from High Churchmen and other enthusiasts 'had been resisted, had withered away or were becoming marginalized to the "lunatic fringe"'. Crucially, 'legislation won toleration for Protestants' when Convocation was prorogued in 1717.[61] The problem here is the difficulty of reconciling this account with those of historians who, as we have seen, argue that the crescendo of the supposed deist movement in terms of numbers and influence occurred in the 1730s. Given that there is little evidence that the deist movement ever existed, debate on the chronology of its victory or defeat is of no great consequence except in one respect, for Porter's 'victory of deism' view is predicated on a thesis of a relatively weak Church. Yet, as we shall see below, there is no consensus amongst historians on the weak Church thesis, and it has been increasingly challenged.

Returning to the Butler-triumphant-over-deism thesis, if, as we know, deist writers were a mere handful over half a century and most of the leading writers died in the years preceding Butler's polemic, should we not consider this a factor in their decline? Tindal, Collins and Woolston all died, for example, in the years 1729–33. Given this rather intractable fact, if we accept that the coterie of deists never managed to attract any significant number of followers or any real broad interest aside from the negative type or sensation hunters, is it surprising that the deist controversy petered out sooner rather than later? We may even say that, even if it had existed, for it to have continued for much longer would have been unlikely. Interestingly, it is rarely mentioned in Enlightenment studies that, even on the Anglican side, there has never been unquestioned acceptance of the idea that the Christian knight Butler single-handedly defeated the deist threat. Mossner long ago argued that even to pose the question in that manner is misleading, and Butler's analogical method was anyway not original.[62]

As we have seen, the evidence of replies to works or propositions is not, in itself, sufficient proof of the existence of one historical reality rather than another potentially contrary one, and the ability of the historical record to portray or be made to portray one rather than another we must surely take for granted. In the eighteenth century, nowhere was this more the case than in the politico-ecclesiastical world, which was capable of systematically raising issues more of concern to itself and its interests than to those of the wider public. As, for example, Walsh and Taylor have noted (not in support of the revisionist thesis I present here), '[r]ecent historians have generally focused on political causes of disturbance in the Church, but this is to ignore the capacity of clergymen, as a highly specialized profession, to worry about issues of morality and theology which did not concern the laity to the same degree'. In short, they could 'overreact' and publicly 'sound the alarm' when not entirely necessary.[63] As Cragg himself long ago put it, 'Church leaders tended to be more aware of their foes than of their friends'.[64] The implications of this realization are important: subjects of public debate and degrees of heat upon them could, therefore, potentially exist more or less independently of public concern.

What, however, constituted a foe of the clergy? This is a question which cannot be given a one-dimensional answer, simply because to ask about foes of the Church and clerical overreaction is to approach the crucial interface between politics and religion. To imagine that in eighteenth-century Britain there were not constituencies of political and religious interest at times happy to describe deism as a threat greater than it really was is to imagine the impossible. Since the late Restoration period and before, the Church-in-danger cry had contained a profoundly political element. This could hardly be otherwise, because the Tory constituency of interest was principally Anglican and often High Church in orientation, and that of the Whig party significantly dissenting in orientation. At the more strident end of the spectrum, that cry could be used, especially by High Church Tories, to associate its opponents with immorality, irreligion and political irresponsibility, and even to cast aspersions on their national loyalty. Perhaps more subtly and certainly more pervasively, the Church-in-danger cry could be raised as a means of prompting declarations of loyalty and so tend to isolate those perceived to be less staunch in their fidelity to Anglicanism. For varied politico-religious reasons, then, the public domain could conjure up a deist threat where non-existed. As Mossner commented some sixty years ago, 'the deist was subject not only to *odium theologicum*, but to legal and popular censure as well. The name of deist became a fashionable bogey indicative of evil character.'[65]

Using external threat as a means of promoting loyalty, unity and even giving identity to the amorphous nature of Anglicanism was a traditional tactic of the Church, traditionally utilizing concepts of popery[66] and the 'Dissenter threat'. It would be very surprising indeed, therefore, if deist writers were not similarly used, for their tenets were clearly anti-Anglican and their arguments certainly inflammatory at times. Such tactics had political value both in times of perceived crisis and in periods of political calm, for in periods of calm the existence (or effective creation) of threat could be utilized as a means of restating the Tory *raison d'être*. The Sacheverell case is perhaps the most well known example of this phenomenon. In 1709 the Tory and High Church Henry Sacheverell preached at St Paul's, emphasizing the dramatic perils facing the Church as a result of the Whig government's policy of relative (that is to say still quite restricted) religious toleration of Dissenters. Not surprisingly, the Commons condemned the sermon as seditious whilst the Tories gave him strong support. The nature of his politico-religious chauvinism, however, widely reported in the press, excited a considerable degree of public support for Anglicanism. Despite strong opposition, Sacheverell was impeached for high crimes and misdemeanour. But this was in fact a climb-down and, if anything, a victory for the Church-in-danger tactic, for his sentence was a mere suspension from preaching for three years and Sacheverell rapidly became a popular hero.

Three years later Sacheverell preached to packed gatherings, his sermons had wide circulation and he was presented by Queen Anne to the living of St Andrew's Holborn. It is also widely recognized that the fall of the Whigs in 1710 was in large part the result of the impeachment of Sacheverell. This was a political-religious lesson never forgotten, in which the power of public opinion to alter political fortunes was never underestimated – we need only recall the successful opposition to the Quaker Tithe Bill in 1737, the riots which forced the withdrawal of Pelham's 'Jew Bill' in 1853, the Gordon Riots against Catholics in 1780, and the Church and King Riots against Dissenters in 1791. So, despite that fact that some lessening of the disabilities under which Dissenters suffered did come about in subsequent decades, Walpole and other political leaders steadfastly refused to repeal the Test and Corporation Acts (the former not repealed until 1829 and the latter until 1828). The Church-in-danger cry, then, had the power to create reputations and bogeys, for we know that the Dissenters certainly never represented the broad threat ascribed to them by Sacheverell, his High Church supporters and sympathetic media organs. The press and interested parties had created a dissenting bogey capable of great political import, and would go on to create others to serve similar ends; indeed, one was already partly created, that of the immoral, irreligious, Church-hating deist. The Church-in-danger cry was not, however, exclusive to Tories, but was to be found in the hands of Whig High Church prelates such as Bishop Gibson, to whom we shall return.

The Sacheverell case, although traditionally given little space in Enlightenment studies, is crucial to our understanding of the conditions under which the Enlightenment developed. It is thus also crucial to our understanding of the conditions under which the creation of Enlightenment shibboleths such as deism were forged and bequeathed to modern historians. As Holmes has commented, in most respects Sacheverell did not undertake any new High Church politico-religious tactic. Inside the 'predictable grooves of the extreme High Churchman', he utilized the 'traditional reliance on political means'. Indeed, it 'is striking how each wave in the "Church in Danger" campaigns of the post-Revolution period began to rise towards its crest at a period when the Whigs were either firmly in control of the government or were threatening to seize control'. The great majority of High Churchmen and even some less conservative Anglican clergy 'still yearned for the closest possible return to the pre-1687 position, when the Church and State still worked in harmony within a regime in which uniformity and unquestioning obedience to authority were the watchwords'. This made the division between High and Low Church or Tory and Whig stark indeed, and the result was the 'prostitution of the pulpit, particularly in Queen Anne's reign, to blatantly party ends'. Many made the Church-in-danger cry 'a regular feature of their sermons. They strove to convince their congregations that the Church not only was in direst peril from the Dissenters, from the new intellectual forces unleashed against it, and above all from the enemy within the gate – from those black sheep, the Low Church bishops and the Whig or moderate politicians.' Indeed, 'Tories were encouraged by the clergy to proclaim their Church's danger from the housetops'. In the constituencies this crude party slogan, 'so easy to spread ... and so hard to eradicate', was even more effective, for '[i]n return for this backing, the bulk of the 9,000-odd parish clergy threw their whole weight behind the Tory cause in Election after Election from 1698 onwards.... by the very nature of their office they were the most effective canvassers any party could possess. But, above all, they were prepared to use their pulpits shamelessly for electoral ends.'[67]

In terms of the development of the Enlightenment and the realization of its 'programme' of liberation from clerical tutelage, what was at stake in the Sacheverell affair? It hardly needs stating that a return to pre-1687 conditions would have been a blow of momentous proportions for progressive aspirations. It is true that Sacheverell and his vast following ultimately failed to bring about any such return, but it is also true that Sacheverell's astute use of public opinion brought about the most serious challenge the English Enlightenment encountered, one which had lasting consequences. Sacheverell was an ambitious man, even arrogantly so, and one way to make fame and fortune – which he certainly did – was to make one's name a household word. From this point of view, his astute use of the media was a landmark in the development of public opinion and print culture.

The foundation of High Church thought was the assumption that the Crown and Church were interdependent and, crucially, that that interdependence was vital to both and also constituted a central element of the English 'constitution'. As Holmes has put it, all around him 'Sacheverell saw men intent on threatening, if not destroying, the sacred links between the civil and ecclesiastical power: and few of his congregations were left in doubt of the potentially awful consequences of such intentions. Once those links were broken the road to republicanism, and even to regicide, would be open.' Thus, as was the norm amongst such thinkers, Sacheverell made no distinction between one form of dissent and another, and was vehemently opposed to the notion of toleration which could only lead to atheism. Whigs and others, 'in the blindness of their spiritual pride [had] ... seemed to assume that the freedom of worship the State had granted to persons of real scruples should empower Deists, Socinians and Atheists to revile, ridicule and blaspheme our most holy faith and Church at their pleasure'.[68] In the hands of such men, the most moderate of Dissenters and insignificant numbers of deists could become grotesquely transformed into movements and national threats, and had been proclaimed so by High Church pulpit-thumpers since the 1690s, and by Sacheverell since at least 1702. His 1709 sermon, however, marked a radical development in the production of the deist myth, and deism too became firmly associated in the public mind with a threat to Englishness. His 1709 sermon, *The Perils of False Brethren,* in good part on account of his impeachment, was to sell close to 100,000 copies. Given that many copies were read aloud and others had multiple readers, this is a very significant figure. Indeed, it has been said that as a 'short-term best-seller' the sermon had no equal in that century: a sermon was now going to be read 'by at least a quarter of a million men and women, in other words by a number equal to the whole electorate of England and Wales'.[69] What is missing from many accounts of his trial and its impact is, however, the power of the media. Too much attention is usually paid to the print figures of the *Perils of False Brethren* and too little to the large numbers of leaflets, pamphlets and copious newspaper coverage of the affair, in which at times England seemed to be at the mercy of the enemies of the Church.

The Sacheverell affair was a personal and media extravaganza the like of which had never been seen, for, while the events of the late seventeenth century had been tumultuous, the Sacheverell phenomenon was not founded on any comparable event, but merely upon one rather predictable sermon. The age of media and public opinion had certainly arrived in the late seventeenth century, but with the Sacheverell affair, the public sphere had matured into something recognizable today. The case reflects the latent tension in early-eighteenth-century society, which was ripe for exploitation. Paradoxically, it was a situation in which the least enlightened played a direct role in the production of the bogey of supposedly the most enlightened, the deists. Sacheverell became the hero of all England, whether urban or rural. He became the white solitary knight steadfastly pitting himself against innumerable foes, and the contemporary descriptions of his rapturous, even tumultuous reception wherever he went are remarkable even without recounting the serious anti-Whig pro-Sacheverell riots in London. On one occasion, in one northern location, 1,700 loaves were distributed to the poor all marked 'Sacheverell', and the rural and urban districts alike boisterously celebrated what was, in effect, Sacheverell's victory in the trial. It is no exaggeration to say – and is accepted so by most historians – that Sacheverell made the Tory campaign for an election possible and also ensured the defeat of the Whigs: '[t]he anti-Whig reaction was nowhere more marked than in those counties and boroughs through which the Doctor had passed'.[70] Such momentous reactions and concomitant political defeat meant the Sacheverell affair produced political lessons difficult to forget. The foremost of these was the vulnerability of the Whigs to the Church-in-danger cry and the possibility of raising it without real evidence of any increase in danger.

To believe the Church-in-danger cry of Sacheverell and his supporters, one would think eighteenth-century England was racked by division and intolerance. Yet most modern historians have recognized that in this period England was above all a society marked by religious diversity, yet relative harmony, a society in which there was also 'a significant unity of purpose between Church and Enlightenment'.[71] According to Porter, after 1688, 'the very statute book incorporated much of the enlightened wish list: freedom of the person under habeas corpus, the rule of law, Parliament, religious toleration, and so forth'.[72] This was, of course, substantially the same description given of Enlightenment England by Voltaire in his *Lettres philosophiques ou Lettres Anglaises* (1734), and he was rather too admiring. So, were the High Church Tories and their varied supporters mistaken in their interpretation of reality? On the other hand, should historians be in the business of declaring the opinions of historical actors invalid? Certainly some believed their own assertions. We may say, therefore, that the historical record contains a series of opinions from which we may choose our reality, and that our interpretation of essential elements of any period should be definitively contingent on our recognition of that fact. In practice, then, we have little choice but to accept that, at times, the politico-religious configuration of the period could result in quite high degrees of 'noise' without evidence of any commensurate battle. Let us examine a case in point, that of the outbreak of anticlericalism in Parliament in the 1730s, supposedly unparalleled since 'Henry VIII's Reformation Parliament' and having deism as one of its contributory causes.[73]

The *Cambridge Modern History* of 1909, hardly a bastion of anticlericalism, describes the politico-religious context of the period in these terms: 'Political considerations dominated ecclesiastical patronage and behaviour; and, while the Church became more and more political, the State became less and less religious'. It was a 'Church occupied chiefly with patronage and controversy.... Episcopal politicians ... learnt the mundane lessons of corruption and venality from the place-hunters of Parliament.'[74] But responsibility for this state of affairs cannot be laid at the feet of any coterie or set of individuals, rather it was in good part the result of the structure of the state–Church relationship. The House of Lords still wielded considerable power and bishops formed an important constituency within it, and, as a consequence, at times their votes could be decisive. In 1733, for instance, the episcopal bench saved Walpole from defeat. As Cragg has commented, the 'appointment of bishops was one of the few ways in which the balance of power could be affected, and it became a matter of prime concern to select men of proven party loyalty. In making appointments, political considerations outweighed all others. A court chaplain of the period remarked that when a bishop "rose by the weight of his character", it was "against all the rules of gravity and experience".'[75] In his own diocese, bishops were very important figures and were expected to promote their party's cause. This status, and the influence and potential earnings from the post, meant that bishoprics were the target for younger sons of the nobility, and lesser but still lucrative prebends and benefices were targeted by the gentry. Given that the gentry and nobility dominated the politics of the period, the unavoidable result was that the higher clergy were often related by ties of family and interest to those sitting in Parliament and their influential party supporters.

Although political parties existed, we should not make the mistake of thinking them to be essentially similar to modern disciplined political parties. They were much looser entities than today's parties and the discipline sought by ministers was too often impossible or hard to come by. The main method of 'encouraging' party obedience was of course patronage, which could come in a variety of forms and be more or less overt or covert depending on circumstance. Patronage was – in Europe as a whole – still an accepted means of influence. That is to say patronage did not equal corruption in the political corridors of early modern Britain, although some forms of patronage might be seen as less legitimate than others. This is an essential understanding, for without it we will have difficulty comprehending the scale and thus the importance of patronage in the public and political life of eighteenth-century Britain. This circumstance provided a key element of the interface between religion and politics. But even patronage could not secure all a minister might desire, especially if the targets were already rich and powerful as was usually the case in the House of Lords, whose members were also guaranteed a seat by right of birth. In this circumstance their fellows, the bishops or 'spiritual lords', could at least be chosen with care for their political reliability, becoming the placemen of ministers.

This blatant mixing of venality, class distinction, politics and religion did not enhance the already jaundiced image of the Church in the eyes of the public. Indeed, in Christian terms, the highly questionable and divisive arrangement was often confirmed by the class-based pew arrangement in Anglican churches themselves. So, while in general terms still loyal to King and the Church, sections of the public could still harbour great resentment at the Church–state arrangement. As Cragg has put it, '[t]here is little doubt that the clergy were unpopular. Neither before nor since has the clerical order been exposed to such general attack.'[76] Nevertheless, as Walsh and Taylor have noted, '[t]here was, however, a powerful strain of popular Anglicanism within English society. Any fashionable stereotype of the Church as an agency of social control neglected or despised by its plebeian constituents needs to be treated warily and set alongside the powerful loyalties which it attracted: loyalties attested to by the great "Church and King" riots from Sacheverell to Priestley, and still more by the innumerable little pro-Church mobbings of Methodist itinerant preachers.' The key point for this discussion should, however, be the significance of Walsh and Taylor's next sentence: 'The existence of that loyalty, however, is easier to define than its meaning. Popular Anglicanism was not primarily theological.'[77] Had or could popular Anglicanism ever be purely or primarily theological? National identity, loyalty and current affairs had, inevitably, always played a most important role in the life of what was the official Church of state and government. If that Church had ever found itself wholly bereft of popular, positive sentiment, that is to say a context either of pure indifference or pure theology in which a sense of Anglican national identity was lacking, then a loud Church-in-danger cry might be justified, whether the supposed danger was identified as popery, Dissent or deism.[78] So, in the broad public and popular realm, the exact theological nature and actual size of any threat to the Church could be less important than its perceived significance in terms of standards of morality, general cultural outlook and national identity. But an important point about public media, known then as now, is that taste, desire, fears, hopes and ignorance can be manipulated. Small news can quickly become big news more or less regardless of the degree of correspondence between the story and reality. As we now know, once taste or habits of media consumption are created, they can serve as a prompt for more media sensationalism and in turn create readerships, influence and income.

In the first half of the eighteenth century, the public's growing hunger for news was fed with a now familiar diet of scandal, political reality and 'current concern' items by the growing numbers of confident political journalists in numerous weekly or monthly newsheets. As Roy Porter has put it, the eighteenth century saw 'the rise and triumph of lay and secular public opinion, the fourth estate'.[79] So worrying was this burgeoning public world that it was felt a government counter was needed. So it was that the *Daily Courant*, the *Free Briton* and the *London Journal*, effectively ministerial mouthpieces, were distributed free by the Post Office and issued free to coffee houses, and their editors were paid considerable sums from state funds.[80] The growing capacity of the press to mount a public critique of the status quo was thus clearly a worry for some, but this is not the same as saying that the Church was besieged by its antichristian enemies. Indeed, most historians accept that indifference and unbelief were, as Porter has recently put it, 'far from the norm'.[81] It is true that some anticlericalism could be loosely termed deistic and antichristian, 'but much of it was not'.[82]

The problem for Whig governments was that the Whig party traditionally represented critics of the Anglican Church and its privileged relationship to the state, yet Walpole and some other leading Whigs realized the ultimate folly of neglecting the Church and allowing it to fall into hands hostile to their political interests. Walpole thus wanted to demonstrate that the Church was at least safe in Whig hands, even if not revered. To his constant chagrin, however, he found that when Church affairs were debated in Parliament, some of his supporters understood it as their right to criticize the Church and continued to take the opportunity to inveigh against Anglican clergy. In those attacks, Whigs were reflecting their own view, but also creating a public impression easily utilized by their orthodox Tory opponents as supposed evidence of their implicit alliance or at least connection with more radical enemies of the Church. This impression is, as we have seen, how some modern historians have interpreted the situation, having taken what seemed to them the noise of the battle as evidence of the real thing.

Part of the underlying problem in this misinterpretation of the historical record has been that the High Church has been considered to have been in great decline in these years, and consequently without significant influence on events or opinions. In addition, on account of the traditional Enlightenment studies focus on radicalism, the very idea of a conservative ecclesiastical lobby having any significant input into the enlightened scene or at least its historical record has been dismissed out of hand. For many years it had been held that the mid and late Georgian Church was dominated by an all-pervasive Latitudinarianism. This view was challenged by J. C. D. Clark in his *English Society 1688–1832* (1985), arguing that 'Tories and Jacobites before 1760, far from being a tiny fringe of fanatics, were a large sector of society. They possessed a powerful and credible ideology.'[83] More recently, Walsh and Taylor have noted that '[i]f the fortunes of High Churchmanship ebbed and flowed, it seems always to have commanded the allegiance of sizeable sections of the clergy'. Indeed, 'the theological (i.e. not ceremonial) tradition of High Anglicanism seems [to have been] strengthening rather than diminishing in the later decades' of the century.[84] The issue of a weak or demoralized or strong or confident eighteenth-century conservative Church goes to the very heart of Enlightenment studies. A strong and/or confident High Church could feel able to exaggerate the deist or 'rational' threat (High Church polemicists had always maintained that Latitudinarianism was a cloak for heresy) with the design of calling its ranks and some of the wavering Latitudinarians to order, and forging increased unity against dissenting campaigns for greater toleration without running any significant risk.

So although anticlericalism did undoubtedly exist, the public and press could still be rallied to the support of popular Anglicanism. Of course deists, those (in the popular portrayal) without Christian morals or allegiance to Church and King, were exactly that, perceived threats to Englishness loosely embodied in Anglicanism. From one historical vantage point, then, it could appear to all intents and purposes as if the Church was besieged on all sides by its enemies, and many clergy were quite happy to subscribe to that version of reality. The paradox is that the public appearance of radical Enlightenment strength was in part predicated upon a Church establishment – or elements of it – that was confident enough to allow that fiction in order to serve its own ends.

There is yet another dimension or shade to our canvas, for as Walsh and Taylor have also noted, although 'historians are confident that "High" Anglicanism existed as a potent force throughout the eighteenth century, they are not always so confident in defining what it was. What makes the taxonomy of church groups particularly difficult is the way in which political definitions became periodically entangled with religious ones ... for many Englishmen in the early eighteenth century High Churchmanship suggested the Tory party at prayer.' Such labels were used for political stereotyping but 'the political use of partisan terminology did not necessarily coincide with the religious usage.... One might be a "High Churchman" in a political sense and not in a doctrinal sense',[85] or indeed vice versa. One such example was Bishop Gibson, a court Whig yet High Churchman. As Cragg long ago put it, if Walpole was sometimes embarrassed by the anticlerical outbursts of his followers, 'his position was easy compared with that of Bishop Gibson of London, his great ally in the management of Church affairs. Gibson was both a staunch High Churchman and a convinced Whig. His difficulties stemmed from the intermediate position in which his party still found itself.' The Whigs certainly believed in toleration, '[b]ut the Whig churchmen themselves regarded the Church as part of the constitutional settlement, as a body of immense political importance whose support must be won for the Hanoverian regime'.[86] This was the basis of the Church–Whig alliance against Dissenter campaigns for greater toleration and Church reform (against tithe collection for example).

Naturally, Gibson deplored much of the anticlerical thought of many Whigs and was therefore viewed as a staunch defender of the Church even against other Whigs. This is an extremely important point, for much of the sparse evidence for the 'reality' of the deist movement is anecdotal, and one such significant source is the life of Bishop Gibson as related by Sykes.[87] As we have seen, Walsh and Taylor, for instance, have said that in the 1730s '[d]eism seemed to have become dangerously fashionable in the *haut monde* and contributed to an outbreak of anti-clericalism in parliament unparalleled, in the opinion of Norman Sykes, since Henry VIII's Reformation Parliament.... The Church leaders of the period sounded shrill notes of alarm.'[88] The evidence adduced for that 'dangerously fashionable' deist movement inciting attacks upon the Church remains, however, at the level of Sykes's anecdote. Walsh and Taylor, it appears, have underestimated the intense interconnections between Church, state, Parliament, press and public opinion and the capacity of those connections to colour the historical record. What may have misled them and others is that Sykes's account of the life of Bishop Gibson is above all a eulogy to a High Churchman who was – as Sykes's account demonstrates – almost fanatical in his zeal against any threat to the Church, urging (unsuccessfully) the imprisonment of deists and unremittingly hostile to both Dissenters and Latitudinarians. Naturally, therefore, Sykes's account highlights at some length the evils of the deist and sceptical threat and focuses on Gibson's heroic role in fighting them.

As Sykes himself recounts it, '[t]he clergy were the objects of a series of sharp and damaging attacks during the latter half of the Parliament of 1727–33, which recalled the Reformation Parliament of Henry VIII in its zeal to attack the stronghold of clerical privilege and abuse'. The 'Church was being attacked on all sides and was steadily losing ground. The Deists were penetrating into the very citadel of revelation ... and the general temper of scepticism and immorality was detaching many of those who had adhered to it outwardly in former times.' According to Sykes, the main champion in the struggle against the tide of hostility was of course Bishop Gibson, cutting a heroic figure in that 'stirring scene'.[89] That 'stirring scene' was of course also a political one, with party-political struggle at its core. Walpole was happy for the Whigs to be seen as defenders of the Church against even a largely imaginary deist threat, but exasperated with Gibson's implacable hostility to Latitudinarians and Dissenters, which in electoral terms was more of a liability. This is also the politico-religious position of Sykes in his biography of Gibson, and Sykes exaggerates the scale of the attack on the Church and its importance, making it appear as if deism was a sizeable threat. We know that anticlerical outbursts by Whigs and their supporters were a commonplace, even if churchmen were apt to exaggerate the scale and content of them with allusions to infidelity and deism. Thomas Secker (1693–1768), subsequently Archbishop of Canterbury, for instance, wrote that 'Christianity is now railed at and ridiculed with very little reserve, and its teachings without any at all. Against us our adversaries appear to have set themselves to be as bitter as they can, not only beyond all truth, but beyond all probability, exaggerating without mercy.'[90]

In 1736, disillusioned with the Whigs' attitude to the Church, Gibson broke with Walpole and, for his own High Church reasons, himself encouraged 'a persistent vein of anticlericalism in Parliament'.[91] By then, however, Gibson had already played a most important part in what Sykes has termed the victory of the dialectic of orthodox divines over deism, 'the most important event of Church history since the Reformation'. It is true, however, that as a propagandist for the Church, Gibson was almost without equal and he contributed to a large degree to the construction of the myth of a deist movement. It has been said that 'the success of his efforts was largely due to the fact that he had addressed himself to the common man.... "At the debate between the Deists and the Christian apologists the public was umpire" ... Because Gibson appealed to the people, therefore his writings became popular.'[92] There is no doubt that Gibson, presiding over the most populous and politically significant diocese in Britain, did manage to reach large numbers of the public with his anti-deist scaremongering, which was designed to frighten Anglican waverers into line and away from Latitudinarianism. His anti-infidelity arguments were transmitted in various writings and numerous sermons, but above all in his pastoral letters, and the printing figures are an extraordinary testament to the scale of the myth of deistic radicalism in the Enlightenment. No fewer than 30,000 copies of his first *Pastoral Letter* (1728) were printed by the Society for Promoting Christian Knowledge. The second edition ran to 27,000 copies and the third edition to 17,000. A further collected edition also ran to 3,000 copies, and some translated into

French for refugees. Many other Anglican and some non-Anglican writers propagated the same theme in numbers of books, tracts and pamphlets. Given that many or most were sold in London and a multiple readership for many copies must be assumed, these figures bear ample evidence not to the reality of deism or any 'radical' Enlightenment, but to the ability of the bogeyman of deism and associated suppositious threats to the Church to reach a popular level.

Dissent and Enlightenment

Any period, past or present, can be assessed in terms of continuity or change, or both, although such choices are not necessarily always conscious. It is only natural for us to look for or highlight new elements that seem to characterize or delineate one historical period from another. But, as Munck in his comparative social history of the Enlightenment has recently reminded us, selecting such elements constitutes little more than a snapshot, a few frames in a long film of untold numbers of frames.[93] Such selective treatment, therefore, can be extremely misleading, serving to minimize, even trivialize vastly greater and more dominant elements of continuity. As has already been argued in the previous chapter, relying on snapshots or what may be called the headlines of history can lead us to believe that the exceptions were the rule, and so to characterize a period in one manner rather than another. Munck too reminds us that – as was certainly the case with the leading English deists such as John Toland – the notoriety of a work or its author is not necessarily an indicator of influence, but more usually an indicator of the limits of acceptability of such ideas and thus their very restricted appeal. So, the old measure of counting the replies to works that challenged hitherto accepted notions is just as likely to measure the lack of acceptability of a work as its 'influence'.[94]

Yet we, myself included, persist in believing there was an intellectual phenomenon in eighteenth-century Europe we term the Enlightenment. Indeed, once we broaden our gaze from the coterie of intellectuals traditionally deemed to personify the Enlightenment, we can see it was a relatively broad intellectual phenomenon cutting across religion and political affiliation rather than being determined by such allegiances.[95] Nowhere was this more apparent than in England and Scotland. The Scottish Enlightenment has for some been seen as an exception to the general European trend, in so far as much of its intellectual thrust emanated from clerical and established milieux. But there is ample evidence to suggest that the Scottish Enlightenment was far less exceptional that has been considered, and that the English Enlightenment hardly constituted a narrow affair restricted to the traditional canonical figures including Newton, Locke, Hume and just a few deists.

There is now almost a consensus that there was no automatic enmity between Enlightenment and religion in eighteenth-century England. It should hardly need recounting that Locke, the empiricist and great campaigner for toleration, and Newton, the unraveller of the laws of gravity, were devout Christians and that science and religion most often happily coexisted. Religion and science were, in fact, seen as complementary to each other, as evident in the work of Boyle and his *Christian Virtuoso: Shewing that by being Addicted to Experimental Philosophy a Man is rather Assisted than Indisposed to Be a Good Christian* (1690). Further, it may even be said that there is more evidence of attitudes to science being influenced by religion than there is evidence for religion being influenced by science. As Fara has noted, natural philosophers were centrally involved in gradual but fundamental changes central to the culture of the Enlightenment. Isaac Newton and his many admirers and adherents legitimated their scientific activities by tying the production of knowledge to the public good. They also asserted that the world had been created by a benevolent God for human benefit, thus the exploration and exploitation of nature was translated into holy commandment. The 'natural philosophers converted their private experiments into a public science by demonstrating their successful domination and manipulation of nature. As they marketed their products, they participated in building a materialist society dependent on their expertise. They used various tactics to enlist public support and capture appreciative audiences, packaging their skills, instruments and knowledge into sellable commodities competing for polite income.'[96] Some of the greatest scientific thinkers of the century were, like Newton, Dissenters. Indeed, Roy Porter has recently described Dissenters, along with sceptics and those resentful of the traditional authority of Church and state, as 'fomenters of the Enlightenment', and underlined the fact that Newtonianism tended to bolster Latitudinarianism as evidence of a constant, divine intervention in maintaining the universe.[97]

The English deist movement

Before the end of the 1770s, Dissenters and dissident Anglicans ranked amongst the foremost writers on political, religious, philosophical and scientific issues. Dissenters themselves were generally predisposed to look positively upon the acquisition of knowledge and many of the general tenets of the Enlightenment. Writing of the late eighteenth century, for instance, Fitzpatrick has noted that

> Dissenting Protestantism, heterodoxy, and enlightenment, were closely interrelated ... Rational Dissenters ... believed that the Reformation was far from complete ... Rational Dissenting religion thus constituted an endless search for truth and understanding. It was distrustful of dogma and received opinion, and it encouraged its adherents to seek enlightenment by free enquiry. This concern for the unfettered pursuit of truth, and willingness to pursue truth into the wilderness of heterodoxy was most marked amongst the English Presbyterians.[98]

Dissenters knew very well that Newton had been heterodox in his ideas and thus felt that the whole Newtonian tradition was – in terms of intellectual endowment – proof of divine favour to such seekers of true religion. For Dissenters, reason and revelation were considered to be complementary in the scientific field; both scientific and theological truths could be understood through the application of reason with revelation providing extra assistance. Another aspect of the congruence of Dissenter thought with the broad progress-orientated aims of the Enlightenment was the belief that reason and revelation had been proved to be consonant with the very latest scientific ideas. In his *Observations on Man, his Frame, his Duty, and his Expectations* (1749), for instance, the dissenting Anglican David Hartley had deduced that the mind was mechanistic, as much subject to the laws of cause and effect as any other part of nature. In addition, he was sure that a benevolent God had at heart the ultimate and unlimited happiness of the human race; thus human actions innately tended towards virtue and happiness. Starting from Hartley's theory of the association of ideas, the dissenting scientist Priestley took the further step of considering the human will to be subject to the same 'mechanical' laws of the mind: the mind desires an object because it provides pleasure, and the highest pleasure of man was to act in conformity with the divine will. Priestley assumed that an innate providence was leading humanity slowly but inevitably to happiness along the path of progress,[99] writing that 'it is in the order of providence, that man, and the world, should arrive at their most improved state by slow degrees'.[100]

The fact that the dissenting community was seen to contain distinguished scientists such as Richard Price and Joseph Priestley was merely more confirmation of the long-standing Dissenter conviction about the place of true religion in the field of enlightenment. Dissenters were not competing for the honour of their sects, but rather stressed the role of free discussion as the route to scientific and intellectual truth. Such convictions, in Fitzpatrick's words, amounted to that 'sense of growing enlightenment, of the possibility of moral regeneration, which is detectable in the European Enlightenment'. Late-eighteenth-century Dissenters were thus naturally also leaders in the call for religious toleration, one of the hallmarks of the Enlightenment.[101] Perhaps the major influence here was Joseph Priestley. In his *Essay on the First Principles of Government*, Priestley argued that Locke had been too confined in his notions of toleration. Priestley was in favour of universal toleration, including Catholics, primarily because in a free society truth would always triumph over error.[102] As we shall see in the next chapter, in France, as in England, the main impetus for broad campaigns to extend toleration in the eighteenth century came from committed Christians rather than from deists or other enemies of Christianity.

Notes

1 The Clarendon Code was composed of four Acts designed to cripple the power of the Nonconformists: the Corporation Act 1661, the Act of Conformity 1662, the Conventicle Act 1664, and the Five Mile Act 1665.

2 In his 'England's Troubles: Exhuming the Popish Plot', in T. Harris, P. Seaward and M. Goldie (eds), *Politics of Religion in Restoration England* (Oxford: Blackwell, 1990), Jonathan Scott argues that much of the seventeenth century can be understood as a continuity of crises – 1637–42, 1678–83, 1687–89 – that were fundamentally about religion. This is, however, to go too far, for there were fundamental interconnections between politics, economics and religion in that century and remained so in the next.

3 G. Holmes, *The Making of a Great Power. Late Stuart and Early Georgian Britain 1660–1722* (Harlow: Longman, 1995; 1st edn 1993), p. 122.

4 E. Mossner, *Bishop Butler and the Age of Reason* (Bristol: Thoemmes Books, 1990; 1st edn 1936), p. 27.

5 T. Halyburton, *Natural Religion insufficient; and Reveal'd necessary to man's happiness* (Edinburgh, 1714), p. 25.

6 R. Porter, *Enlightenment Britain and the Creation of the Modern World* (Lon-

don, Penguin, 2000), p. 112.

7 Ibid., p. 115. In his *Reason, Ridicule and Religion.The Age of Enlightenment in England 1660–1750* (London: Thames and Hudson, 1976), John Redwood adopts a similar descriptive or circumstantial approach.

8 D. Daily, *Enlightenment Deism. The Foremost Threat to Christianity* (Pennsylvania: Dorrance, 1999), p. 53.

9 Porter not only cites Wollaston as a deist, but also the dissenting John Trenchard (*Enlightenment Britain*, pp. 31–2) – on whom see below. Without adducing any evidence, T. Munck (*The Enlightenment. A Comparative Social History 1721–1794*, London: Arnold, 2000, pp. 31–2) too claims Trenchard as a deist, as does J. C. D. Clark (*English Society 1688–1832. Ideology, Social Structure and Political Practice during the Ancien Régime*, Cambridge: Cambridge University Press, 1985, p. 438). Similarly, J. Champion (*The Pillars of Priestcraft Shaken*, Cambridge: Cambridge University Press, 1992, pp. 137–8, 160–1, 177–9) claims Robert Howard, Trenchard and John Dennis – on whom see below – as deists or freethinkers, as does M. Goldie ('Priestcraft and the Birth of Whiggism', in N. Phillipson and Q. Skinner, eds, *Political Discourse in Early Modern Britain*, Cambridge: Cambridge University Press, 1993). I will not comment on the old claims that the Unitarians Newton and Locke were deists; these claims belong to a much earlier, now widely discredited view.

10 R. Howard, *The History of Religion. As it has been manag'd by Priestcraft* (London, 1709), pp. 283, 288, 321–2.

11 Champion, *Pillars of Priestcraft Shaken*, pp. 137–8.

12 Howard, *History of Religion*, pp. 278, 291, 302.

13 On Howard's Unitarianism see, for example, where he writes of the 'Being and Unity of God' (*History of Religion*, p. 315).

14 Champion (*Pillars of Priestcraft Shaken*, pp. 16–1) has argued that Dennis is a deist or freethinker.

15 J. Dennis, *Priestcraft distinguished from Christianity* (London, 1715), preface, p. 3; text, pp. 1–2, 8–9, 31–2, 39. The analysis contained in this work is much the same as in his *The Danger of Priestcraft to Religion and Government, with some Politick Reasons for Toleration* (London, 1702).

16 Champion (*Pillars of Priestcraft Shaken*, pp. 160–1) has claimed Trenchard as a deist or freethinker.

17 Porter claims John Trenchard is a deist (*Enlightenment Britain*, pp. 31–2), as does Munck (*The Enlightenment*, pp. 31–2), and also Clark (*English Society*, p. 438).

18 J. Trenchard, *The Natural History of Superstition* (London, 1709), pp. 6, 8–9.

19 S. Lee (ed.), *Dictionary of National Biography* (1899), vol. 57, pp. 198–9.

20 Champion, *Pillars of Priestcraft Shaken*, pp. 99–100.

21 P. Gay, *The Enlightenment. An Interpretation. Vol. 1: The Rise of Modern Paganism* (London: Norton, 1995; 1st edn 1966), p. 327.

22 R. Evans, *Pantheisticon. The Career of John Toland* (New York: P. Lang, 1991), pp. 1, 20.

23 Goldie, 'Priestcraft and the Birth of Whiggism', p. 212. See also M. Goldie, 'The Theory of Religious Intolerance in Restoration England', in O. P. Grell, J. I. Israel and N. Tyacke (eds), *From Persecution to Toleration. The Glorious Revolution and Religion in England* (Oxford: Clarendon, 1991).

24 See J. G. A. Pocock, 'Post-Puritan England and the Problem of the Enlighten-
    ment', in P. Zagorin (ed.), *Culture and Politics from Puritanism to the Enlight-
    enment* (Berkeley: University of California Press, 1980).
25 J. Locke, *A Letter Concerning Toleration* (London, 1689), p. 26. On the limita-
    tions of Locke's views on religious toleration see J. Israel, 'Spinoza, Locke and
    the Enlightenment Battle for Toleration', in O. Grell and R. Porter (eds), *Tolera-
    tion in Enlightenment Europe* (Cambridge: Cambridge University Press, 2000).
26 G. Bennett, 'Conflict in the Church', in G. Holmes (ed.), *Britain after the Glori-
    ous Revoloution 1689–1714* (London: Macmillan, 1982; 1st edn 1969), p. 155.
    On the need for 'political conflict as an interpretive foundation of
    historiography' in studying religion in Restoration England, and so ending 'the
    long-standing divorcement between intellectual and political history', see
    R. Ashcraft, 'Latitudinarianism and Toleration: Historical Myth versus Politi-
    cal History', in *Philosophy, Science, and Religion in England 1640–1700* (Cam-
    bridge: Cambridge University Press, 1992), p. 167.
27 D. E., *The Prodigious Appearance of Deism* (London, 1710), pp. 4–7.
28 W. Stephens, *An Account of the Growth of Deism in England* (London, 1696),
    pp. 3–6.
29 See, for instance, Goldie, 'Priestcraft and the Birth of Whiggism', pp. 215–16,
    224.
30 On Goldie see his 'Priestcraft and the Birth of Whiggism'.
31 On eighteenth-century Unitarianism and politics see the useful discussion in
    D. Nicholls, *God and Government in an Age of Reason* (London and New
    York: Routledge, 1995), ch. 3.
32 On Newton's analysis of priestcraft see, for instance, my edition of *Isaac New-
    ton's Observations on the Prophecies of Daniel and the Apocalypse of St John*
    (Lampeter: Edwin Mellen Press, 1999).
33 J. A. Herrick, *The Radical Rhetoric of the English Deists. The Discourse of
    Skepticism, 1680–1750* (Columbia: University of South Carolina Press, 1997),
    p. 4.
34 Champion, *The Pillars of Priestcraft Shaken*, p. 101.
35 For an appreciation of Toland written within living memory of his life, see the
    biography of him prefaced to Toland's posthumous *A Critical History of the
    Celtic Religion and Learning* (London, 1740), esp. pp. 6–7.
36 J. Toland, *An Apology for Mr Toland* (1697), quoted in Evans, *Pantheisticon*,
    p. 24.
37 On the difficulties of defining republicanism, and locating archetypal republi-
    can currents in the period 1680–1720, see D. Wootton, 'The Republican Tradi-
    tion: From Commonwealth to Common Sense', in D. Wootton (ed.),
    Republicanism, Liberty, and Commercial Society (Stanford, Calif.: Stanford
    University Press, 1994).
38 For more discussion of the difficulties of terming Toland a republican see, for
    example, R. Sullivan, *John Toland and the Deist Controversy* (Cambridge,
    Mass.: Harvard University Press, 1982), p. 149.
39 On Toland's concern for the Protestant succession see also the biography of
    Toland prefaced to his *Critical History of the Celtic Religion*.
40 John Toland, *Vindicius liberius: or M. Toland's Defence of Himself, against the
    Lower House of Convocation* (London, 1702), pp. 26–7, 162. On Toland's

extemely wide definition of Christianity see Evans, *Pantheisticon*, pp. 146–7.

41 P. Harrison, '*Religion' and the Religions in the English Enlightenment* (Avon: Cambridge University Press, 1990), p. 87, and Evans, *Pantheisticon*, pp. 14–15, also describe *Christianity not Mysterious* as a work aimed at reform of the Protestant Church. Evans (p. 15) notes that Toland, on account of his religious concerns, cannot be written off as a 'sceptic or simple deist'; so too does Sullivan in his *John Toland and the Deist Controversy*.

42 J. Toland, *Christianity not Mysterious* (London, 1696), preface, pp. 9, 21; text pp. 168–76. On Toland's belief that Christianity demonstrated the immortality of the soul and for more on the condemnation of superstition and idolatry see Toland's *Letters to Serena* (London, 1704).

43 See, for instance, Henry Ainsworth's *An Arrow against Idolatry. Taken out of the Quiver of the Lord of Hosts* (1611).

44 Convocation of Canterbury, *A Representation of the present state of Religion, with regard to the … growth of infidelity, Heresy, and Profaneness* (London, 1711), p. 5.

45 Toland, *Christianity not Mysterious*, pp. 159–63, 168–71.

46 For more on the topic of censorship in England see F. S. Siebert, *Freedom of the Press in England 1476–1776* (Urbana: University of Illinois Press, 1952).

47 Herrick, *The Radical Rhetoric of the English Deists*, pp. 6, 10, 12, 205, 211.

48 W. Ward, *Christianity under the Ancien Régime 1648–1789* (Cambridge: Cambridge University Press, 1999), p. 162.

49 On secret societies see, for instance, M. Jacob, *The Radical Enlightenment. Pantheists, Freemasons and Republicans* (London: George Allen and Unwin, 1981).

50 Herrick, *The Radical Rhetoric of the English Deists*, pp. 35–6.

51 Ibid., p. 67; see also D. Berman, *A History of Atheism in Britain* (New York: Croom Helm, 1988).

52 See, for instance, Charles Blount, *The First Two Books of Philostratus, concerning the life of Apollonius Tyaneus* (London, 1680).

53 In his *Radical Rhetoric of the English Deists*, Herrick cites following deists: Joseph Addison, Annet, Peter Blount, Thomas Chubb, Collins, Shaftesbury, Henry Dodwell (the younger, d. 1748), Morgan, Tindal, Toland, William Woolaston and Thomas Woolston.

54 R. H. Popkin, 'The Deist Challenge', in Grell, Israel and Tyacke (eds), *From Persecution to Toleration*, p. 196.

55 G. R. Cragg, *The Church and the Age of Reason 1648–1789* (London: Penguin, 1962), p. 161.

56 Ibid., p. 162.

57 Sullivan, *John Toland and the Deist Controversy*, pp. 7–9.

58 Ibid., pp. 9–10.

59 Ibid., p. 109.

60 Cragg, *The Church and the Age of Reason*, p. 165.

61 Porter, *Enlightenment Britain*, p. 98.

62 Mossner, *Bishop Butler and the Age of Reason*, pp. 79, 152, 177, 238.

63 J. Walsh and S. Taylor, 'The Church and Anglicanism in the "Long" Eighteenth Century', in C. Haydon, J. Walsh and S. Taylor (eds), *The Church of England c.1689– c.1833* (Cambridge: Cambridge University Press, 1993), p. 21.

64 Cragg, *The Church and the Age of Reason*, p. 129.
65 Mossner, *Bishop Butler and the Age of Reason*, p. 27.
66 On the use of anti-Catholicism by the Anglican Church in the eighteenth century see, for example, C. Haydon, *Anti-Catholicism in Eighteenth-Century England, c.1714–1780* (Manchester: Manchester University Press, 1993), pp. 253–4.
67 G. Holmes, *The Trial of Doctor Sacheverell* (London: Methuen, 1973), pp. 32, 43–5, 47. For more on the place of the state within the thought of High Churchmen see, for instance, Grell, Israel and Tyacke (eds), *From Persecution to Toleration*.
68 Holmes, *The Trial of Doctor Sacheverell*, pp. 51, 55.
69 Ibid., p. 75.
70 Ibid., pp. 240–1, 254.
71 K. Haakonssen, 'Enlightened Dissent: An Introduction', in K. Haakonssen (ed.), *Enlightenment and Religion. Rational Dissent in Eighteenth-Century Britain* (Cambridge: Cambridge University Press, 1996), p. 3.
72 Porter, *Enlightenment Britain*, p. 14.
73 Walsh and Taylor, 'The Church and Anglicanism', p. 21.
74 A. Ward, G. Prothero and S. Leathers (eds), *Cambridge Modern History. Vol. VI: The Eighteenth Century* (Cambridge: Cambridge University Press, 1934; 1st edn 1909), pp. 78, 80.
75 Cragg, *The Church and the Age of Reason*, p. 120.
76 Ibid., p. 127.
77 Walsh and Taylor, 'The Church and Anglicanism', p. 27.
78 In his *Anti-Catholicism in Eighteenth-Century England*, Haydon has shown how the Church-in-danger cry was directed at popery and Dissent by the elite and the clergy in order to foster greater allegiance to the Church and a sense of Anglican national identity.
79 Porter, *Enlightenment Britain*, p. 23.
80 D. Jarret, *Britain 1688–1815* (London: Longman, 1977), p. 198.
81 Porter, *Enlightenment Britain*, p. 97.
82 Walsh and Taylor, 'The Church and Anglicanism', p. 26.
83 Clark, *English Society*, p. 279.
84 Walsh and Taylor, 'The Church and Anglicanism', pp. 32–3.
85 Ibid., p. 34.
86 Cragg, *The Church and the Age of Reason*, p. 120.
87 N. Sykes, *Edmund Gibson, Bishop of London 1669–1748. A Study in Politics and Religion in the Eighteenth Century* (London: Oxford University Press, 1926).
88 Walsh and Taylor, 'The Church and Anglicanism', p. 21. Sykes's description of parliamentary anticlericalism is still cited as evidence of the challenge of deists. See, for example, N. Aston, 'Anglican Responses to Anticlericalism: Nonconformity and the Ideological Origins of Radical Disaffection', in N. Aston and M. Cragoe (eds), *Anticlericalism in Britain c. 1500–1914* (Stroud: Sutton Publishing, 2001), p. 118.
89 Sykes, *Edmund Gibson*, pp. 149, 247, 289–90.
90 Quoted in Cragg, *The Church and the Age of Reason*, p. 127.
91 Ward, *Christianity under the Ancien Régime*, p. 240.

92 Sykes, *Edmund Gibson*, pp. 241, 253.

93 Munck, *The Enlightenment*, p. 108.

94 Ibid., p. 134.

95 For discussion on various aspects of Dissent and Enlightenment see, for example, Haakonssen, *Enlightenment and Religion*; and M. Fitzpatrick, 'Heretical Religion and Radical Political Ideas in Late Eighteenth-Century England', in E. Hellmuth (ed.), *The Transformation of Political Culture. England and Germany in the Late Eighteenth Century* (Oxford: German Historical Institute, 1990).

96 P. Fara, '"Master of Practical Magnetics": The Construction of an Eighteenth-Century Natural Philosopher', *Enlightenment and Dissent*, 15 (1995), p. 55.

97 Porter, *Enlightenment Britain*, pp. 47, 135–6.

98 Fitzpatrick, 'Heretical Religion and Radical Political Ideas', pp. 341–2.

99 On Priestley's theory of progress see his *The Doctrine of Philosophical Necessaity Illustrated* (London, 1777).

100 J. Priestley, *A General History of the Christian Church from the Fall of the Western Empire to the Present Time* (4 vols, Northumberland, USA, 1802–3), vol. 2, p. 25.

101 On Dissent and toleration see also M. Fitzpatrick, 'Toleration and Truth', *Enlightenment and Dissent*, 1 (1982).

102 Fitzpatrick, 'Heretical Religion and Radical Political Ideas', pp. 343, 357.

4

France: the revolt of democratic Christianity and the rise of public opinion

This chapter focuses on the emergence of religious toleration in France and the degree to which it was brought about by broad politico-religious struggle rather than by the philosophes.[1] The discussion will, therefore, not provide the usual Enlightenment studies degree of focus upon the philosophes. Much of the research necessary for a revision of the role of the philosophes in France has been accumulating for several decades, but there has not yet been an attempt to bring together the various strands and integrate them into a critique of their role. Albeit slowly, from the mid 1960s a revision of the status of Pierre Bayle as a Calvinist fideist (discussed in earlier chapters) rather than an early philosophe has gradually gained acceptance.[2] Again rather slowly and mostly from the 1980s, there have been efforts to demonstrate that Christianity occupied a more important place in the development of the French Enlightenment than had hitherto been accepted.[3] In particular there has been increased recognition of the role of Jansenism, especially in the landmark suppression of the Jesuits.[4] Much of the tale I recount in this chapter is, therefore, already well-known and I am indebted to the research of a number of scholars (some of whom have already been cited in earlier chapters) including R. Barny, C. J. Betts, P. R. Campbell, A. Kors, P. J. Korshin, Elizabeth Labrousse, M. Linton, J. McManners, W. Rex, P. Riley, J. Shennan and D. Van Kley. I present here a synthesis of various scholarly contributions from the above authors. The conclusions I draw regarding the need for a thoroughgoing re-evaluation of the role of the philosophes in the development of central tenets of enlightened thought such as religious toleration are, however, my own.

France: the revolt of democratic Christianity
Bourbons, Huguenots and Jansenists

Traditionally, France has been seen as one of the great examples of absolutist rule. Hence, comparison of its political life with England, where Parliament was challenging and limiting the monarchy in fundamental respects, has been understood as comparing the proverbial chalk with cheese. The consensus on the character of French absolutism, however, has now broken, and many now accept that the claims of French monarchs to absolute rule must be accepted within the same methodological framework applied to the rest of historical studies. That is to say their claims must be first and foremost accepted as claims rather than reality. In his *Myth of Absolutism* (1992), Nicholas Henshall has summed up much of the argument for a more limited view of the 'reach' of French absolutism.[5] He demonstrates that the Bourbon monarchs were forced to patronize, negotiate and cajole their noble *parlements* into cooperation. Indeed, as Shennan conclusively demonstrated even in the 1960s, French monarchs at times faced the concerted defiance of the Parisian and provincial *parlements*, whose members understood themselves to be acting in the wider interests of the people of France.[6] Absolutism was thus an aspiration rather than an achievement. The problem, however, is that this crucial understanding has not been assimilated into the assumptions and theoretical outlook of Enlightenment studies. This is in good part because the myth of absolutism has been a happy circumstance for a variety of outlooks. For pro-Bourbon thinkers the notion of absolutism can be seen as a confirmation of the power and grandeur of the dynasty. For the English political class from the seventeenth to the nineteenth century, the concept of French absolutist tyranny was a useful aid to various fundamental political projects often including the bolstering of British nationalism. Finally, for some historians of the Enlightenment, French absolutism was a useful negative contrast to the 'progressive' philosophes fighting the old regime. Of what relevance, however, is the question of absolutism to the study of religion in the Enlightenment? Any adequate answer to this deceptively simple question requires investigation on various levels. The level that is of most interest to this chapter, and arguably the most fundamental, is that of the unavoidable political conflict brought about by the simple struggle for religious liberty in eighteenth-century France, which is where our discussion will begin.

France too had its presbyterians, the Calvinist Huguenots,[7] whose Church naturally seemed to embody a polity in direct contrast with that of absolutism. Allied with the monarch, French orthodox Catholicism – the state Church and staunch advocate of the divine-right-to-rule theory – had an interest in ensuring that the Huguenot representative polity was not allowed to corrupt the Gallican (French Catholic) Church or the noble *parlements*. That fear was not groundless paranoia.

Although they were a minority and principally confined to the south, the Huguenots had from the beginning been implicitly political, and the result was the sixteenth-century Wars of Religion. At great cost in human and economic terms the Wars of Religion had resulted in Huguenot defeat, in which the integrity of the monarch's right to rule was protected but peace obtained via enshrining some restricted rights to Huguenot worship in the Edict of Nantes (1598). But from the beginning, the Edict was a means of control, and in any case was continually breached to the detriment of Huguenots. To imagine, then, that any French monarch aspiring to absolutist rule could altogether forget the potentially seditious political views of the Huguenots would be to imagine a shortsighted monarch. When the great mid-seventeenth-century crisis of revolt and rebellion across Europe subsided, it was (with the exception of England) mostly in favour of centralizing monarchical rule. Under such circumstances, it was only natural that a Bourbon monarch would want finally to remove the lingering problem of the Huguenot south. If Louis had been primarily motivated by his piety, it seems strange that he went ahead with the revocation of the Edict in 1685.[8] At this time the Huguenots were unofficially proposing union with the Catholics, and the Assembly of the Clergy of France – the hierarchy of his own Church – was also discussing a conciliatory profession of faith.[9] Seen from another viewpoint, 1685 was at the same time a very auspicious time to launch such a project, for in that year Catholic James II was installed on the English throne. As Labrousse has noted, it would be thus quite incorrect to view the Revocation as religious in inspiration, as the final thrust of the Counter-Reformation.[10]

The Revocation of the Edict of Nantes resulted in the most brutal military persecution, forcing the mass exodus of Huguenots from France.[11] Flight, however, was forbidden and punishable by a catalogue of horrors culminating in condemnation to galley slaving or execution. This inhuman attitude to emigration – partly in order to limit the economic cost of the loss of many enterprising and skilled citizens – was certainly too much for some Catholics. Even some officials charged with the responsibility of apprehending those who had attempted to flee connived to allow Huguenots to escape the country. It is most important, however, to remember that the Revocation of the Edict did not mark the beginning of renewed persecution. For two decades before 1685, Louis had been brutally persecuting the Huguenots, who continued to refuse to accept the right of the King to suspend their worship, as they again did in 1683.[12] Even though the Huguenots as a mass had remained explicitly faithful to the King, his propagandists and the Church persisted in depicting the Huguenots as a foreign body and thus an internal threat which had to be dealt with. The Huguenots were portrayed as enemies of Christ, subversive and republican, using the fact of their representative assemblies as evidence and linking them to the still alarming memory of the English Revolution in which Calvinists had played such a conspicuous role.

Their persecution, therefore, aroused relatively less overt sympathy than might have otherwise been the case. The Bourbon dynasty could at least initially, therefore, feel that it had successfully eradicated any potential political threat from the Huguenots. But, as Christians were just beginning to learn from hard experience, persecution rarely achieves its goals. Even though the persecution continued, the Huguenots slowly re-established their organization underground, and as the eighteenth century wore on and sentiment for toleration grew under the hammer of French Catholic infighting, the Huguenots became a thorn in the conscience of the nation. In the short term, the Revocation naturally produced anger in Protestants and more liberal Catholics and a greater degree of cynicism about the possibility of established Churches respecting individual belief. Most dramatically, the anger boiled over into insurrection in the Camisard Revolt (1702–4), which, although desperate and bloody, ultimately failed because of the lack of active sympathy for it amongst the majority of the Catholic population.

There is no doubt, as other historians have confirmed, that the Revocation and its aftermath did contribute towards anti-clericalism, for the Church was often viewed as more culpable for the inhuman reality of intolerance than the state. Formerly perfectly respectable citizens, between 2,000 and 3,000 Huguenots slaved on

the galleys of France under Louis XIV and XV, under the most atro-
cious conditions and savage rule where death was cheap. These
men, of course, were connected to French society by many ties.
They had wives, daughters, sons, brothers, sisters; they often had
Catholic relatives through inter-marriage; they had business, religious and social connections; which is to say that the experience of
3,000 men became the experience of many, many times more
Huguenots and Catholics.

To note, therefore, as some have done, that the Huguenot question was shelved as a political question relatively soon after the
Camisard Revolt is only to note that the Huguenots had in part
been physically removed, their Church bloodily driven underground and any political influence they ever disposed of destroyed.
This statement of the bare facts, however, has only a limited bearing
on the question of whether the events of 1685–1709 had influence
on subsequent politico-religious thought. For how can one measure
the possible influence of such events when defence of the Huguenots
or attacks upon Gallican and royal intolerance could only be made
public at great risk? To defend the Huguenots publicly was to risk
being accused of sympathy with the enemies of France, notably
England. Thus, we might be able to say that the Huguenot issue was
'shelved' as a political question, but the influence of the
persecutions on those already not well disposed towards the
Gallican hierarchy and its relationship with the monarch is entirely
another matter. So, while we can assert that no deist movement or
indeed any tangible increase in 'public' deism resulted from
humanitarian outrage at the treatment of the Huguenots, it does
not mean those events were without influence inside France. It only
means we cannot measure it to any significant extent.

Not all or even many of the philosophes at the time of the Revocation and Camisard Revolt greatly sympathized with the Huguenots, for we know that some such as Voltaire were staunchly
anti-Huguenot and pro-absolutist. Those who did sympathize were
hardly likely to go public about it, and anyone wishing to criticize
Christian intolerance in public had need of a much less potentially
dangerous topic than the Huguenots. Consequently, the
philosophes cited the sixteenth- and seventeenth-century Wars of
Religion – or rather wars with a religious pretext – as the height of
Christian barbarity. They wished to emphasize the religious nature
of those wars in order to attack the 'medievalism' of the contempo-

rary established Churches and governments. If the philosophes often used those earlier wars of religion as examples of the iniquity of religion rather than more contemporary events, it did not mean that more contemporary events – such as the Revocation – necessarily had less impact upon them. The philosophes of course wished to arouse the maximum impact in their readers, and the religious form of the Thirty Years War was, in polemical terms, material of the first order for their attempt to demonstrate the backward nature of the hierarchical Church. A critique of relatively distant times which most – privately, even some monarchs – could agree with was far less objectionable to the censor and ran less risk of state retribution than a similarly sharp critique of relatively recent or contemporary and therefore still sensitive issues such as the Revocation. Unsurprisingly, we know that even in the writings of those of the enlightened elite who condemned such events, the Revocation and its aftermath assumed a relatively low profile. Clearly, then, using the writings of the philosophes as simple mirrors with which to detect formative influences acting upon them is at least problematic.

Thus the 'shelving' of the Huguenot question, that is to say its lack of influence, will seem to be compounded by the relative lack of public polemics on the issue. Such authorial prudence was of course hardly uncommon in Europe. We need only to look at the late-eighteenth-century Italian peninsular, for instance, where philosophes usually avoided the question of the Church. Similarly in England, Dissenters continually railed at the Anglican Church but rarely named it explicitly and so seemed to damn all Churches. There is, then, good reason to approach many of the polemical works of the philosophes with some caution if one is interested in the influences bearing upon the formation of their thought. It is reasonable, surely, to assert that contemporary politico-religious reality played a prominent role in determining the outlook of the philosophes. As a consequence, it is difficult to escape the recognition that historians should devote considerable attention to the greatest politico-religious division within eighteenth-century France, that within the Gallican Church between Jansenists[13] and orthodox Catholicism. Until the Revolution, the Bourbons, their governments and the Gallican prelacy made repeated attempts to crush Jansenist dissent in the Church.

The Enlightenment and religion

The *Nouvelles ecclésiastiques* and Bourbon miscalculation

It is striking that the similarity between Calvinism and Jansenism is so seldom remarked upon. Jansenists wished to return the Church to its primitive, Augustinian purity, rescuing it from its medieval corruptions and reforming it. Most importantly, they usually felt they did not need official sanction to carry out God's work and were prepared to defy actively the hierarchy of Church and state. It was not surprising, therefore, that the Archbishop of Paris observed that the King 'wants no conventicles;[14] a headless body is always dangerous in a state'. For Louis XIV the Jansenists were 'a sect inimical to all lordship'.[15] From the English Civil Wars, above all, Louis had learnt that episcopacy and monarchy stood or fell together.

The thought of Cornelius Jansen (1585–1638) had already been condemned by Pope Innocent X in 1653. Notwithstanding this, Jansenists persisted and became involved in a bitter controversy with the elite defenders of Roman orthodoxy, the Jesuits. It was clear by the early eighteenth century that the papal denunciations and victimizations – reinforced in 1705 by the Bull *Vineam Domini* – had been ineffective and that the number of adherents to the ascetic-reforming tenor of Jansenism was growing rather than diminishing. This was only too evident to Louis XIV, and rather too near to home, in the form of the staunchly Jansenist abbey at Port Royal in Paris. With the Huguenot cause also still visible and rumbling on sporadically in the form of the Camisard Revolt (which, although suppressed in 1704, stubbornly refused to be finally quelled until 1710), Louis's patience evidently came to an end in 1709. In that year he ordered the physical eradication of Port Royal (which he had already sentenced to slow death since 1679 by the prohibition of a new intake). The abbey was demolished, its inmates divided and transported to other unsympathetic houses, its graves emptied and the land ploughed to remove all traces of its existence. This sparked a train of events that, over the next fifty or so years, produced bitter divisions and frontal assaults on royal and Roman 'despotism'. On one side were the episcopate, King and government, and on the other Jansenists, popular support and the *Parlement* of Paris and other provincial *parlements*. What interests us here is how the views of reforming clergy and their supporters effectively became politicized, and evolved into an anti-absolutist reforming ideology, which at times shaded into enlightened thought.

Louis's police knew that there was a market for Jansenist books and they battled against it at the frontiers, yet they had not understood the extent of the continued support for Jansenist ideas. Jansenist controversy broke out again in Paris in 1710, and Louis, exasperated, requested yet another Bull from the Pope condemning and prohibiting Jansenist views. If any single action of Louis's can be isolated as decisive in the final erosion of Bourbon prestige and the turning of public opinion against Church and state, his request for a Bull from the Pope and the reaction to it is without comparison. As we will see, with some justification, it has been said that the resultant Bull and the reaction it provoked was a spur to the politicization of Diderot and other philosophes.[16]

In 1713 Pope Clement XI issued the Bull *Unigenitus*, which condemned as heretical all the main elements of Jansenist thought. Amongst the propositions condemned were those recommending the reading of the scriptures, those promoting more active participation in Church affairs by the laity, those which implied that the Church existed independently of its hierarchy, and those claiming that the coercive stifling of dissent was illegitimate and unjust. The conflict over the imposition of *Unigenitus* was to reveal just how deep were the divisions within the state and Gallican Church, and how the title of absolutist monarch has so misled posterity. The *Parlement* of Paris was a bastion of aristocratic privilege against royal pretensions. That *Parlement*, in fact, had jurisdiction over a large part of France centred around the capital, and the prospect of deepening royal control over the religious life of the country was viewed by it with great concern. Its members understood only too well the political implications of such a state-inspired religious gag (*Unigenitus*), as did some of the members of regional *parlements*: the suppression of religious dissent could be utilized as a disguise for the oppression of those opposed to the monarchy on other issues.

In a country in which an Estates General (i.e. a body comprising representatives from the Three Estates: clergy, nobility and lower orders) had not been called for about a hundred years, the *Parlement* of Paris had gradually become a symbol of resistance to royal absolutist tendencies. So, despite the fact that the *Parlement* was aristocratic in nature, without any other effective political voice, the lower echelons of society were at times ready to follow its lead in defying Louis's perceived authoritarianism and excessive fiscal demands. The *Parlement* of Paris could not, therefore, be ignored, suspended, dispersed or otherwise persecuted without potentially great political risk. Hence Louis exerted as much pressure as possible in order to coerce the *Parlement* into acquiescence to his wishes, and only reluctantly applied more forceful means. But the implications of *Unigentus* constituted an issue on which the *Parlement* would not lightly yield its power to officially register – that is to say legitimize – royal decrees. Not surprisingly, the *Parlement* of Paris, despite loud threats from the King, refused to register the Bull until it was accepted by the Gallican episcopate. In the event, the final acceptance of *Unigenitus* by the episcopate was the outcome of only a partial meeting of prelates, for even amongst the bishops themselves there were some who did not feel able to give their assent to the Bull. Naturally, the *Parlement* declared that meeting insufficient to legitimate the Bull. The scale of the uproar against *Unigenitus* can be partly estimated by the fact that debates on *Unigenitus* reduced the University of Sorbonne to chaos and some 200 books and pamphlets were written against it in 1714 alone.

For sympathizers of the Jansenist cause, the French state and its Church were now more closely identified with the tyranny of Rome. Even worse, perhaps, the Archbishop of Paris forbade the publication of the *Unigenitus* within his diocese. In 1715 Louis died as he was planning to force acceptance of the Bull upon reluctant clergy. There is little doubt, as McManners has recently noted, that for Louis, Jansenism was a republican party inside the state Church. Yet it has been estimated that the imposition of *Unigenitus* upon France only served to create a million more Jansenists.[17] But it would be inadequate to leave the latter statement as it stands. The political nature of the *Unigenitus* dispute ensured that Jansenism was not only broadly identified as a doctrine of salvation and resistance to Rome. By 1715 it had already become a politico-religious ideology and hence France had acquired an enduring party of resistance to the Crown's pretensions. Unsurprisingly, then, if Louis had been unpopular before *Unigenitus*, he was certainly more so afterwards. On his death there were celebratory bonfires in the streets of Paris, and the Jesuits – the staunch allies of Rome and the declared opponents of Jansenism – were universally condemned by what was effectively an anti-Jesuit coalition.

France: the revolt of democratic Christianity

After the death of the King, many clergy who had formerly accepted *Unigenitus* recanted, including some bishops and the University of Sorbonne. Anti-*Unigenitus* publications continued to roll off the presses, reaching a thousand titles by 1730. In 1718 the Archbishop of Paris, Noailles, made his appeal against *Unigenitus* public and 10,000 copies of it were sold and many more supported his appeal. In 1718 three-quarters of the Parisian clergy rallied publicly against *Unigenitus*.[18] The movement brought into being by the royal imposition of *Unigenitus* peaked in 1719–20, but struggle against the Bull continued, providing core elements of Jansenist politico-religious ideology for ensuing decades.

The next important phase of development of Jansenism from spiritual rebellion to political ideology came in 1727–28. Again, the spur to change was traditional in form – intra-confessional conflict – which has led to it being ignored by many historians searching for a more modern-looking challenge to the old regime. But, of course, it is not the origin of a tale that counts, but its telling and its reception. In 1727 a Jansenist bishop, Jean Soanen, was suspended and exiled to a remote abbey for issuing a pastoral letter denouncing *Unigenitus*. This came on top of other suspensions and exiles of lesser clergy, for the government continued to be determined in its resolve to whittle down the anti-*Unigenitus* movement by steady persecution of individuals. Soanen's case was distinguished by the publication in Paris of a legal brief denying the legality of his treatment. In itself this is not so remarkable. But, crucially, we know that the brief – *The Consultation of the Fifty* – was signed by fifty advocates of the Parisian *Parlement* and orchestrated by other members. As far as can be presently determined, this was the first time that the leadership of the Jansenist cause was concentrated in the hands of laymen, and it demonstrates a significant Jansenist presence in the *Parlement* of Paris prior to the 1730s. This circumstance thus marks Jansenism's maturation from a spiritual movement to a political ideology in which the Doctrine of Grace, which supposedly formed the heart of Jansenism, took a very second place to struggle against royal tyranny. In the words of McManners, from this point it became quite usual to become a Jansenist without any real interest in the Doctrine of Grace.[19]

In purely religious opposition, then, the Jansenist movement actively encouraged resistance to Roman tyranny in the Church and a more personal approach to religion via individual study of the

Bible, which was actively discouraged by orthodox Catholics. In *political* opposition, in the struggle to embrace greater religious freedom in Bourbon France, the Jansenist-led *parlements* fought against what Jansenists themselves termed tyrannical rule.[20] There are many avenues by which historians can discount potential similarities, but, in terms of the catalysts to intellectual change, the parallel of the French Jansenist conflict with the transformation of seventeenth-century English dissenting struggle into the Whig political outlook is too compelling to dismiss easily.

Taking the Jansenist movement in a more political direction also meant relying more heavily on lay support. In turn, this meant that the public should not be allowed to lose sight of the issues. It is at this point (1728) that 'one of the most effective and well-organized underground propaganda sheets of all time' emerged in the form of the *Nouvelles ecclésiastiques*.[21] This publication, condemned as reactionary by almost all philosophes (with the part exception of Rousseau), rapidly established itself as a reliable journal of record and promoter of sharp polemic far beyond the ranks of ecclesiastical Jansenism. Its authors were never identified nor its presses ever silenced until it ceased publication in 1803. Its political integrity as a mouthpiece against tyranny provoked an intense loyalty of readership. It has been described 'as far from being an elementary broadsheet for the naive: a masterly vehicle for propaganda'.[22] The problem with assessing the political importance of the *Nouvelles ecclésiastiques* has been much to do with its title, which has led many historians to dismiss or underrate its importance simply on account of the ostensible failure of the journal's titular form and pious tenor to embody secular progressivity.

As Doyle has succinctly put it, with a prestigious lay leadership[23] and the advent of the *Nouvelles ecclésiastiques*, 'defeating Jansenism was no longer simply a question of Bullying parish priests or other clergy'.[24] The advocates who had written the *Consultation of the Fifty* took the lead by writing briefs for those priests who were determined to appeal against the imposition of *Unigenitus*. The term 'brief' here is the appropriate description for their writings simply because then legal arguments against *Unigenitus* were dominant. By 1730 these arguments even began to challenge the foundations of royal absolute authority by declaring that laws were based on a *contract between governors and governed*. Ministers quickly attempted to suppress such appeals, but that only enraged the corps of advocates and the *Parlement* and a full-scale strike of the bar was declared in 1732. By 1727 Paris had already become a Jansenist stronghold, and, according to one contemporary, the Jansenists were supported by most of the bourgeoisie and the poor. By 1731 the same observer considered that about 75 per cent of the rank and file of the Parisian police were to be counted as Jansenist supporters.[25] What proportion of that figure were fully Jansenist in theological terms is a secondary, if not irrelevant, question. The central point here is that the King's policy of repression and persecution had aroused hostility to the government far beyond purely religious circles, and political and religious Jansenism were now virtually inseparable. As now at least partly recognized by some writers,[26] public opinion, spearheaded by the *Nouvelles ecclésiastiques,* constituted a radical opposition to royal absolutism hitherto unseen in the heart of urban France.

But how can we mention social contract theory without thinking of Rousseau's *Du contrat social* (1762)? It would of course be an unfounded assertion to claim that political Jansenism prefigured Rousseau's political thinking. It would, however, be just as unfounded to argue that Rousseau's ideas were wholly original. Contract theory had been present in European thought in one form or another since the Middle Ages. What helped make contract theory notable in the eighteenth century was that the political conceptions of Bourbon kings became more obstinately absolutist in nature just as resistance to royal aspirations was becoming more widespread and stubborn. Thus what was in essence an old idea, but one now linked to widespread active resistance to absolutism, could seem shocking in 1730s Paris and appear to the opponents of despotism as the obvious and major ideological choice available to them. With respect to Rousseau and his enlightened contemporaries, then, we can say that had not one of them advanced something like his *Du contrat social*, we should be very surprised indeed (on Rousseau and his General Will see below). So, to sum up, a religious dispute engendered or facilitated a political alliance between nobles, bourgeoisie, artisans, the poor and the clergy. Public opinion in Paris had rarely, if ever, been so powerful. Noble *Parlement* members and the poorest social layers, usually in unsympathetic relationship, now found themselves in staunch unison against the greater enemy. The idea, then, that exclusively top-down models of intellectual influence and discrete categories of religious, political and philosophical thought can be used to understand eighteenth-century Europe is not a tenable one.

Now we must talk of miracles and convulsions. In the late 1720s there were reports of miracle cures of the pious in the parishes of Jansenist priests. These miraculous events – including convulsions and speaking in tongues – continued, with some level of popular acclaim, into the 1730s. In any truly popular movement, there will inevitably be a variety of forms of expression of its hopes and beliefs. It would have been unthinkable that the more pious Jansenists would not express some traditional elements of Catholic religiosity, even though Jansenists usually combatted what they regarded as excessive superstition. Indeed, even some more religiously orientated Jansenists thought the miraculous 'cures' to be an embarrassment. Scholarly modernity hunters have of course also recoiled with distaste at these events and have turned their heads elsewhere for the roots of modernity. Those who look for pure revolutions, movements or trends, however, will of course never find them. Most historians have also wished to forget the fact that, for instance, Sir Isaac Newton had to be dissuaded by his friend John Locke from going to view the miracles of the French (Huguenot) Prophets in England. Perhaps the most disappointing aspect of the 'embarrassment' caused by such Christian 'enthusiasm' is that some academics have seemingly failed to notice the implications of the fact that the convulsion meetings in Paris were suppressed by the state in 1732. The context here is crucial. The popular miracles were part of a much larger political protest arising from *Unigenitus* which, in the autumn of 1731, was approaching a level at which the 'public life of the capital, and with it the mainsprings of political authority in the entire kingdom', would be reduced to chaos.[27]

For our purposes, it does not matter whether the King, ministers, *Parlement* members or the authors of the *Nouvelles ecclésiastiques* believed in the authenticity of the cures or not. The important point is that they all understood the political dimension of the events. We know that the editors of the *Nouvelles ecclésiastiques* could not risk outright condemnation of the miraculous events even if they felt they ought to do so. It would be far safer, in terms of the popular dynamics of the movement, to turn the events against the King's tame prelacy by demanding that the Archbishop of Paris begin procedures for the authentification of the miracles. When he refused to do so, and instead condemned the cult, we are given just a glimpse of the active and fascinating psychological symbiosis of popular politics and religion: his refusal led to a dramatic rise in the number of reported cures. Thus modern historians have often failed to realize that the 'embarrassment' of the miraculous cures was, in effect and above all, a political embarrassment for the government. As one placard read after pilgrims had been turned away from one famous miracle site by a huge show of force: 'God Take Note, By Royal Command, Miracles In This Place Banned'. Even after 1732, attacks on Jansenist convulsionaries could excite great outrage. In 1736 such attacks by the government excited a storm of pamphlets. In this manner miracles were brought to the aid of anticlericalism (directed principally at the episcopate) and anti-despotism, which, in those years, were difficult to tease apart. Quite unsurprisingly, therefore, in that period French Jansenists made parallels between Louis's religious persecution and that of the English kings.[28] For them the fact that one king was Catholic and the other Protestant was of little account. The notion of divorcing powerful anticlerical movements from traditional piety, it seems, is not a helpful one within Enlightenment studies.

The uncertainties of the regency period and the mass support given to Jansenists in the 1720s made any general attempt to enforce *Unigenitus* potentially very dangerous. But in the 1730s zealous orthodox clerics took the initiative and began a determined campaign of sacrament refusal to those accused of Jansenism. Although the refusal of sacraments was already an established weapon in the orthodox battle against Jansenism, in the politico-religious hothouse that was eighteenth-century Paris many less religious Jansenists viewed it as one more facet of heartless Bourbon despotism. The denial of one sacrament, however, that of extreme unction, was unmatched in its psychological ferocity: denial of this, the last sacrament, meant that a sinner died unabsolved of sin, so putting into jeopardy his or her participation in final Salvation. The evocation (the removal to a higher court) of an appeal to *Parlement* against this perceived abuse of spiritual power was one of the important issues contributing to the judicial crisis of 1731–32. As we shall see, it has been claimed, with some justification, that the 'roots of later Parisian anticlericalism' are to be found in the bitterness and events brought about by the refusal of sacraments, especially in the 1750s.[29] In accounts of Enlightenment thought, the bitterly volatile mood of Parisians in, for instance, the years 1749–50 is usually not deemed worthy of mention. Yet it seems to me a profound mystery how the French Enlightenment can be understood without some comprehension of the political condition of what was then France's political and intellectual fulcrum.

In the year following December 1749, there were at least thirty riots in Paris. It has been said that these were the result of over-zealous police activity. It has also been conjectured how far they were connected to each other. Pending more research, it seems we cannot provide a full answer. But this should not lead us to dismiss the value of these occurrences in charting intellectual change. The principal point is that the riots were directed against what was perceived to be a despotic establishment. Even if the riots served to briefly divorce *Parlement* from the lower orders, such an advanced condition of political alienation helps us understand how continued religious 'tyranny' could serve to politicize religion, for the response to religious tyranny was certainly a feature of the build-up to the riots.

The revolt of the 1750s

Beginning in 1749, there began in Paris a renewed and more con-certed campaign of sacrament refusal. Suspected Jansenists were re-fused the last rites unless they could prove their orthodoxy by producing a certificate, a *billet de confession*. This was a certificate signed by the priest to whom they had last confessed. The first vic-tim, Charles Coffin (1676–1749), college principal and rector of the university, thus died unshriven. The result was a political disaster for the Church and government, for the government was widely understood as a staunch supporter of the unjust and oppressive ac-tions of the orthodox Church. Four thousand attended Charles Coffin's funeral, which was, in effect, a demonstration against the polity of the Church and the state and, moreover, against a Church leadership known at that time to be defending its great wealth against taxation. After the occurrence of other cases and the inevita-ble involvement of the *Parlement* in their defence, in late 1751 there began a judicial strike against the government's refusal to heed *Parlement*'s appeals which was more unanimous and determined than that of 1732. Even when *Parlement* was forced to resume its functions by direct royal orders, it was showered with appeals against the refusal of sacraments. It is at this point that we reach a watershed in the development of opposition to Bourbon oppression, in good part a result of the confidence given to *Parlement* from the fact that it received unprecedented support from its provincial counterparts. Parisian Jansenism was thus the political lever which awoke unheard of confidence and unity in the opposition against the Bourbon dream of absolutist rule.

In spring 1752, when the Archbishop of Paris refused to recognize the jurisdiction of *Parlement* in appeals against the refusal of sacraments, *Parlement* took the unprecedented unilateral action of impounding the bishop's temporalities and forbidding parish priests to withhold sacraments. It published this prohibition, posted it up all over Paris, and sold an amazing 10,000 copies. Many bought copies of the prohibition to frame for displaying at home and work, and in turn it prompted a hail of pamphlets supporting *Parlement*'s case. As the Marquis d'Argenson wrote, '[t]here now reigns in Paris a fermentation almost unparalleled since the civil wars ... our amiable prince – once so well loved – is hated, and the government scorned: all this presages baleful happenings to come'.[30]

In early 1753, by means of evocations and threats, the King managed to override *Parlement*. But the mood of Paris, as indicated by *Parlement*'s response, was determined and confident, for how could Paris be governed without the allegiance of its people and its judiciary? Without *Parlement* there was no judicial process, and without that how could the King 'authenticate' new taxes? Thus, in reply, *Parlement* sent new remonstrances to the King. Constituting a propaganda coup of central importance, these so-called Grand Remonstrances were also sold to the public, 20,000 being sold in just a few days. The dramatic sales figures (even more dramatic when multiple readership for each is calculated) reflected the radical contents. The Grand Remonstrances catalogued the crimes of the episcopate against the people and the Crown and claimed an 'exalted role' for the *Parlement* in the preservation of the King's realm.[31] As McManners has explained, the document defined authority 'to exclude arbitrary power'. Even in court and army circles royal policy met with disapproval, and some officers even refused 'distasteful' orders.[32]

Not surprisingly, the King refused to receive such an indictment of his rule, and it was this that prompted *Parlement* to publish the Grand Remonstrances and go on strike. In turn, Louis exiled

Parlement and replaced it with his own tame judicial chamber. Louis's government was in a very difficult situation, embroiled in dispute which threatened to further inflame Paris and provincial centres and one which it was almost impossible to win without concessions. To sum up, astonishingly – from the perspective of traditional Enlightenment studies – royal and governmental authority was publicly challenged by its own *parlements*, and with mass support, all united by Jansenist politico-religious ideology. Why had Louis exiled *Parlement*? He had no choice but to remove the spectacle of public defiance of royal authority from Paris. Why did he not simply arrest its members and so decisively end their defiance? Simply because the political condition of Paris was too unstable. He did not dare risk further inflaming an already very serious situation in which the legitimacy of the government had already been reduced to a dangerously low level. As ever in financial difficulties, his own newly created tame judicial chamber could not provide the requisite legitimacy to raise new taxes. To calm the situation and resume normal judicial business, the *Parlement* had to be recalled with some form of words to disguise the weakness of the government in the face of the Jansenist challenge.

Parlement was thus recalled with ambiguity and an avoidance of the original issues, which in the circumstances was all but a royal capitulation. In another tacit retreat, this was followed with a royal decree of silence on *Unigenitus*. This form of settlement allowed Louis to save face by continuing his refusal to receive the Grand Remonstrances. But the strength of the Jansenist challenge was more than anything evident in the fact that Louis invited *Parlement* to deal with any breaches of the decree of silence on the issue of *Unigenitus*. This decision was a turning point of the greatest magnitude: *Parlement* now had an opening through which it could assert its authority in the government of the Church, something supposedly unthinkable in an absolutist regime. Those who persisted in trying to refuse sacraments now faced exile or would be forced into resignation. *Parlement* quickly made its new authority felt when orthodox clergy, with the support of the Archbishop of Paris, continued to refuse the last sacraments to suspected Jansenists. In response, amongst other actions, *Parlement* brought about the exile of one of Louis's most staunch and powerful defenders, the Archbishop of Paris himself. In 1755 the last rites were refused to Lady Drummond, the wife of the Duke of York. Quick to respond, the

Parisian magistrates even waived the monopoly rights of *curés* in their parishes, allowing Jansenist or more liberal priests to administer sacraments. It is true that the Jesuits were still the greatest hate figures of the day and extra police protection was provided for Jesuit houses, but by this time orthodox clergy were in general so universally reviled that 'priests no longer dared to walk the streets in clerical dress'.[33] Some priests were indeed attacked, and if a priest refused the last rites and news spread to the street, ugly crowd scenes could result, in which priests were at considerable physical risk.

It is difficult to believe that, in examining these events, it is possible to adhere to the myth about French absolutism. Clearly, at least, there was a great deal of difference between royal and governmental rhetoric on the absolutist power of the King and actual reality. Indeed, in these years the *parlements* of France (although we must remember that some provinces did not have *parlements*) asserted themselves as representatives and defenders of France. In the Remonstrances of 1755, for example, it was stated that 'the *Parlement* of Paris and ... the other *parlements* form a single body and are only different divisions of the royal *Parlement*', and the *parlements* of Rouen, Rennes, Bordeaux, Toulouse, Metz, Grenoble and Aix all concurred. As Shennan has expressed it, 'this idea of a united magistracy implied less a royal court than a nation-wide institution with positive powers of its own, virtually independent in the exercise of them'.[34] In a practical manner, therefore, the *parlements* were struggling for some form, albeit limited, of representative government. This desire was, of course, reflected in their writings. It is apparent, for example, from the title of perhaps the most sophisticated treatise on the historic rights of the nobility to share in government by Louis Adrien Le Paige (1712–1802), *Lettres historiques sur les fonctions essentielles du Parlement; sur les droits des pairs, et sur les loix fondamentales du royaume* (1754). In these years other Jansenists wrote in a similar vein. In various pamphlets Claude Mey and Gabrielle Maultrot did not deny the authority of the King. If, however, the King could not be trusted to rule justly and within the law, they claimed that his own subjects and their institutions must be able to do so for him. As Doyle has expressed it, this meant that the *parlements* 'were elevated beyond their traditional role of defenders of the Gallican liberties, into the voice of the nation; and Jansenism can be seen as one of the sources of the idea of representative government in France, fully three decades before it came to fruition'.[35]

Aristocratic in outlook, it could be said that the *parlements*, in putting forward demands for representative government, were fighting for their own traditional corner, the role of nobility in government. There is no doubt, however, that in the context of eighteenth-century Bourbon France, such ideas were radical indeed and not solely on account of their subject matter. They were seen as dangerously radical because Paris (and many other urban centres) was dominated by political Jansenists, and thus the arguments of such works as the *Lettres historiques* were understood as the form of words which in the practical world united dangerously large sections of the nobility, many clergy, the bourgeoisie and the poor against royal tyranny. It only adds to the fascination of Enlightenment Europe when we note that this was a situation peculiar to France. In England the House of Commons was understood to be a legitimate brake on royal aspirations, yet in the Italian peninsula royal absolutism was usually seen by the enlightened and many more as a progressive political form against theocracy and quasi-feudal noble tendencies. Given this diversity of political forms and circumstances within Enlightenment Europe, we cannot, obviously, condemn French philosophes such as Voltaire as non-enlightened for their support of absolutism. But by the same token, neither can we easily categorize as entirely non-enlightened the many intellectuals who saw the *parlements* as the voice of political and religious progress against old regime despotism.

For the King and episcopate, *Parlement*'s defiance and the declarations of its rights to represent the nation were of course seen as dangerous invitations to challenge the political status quo of France and orthodox Catholicism. From its own point of view, *Parlement* was asserting what it saw as its right to save France from despotism and reassert its noble political and material rights. From the point of view of the lower orders, *Parlement* was leading the struggle against royal tyranny for representative government on behalf of those less able to defend themselves. From the point of view of the philosophes, the Church – the abettor of superstition and ignorance – was tearing itself apart and in the process travelling some of the road the philosophes would have liked to travel had they the forces and organizational strength. We already know that historical reality is multi-layered, and as we shall see below, for some modern historians an unexpected layer fulfilled important elements of what is usually regarded as the programme of the philosophes. Far from detracting from the Enlightenment, this admission helps us to come to terms with the dilemmas and opportunities which confronted the enlightened, and in so doing we can enrich our understanding of how the Enlightenment was experienced by its participants.

That the nobility could lead a challenge to royal power in a religious form, and in so doing draw the lower orders behind it, was of course nothing new in early modern Europe. This had been one feature of the Reformation, as competing princes often fought under the banner of religion, of which the Huguenot revolt was an important example. The great difference, however, was that the Jansenist conflict erupted at the heart of urban France in which print culture was burgeoning and major discontent with Bourbon rule existed in both the upper and lower orders.

To resume our account: again, despite the noble nature of *Parlement*, the advocates of Paris became more influential as opponents of despotism and champions of Jansenism than the Jansenist clergy themselves and rivalling even the *Nouvelles ecclésiastiques*. As bystanders to these events, enlightened figures such as Voltaire could only observe and draw the obvious lesson: the struggle between defenders and attackers of old regime tyranny seemed to be entering a decisive phase; without intervention the philosophes would remain isolated. Hence it was in the 1750s, when the noise of battle was audible over most of France, that Voltaire launched his polemic against the infamy of the Church. We can also suggest that as the *billet de confession* conflict encompassed the greatest political conflict of those years, part of the infamy Voltaire had in mind at that time was that of the *billet de confession*. More pertinent, however, was that the enormous impact of the *billet de confession* conflict politicized religion as never before. Crucially, the explicit anticlericalism of the confrontation gave philosophes such as Voltaire the opportunity – that is to say the audience – for a much wider offensive against the Church. These were, in terms of the history of Church and state, remarkable times. As had been effectively happening in England since 1689, the confessional state was buckling under the weight of its own opprobrium and lack of relevance to politico-religious reality. The problem for the Bourbons was that, whether they liked it or not, the concept of the confessional state in France was more intimately linked to general political legitimation than in England. This meant that serious defeat for the regime in religious matters constituted a potentially grave threat in matters of state, and could not but signal the weakness of the regime and presage further political challenge. When that challenge came in 1756, it came from Jansenist lawyers in the form of a direct political challenge to the foundations of absolutism. In that year they prompted a federation of *parlements* and called upon France's princes and peers for support.

The next high point of Jansenist struggle was undoubtedly that against the Jesuits. Yet the suppression of the Jesuits has been considered one of the great ideological measures of the Enlightenment. For Jansenists, the Jesuits – ultra orthodox and only responsible to the Pope himself – were the casuistical abettors of Roman and French tyranny. For the philosophes, too, the Jesuits were archenemies, and they felt that the suppression of the *Encyclopédie* in 1752 and 1758 was Jesuit-inspired. Not surprisingly, in these years of growing antipathy to state and Church, numbers of anti-Jesuit publications emerged from the milieu of the *parlements* and even clerics of the University of Paris attacked the Jesuits. They were widely accused of acting only on behalf of Rome and in their own interests, and consequently against the interests of the monarchy, the nation and true Christianity. In 1760, upon its release all over France, one anti-Jesuit manifesto sold 12,000 copies.[36] One of the most significant Jansenist anti-Jesuit publications of this period was Christophe Coudrette and Louis Adrien Le Paige's four-volume *Histoire general de la naissance et des progress de la compagnie de Jésus en France* (1761). Notions of 'nation' should also cause us to consider the role of broad politico-religious struggle in the formation of nationalism. As we shall see in Chapter 6, it can hardly be denied that politico-religious struggle was decisive in bringing about a massive widening of the public sphere in England and France. Yet, as Van Horn Melton has observed, 'the rise of the public sphere can no more be separated from the origins of nationalism than it can be divorced from the development of capitalism'.[37]

Popular victory against the Jesuits and the call for toleration

Following the expulsion of the Jesuits from Portugal in 1759 and the call by the *Nouvelles ecclésiastiques* for the abolition of the Jesuits, French Jansenists felt confident enough to contemplate a struggle for their suppression in France. In response to a financial scandal, in which the Jesuits were under attack by the court of Marseille, the Jesuits took the fateful decision to appeal to the *Parlement* of Paris. This was presumably in the hope of royal intervention. The appeal, of course, failed, and did so in the most spectacular and politically significant manner. By 1761 the authority of the Crown on this issue was 'manifestly crumbling'[38] and, as in Paris, some provincial *parlements* began closing Jesuit houses. Louis, in an attempt to rescue the situation, proposed reforms of the Jesuits. But his proposals were too limited for *Parlement* and too radical for Rome, and in any case only ensured that provincial *parlements*, whether they wanted to or not, were forced to debate and decide where they stood on the issue. In 1762 the *Parlement* of Paris promulgated its definitive decree abolishing the Jesuit order. The political importance of these events cannot easily be overestimated. Major unilateral intervention in the government of the King's Church was unheard of and politically very ominous indeed, for the King had, in practice, literally lost control of part of his state machine.

The leading Jansenist Le Paige used a network of provincial contacts to spur other *parlements* into action and by the end of 1763 all but three *parlements* had condemned the Jesuits in similar terms. Louis had to fight for his political credibility or concede, but to attempt to reverse the closures risked a political storm from which he and his government may not have emerged. By November 1764, by royal declaration, the Jesuit order had ceased to exist in most of France. Such a signal victory over the Jesuits, famed for their education of the European elite and dedication to maintaining Roman orthodoxy, could hardly be ignored by the philosophes. It was inconceivable that they could silently ignore the victory; something had to be said. This was the momentous context in which d'Alembert claimed the suppression of the Jesuit order as a victory for the influence of the philosophic spirit, that is to say the thought of the Enlightenment. In his *Sur la destruction des Jésuites en France*, he characterized the Jansenists as intolerant supporters of superstition who hated the Jesuits only on account of an obscure and fanatical theological wrangle. Yet he could hardly have been ignorant of the great popular politico-religious struggles that finally gave sufficient power to the *parlements* to unilaterally suppress the Jesuit order.

That, under the circumstances, d'Alembert's claim for the role of the philosophes was outrageous, few historians would deny, and his hatred of Jansenists is evident in his correspondence with Voltaire. But to stop there is potentially to miss an important point. D'Alembert and other philosophes were of course well aware of the politico-religious nature of the wide forces which brought about the downfall of the Jesuits. The animosity of the philosophes to the Church in general, and their recognition that the Church would never be a determined ally in the fight for enlightenment, prevented them from taking a leading role beside Jansenists in the struggle to terminate the Jesuit order. Although there were certainly good grounds for being pessimistic about the willingness of the Church to struggle systematically for enlightenment, it can be justifiably argued that the philosophes significantly underestimated the potential for sections of Christianity to embrace elements of enlightened thought. But two things are for sure: the Jansenist victory over the Jesuits was stunning and of great political importance; and the very weakness of the philosophes – their lack of numbers, cohesion and consequently social and political presence – made it essential that enlightened thought claimed a place in that victory. In such upheavals the alternatives – silence, or a pat on the back for Jansenism (which they would never have performed in public) – were not acceptable: to avoid eclipse on this most central of Enlightenment issues, the philosophes had to claim their place in the sun.

It is hardly a coincidence, therefore, that in 1762 – the same year as the Parisian *Parlement*'s decree against the Jesuits – Voltaire launched his campaign against the injustice visited upon the Calas family by the *Parlement* of Toulouse. The father of the Calas family, unjustly accused of murdering his son because of his engagement to a Catholic, was broken on the wheel. There can be no doubt that Voltaire's propaganda campaign and his lobbying of influential contacts performed an important role in the rehabilitation of the memory of Calas in 1763 and placed the blame squarely on religious intolerance. The struggle against religious intolerance was of course the very context of the wide struggle for the suppression of the Jesuits. To put it plainly, Voltaire could hardly fail to attract significant support for his campaign: as we shall see below, we know that Jansenists too were against the continued persecution of the Huguenots. Voltaire would thus have been very shortsighted indeed if he had not then continued to intervene in such an unprecedented circumstance of Church and state. For, in 1762–63, who knew where the new do-it-yourself reform movement within Church and state might lead? Not surprisingly, then, his *Traité sur la tolérance* appeared in 1764. Again, in order to avoid the danger of being outflanked by religion itself, a public intervention for the philosophic spirit was required even if it was planned to restrict the sale of the *Traité* to the elite only.

Daniel Mornet, in his *Les Origines intellectuelles de la Révolution Française*, has termed this moment of intervention by the philosophes the beginning of the philosophes' exploitation of the victory over the Jesuits.[39] As a consequence of the suppression of the Jesuits, in subsequent years the philosophes were able to gain a wider audience for their ideas and demands. This was an unprecedented period in which the animosity of public opinion and that of the *parlements* to the government allowed more radical opinion to be broached publicly with less risk attached. Thus public opinion and the diffusion and acceptance of elite intellectual writings went in tandem, or more aptly, in symbiosis. If, of course, historians wish to take (or mistake) the headlines of history for reality, then Voltaire's *Traité sur la tolérance* could be portrayed as creating public opinion. From another point of view, the *Traité* – which was aimed only at a tiny elite and was not given wide public release – was a reflection, a response to new conditions, rather than an initiator of them. The plan was to keep the work out of the booksellers' hands and to distribute it directly to well-placed ministers and magistrates as well as to a few discreet friends. It was only natural that, once the victory over the Jesuits had been digested and seen to be without repercussions, liberal public thought turned to continuing instances of brutal Church–state intolerance and the plight of the Huguenots. As McManners has put it, 'the force of public opinion [was] repudiating the past'.[40] From this perspective, any attempt to write the history of the Enlightenment solely from the viewpoint of active radical thought and a passive receptive public will produce potentially serious distortions.

The philosophes were generals without troops. Yet the nature of the historical record and the ideological position from which it has been traditionally viewed has meant that most accounts of the Enlightenment focus on the views of the generals, and overlook or minimize the significance of the broader ideological battles against the old regimes. It is rather strange to track how far the philosophes influenced practical government and to conclude – as all have – that they had very little impact on government, yet pass over the momentous Jansenist suppression of the Jesuits as a mere sign of the enlightened times. The Jansenist victory over the Jesuits in France was decisive in the final papal supression of the Jesuit order. Yet to exclude the philosophes from this general picture would be equally mistaken, for that victory provided them with an unexpected weakening of orthodoxy and, in practical terms, a widened ideological terrain in which to propagate their own ideas. The destruction of the Jesuits marked the peak of Jansenist influence and organizational strength. Nevertheless, in the following years, Jansenists were still active in the struggle against religious oppression, if a little less visibly so than hitherto. Yet, for d'Alembert and other philosophes, Jansenists remained backward religious fanantics, and the philosophes continued to underestimate the possibility of Catholic tolerance.

We know that, famously, the philosophes wrote in favour of toleration. But the fact that, from the mid-century, they were essentially commentators on the outside of a broad *de facto* or organic tendency towards religious toleration cannot be disguised.[41] Indeed, Campbell has noted in his *Power and Politics in Old Régime France* (1996) that, by the accession of Louis XVI (1754), the idea that citizenship conferred the right to religious toleration had gained ground amongst the reading public.[42] There is a very big difference between the actual unfolding of events and the claims and treatises of progressives. Thus, for instance, we ought to be cautious of claims that there was a 'sea-change' in the mid eighteenth century towards toleration, when even many members of the Catholic clergy endorsed demands for toleration.[43] This 'sea-change' was very likely a reflection of earlier, more fundamental processes. But, nevertheless, broad tendencies and elite writings cannot be separated without serious damage to the integrity of intellectual history: they were facets of the same politico-religious reality and we cannot possibly comprehend the philosophes if we effectively decontextualize them. History might be multi-layered, but is always interconnected and interactive. Thus the philosophes were at the same time part of the process of change and, within elite progressive circles, an organic reflection of it.

We know that even before the mid-century, the proscription of Protestantism was not always adhered to. In the army, for instance, in order to keep recruitment at acceptable levels, Protestantism was officially accepted. Tolerance was also evident in civil society. Huguenots were not always strictly excluded from public office as the law dictated; in many places their expertise could not be dispensed with.[44] The years 1744–45 saw the last effort to ensure that disabling laws against Huguenots were properly enforced. As they did not officially exist, Huguenot cemeteries were illegal, yet often unofficially tolerated, and even some *intendants* (regional governors) refused to enforce orders for the brutal persecution of those attending outlawed religious assemblies. Indeed, as early as 1715 a government circular complained with some justification that the laws against Protestants were not being enforced on the ground. Worse still for the Bourbon efforts to eradicate the Huguenots, peaceful tolerance was evident in some mixed Catholic–Protestant communities. Unsurprisingly, the historical record rarely gives us proof that these Catholics actively denounced intolerance, for this sentiment was still contrary to French law. But from the bare facts we know that they were at times certainly defying the laws of the land. There is no doubt that many Catholics did approve or at least accept state–Church intolerance, but there were many more who did not, many of whom had lived close to or within Huguenot communities for generations and had long accepted toleration as a way of Christian life.

As the mid-century approached, intolerant persecuting bishops were fewer in number and, if anything, Catholics were less inclined to accept or favour persecution. We know that, for instance, in one area in the 1750s Catholics and their *curés* combined to protect their Calvinist neighbours. Within the French Catholic Church in the same years there also arose a sharp debate on the issue of intolerance. Significantly, those writers defending the toleration of the Huguenots included Jansenists, who even opined that the Reformed religion was more conducive to good moral conduct than Catholicism[45] – something the philosophes echoed. The 1750s saw several liberal Catholic and Jansenist pro-toleration publications, including those of Abbé Yvon, J. Ripert de Monclar and Abbé Quesnel.[46] Perhaps most notably, in 1758 the Jansenists Maultrot and Tailhé published their *Questions sur la tolérance chrétienne* (printed again two years later as *Essai sur le tolérance chrétienne*), in which they denounced the persecution of Protestants. As O'Brien has illustrated, there were important components of Jansenist Church thinking which militated against intolerance. These included their model of

Church polity, which 'was drawn from the early church of the New Testament and the Fathers, which in principle and in practice seemed less given to summoning the state's power than the contemporary church'. Jansenists were of course still Catholics, so voicing solidarity with Protestants had not always come naturally. It was experience of decades of struggle against orthodox intolerance of Jansenism that overcame such reluctance, especially 'the notorious attempt ... to pursue Jansenists on their deathbed by means of the *billet de confession*'.[47]

In November 1748 Montesquieu's *Esprit des lois* appeared and Jansenists and the *Nouvelles ecclésiastiques* were hostile to much of it, so much so that Montesquieu felt forced to defend himself publicly. The editor of the *Nouvelles ecclésiastiques* (at that time, Fontaine de la Roche) and most other Jansenists considered the *Esprit des lois* a thinly disguised antichristian writing in support of natural religion. We know, however, that Jansenist thought on toleration was by this time well developed, for the *Nouvelles ecclésiastiques* quoted substantial parts of the *Esprit des lois*'s chapters on religious tolerance, and they were not shy to berate the author for his limited conception of toleration. Montesquieu had argued (*Esprit des lois,* bk 24, ch. 5) that the Protestant religion suited a republic better than a monarchy and thus should not be permitted in France. Maultrot and Tailhé replied by citing the rather obvious example of the Catholic Republic of Venice.

Although preceded by other philo-Jansenist tracts arguing for greater toleration, the appearance of Maultrot and Tailhé's *Questions sur la tolérance* caused some sensation. It was the first obviously learned pro-toleration Jansenist tract which commanded wide support amongst Jansenists and the general public, and was consequently soon placed on the papal index of prohibited books. As O'Brien has commented, it was 'an important step towards a modern idea of tolerance ... the first significant attempt by eighteenth-century Jansenist authors to establish a Christian rationale for civil tolerance'.[48] Their arguments were based in part on the need to respect the personal relationship of the individual with God, but also – in enlightened fashion – incorporated natural law and political pragmatism. Maultrot and Tailhé brought a variety of thinkers to their aid, including Bayle and even Montesquieu. The Jansenist debate on toleration, then, should be seen as the eventual reaction to the intractable religious reality of France: no matter what was done, the Huguenots were a permanent, integrated and often respected section of French life. As we now know, thankfully, in the long term (and despite politically inspired lapses) social integration tends towards toleration.

In the early 1760s with the defeat of the staunchly intolerant Jesuits and the hatred of an intolerant Church by large numbers of Jansenists and sympathizers, many in government circles knew that something had to be done. With the recent and very disturbing evidence of how Church and state could be rocked by determined religious opposition, to continue persecution as if it were still 1685 was to court potential disaster. Yet this realization did not mean that intolerance could be abandoned easily. The Crown knew that to concede an element of plurality in a supposedly absolutist state was to invite further representational demands. The episcopate, too, was certainly not going to agree to pluralism within the Church. But, nevertheless, it was clear something would have to be done.

It is at this point that historians often experience difficulty. How will we ever know the precise logic of governments and hierarchies at such moments? It is, of course, a simple fact that many delicate decisions and the grounds for them were not deemed suitable for the ears of the public and indeed of many servants of the Crown or hierarchy. The 'real' tale, in terms of the written record, is often not recorded. Thus it is quite problematic to argue that historical accounts can always avoid informed speculation outside the historical record. We can say, then, on the basis of the facts, that the forces for inertia in the French Church and state of the 1760s were at least a degree greater than those for radical change. But it is most unlikely that many of those who saw change as inimical to their interests were not sharply aware of the desirability of some easing of the situation, even if only to stave off temporarily the likelihood of future change.

We do know, however, that in 1766 the papal nuncio in France sent a report to Rome emphasizing the difficult situation that Calvinists faced. Their own marriage ceremonies were not recognized by the Church and they would never have undertaken a heretical Catholic marriage ceremony. For the Gallican Church, then, Protestants faced a choice of celibacy or concubinage. The nuncio added that this was a situation which had to be dealt with and could not be avoided by reaffirming the official French line that the Huguenots did not exist. But the nuncio's letter does not reveal the full extent of the apprehension of the French state on the question of religion, for we know that other, wider discussions took place in France.[49] In 1767 the royal councilor Gilbert de Voisins recommended reinstating some of the civil and religious rights of which the Huguenots had been deprived for so long: civil marriage, the right to entrance to most professions, and the right to the presence of their own pastors for discrete worship. It is indicative that, in the same year, the Sorbonne suffered intense ridicule for its condemnation of arguments for toleration.

If there were many in state and Church who now feared for the future of an intolerant regime, there were many who feared the religious and political consequences of conceding toleration, perhaps none more so than the King himself. Thus, although the debate on reform continued, two decades were to elapse before reform proposals were decreed and implemented. But, as we have seen, reality and law do not always coincide. The crushing defeat of Church and state in the unilateral action of the *parlements* to abolish the Jesuit order had naturally brought about a profound change in the confidence of some *parlements* to defy official policy and initiate religious liberalization. Yet unilateral action remained a very risky option indeed, for, if the government thought it propitious, it could still adopt a hard line against disobedient *parlements*. In 1763 a new archbishop came to the see of Toulouse, Archbishop Brienne, who favoured toleration. The arrival of Brienne – and perhaps also the memory of the shame of the Calas case – eventually persuaded the *Parlement* to overcome its fears of unilateral action and it decisively turned towards toleration in 1769.[50] Perhaps the most important point here is that what was happening in Toulouse was happening in many places.

By the beginning of the reign of Louis XVI (1774), the groundswell towards effective – if not always legal – toleration meant that almost everywhere Huguenots found themselves living side by side with Catholics in greater harmony and with fewer disadvantages. Indeed, some Protestant families, the Masson family for instance, were so prosperous that the government and others paid them deference. It was true that brutal persecution undoubtedly initiated by Catholic clerics still occurred in a few places. It is also indisputable that the emerging general toleration could not have possibly come about without the agreement or at least acquiescence of many of the Catholic parish clergy. How far it was agreement or resignation to a *de facto* situation is difficult to judge. Unsurprisingly, persecuting bishops were certainly becoming less numerous. Nevertheless, hard-line prelates in the Assemblies of the Clergy called continually – up until the 1787 Royal Edict of Toleration – for the government's enforcement of the laws against Huguenots.[51] But the Assemblies had little power to change reality, for the government had little stomach for an escalation of political alienation which would have certainly been the result of any renewed persecution.

Another illustration of how the reality of effective widespread toleration was imposing itself is provided by the circumstances in which Amelot, a government minister determined to ingratiate himself at court by enforcing the laws against the Huguenots, quickly abandoned his plans. Within a few months of taking office, he realized the extent of *de facto* toleration and the impossibility of turning the clock backwards and consequently abandoned his plans. The interesting thing here is that on this issue Amelot heeded the advice of the military commander of Languedoc, the Comte de Périgord, who was pro-toleration. On the advice of Périgord, he sent orders to all the intendants to leave the persecuting legislation unenforced and endorsed an agreement Périgord had made to tolerate Desert (unofficial Protestant) marriages. Neither government ministers nor military commanders could overturn the weight of reality. The call for the legalization of Protestant marriages was now almost universal. Thus the *philosophe* Condorcet's call for legalization in 1779 can hardly be seen as a radical proposal, especially given the fact that even Albert, the Lieutenant-General of the Paris Police, was pro-toleration. Already, in 1776, in his *Un projet d'edit de tolérance*, Albert had argued in favour of the legalization of Protestant marriages. After the victory against the Jesuits, broadly Jansenist issues had occupied less space on the agenda of the *Parlement* of Paris. Jansenist members nevertheless remained active in the demand for toleration, arguing, as Robert de Saint-Vincent did in 1787, that 'those who destroyed Port-Royal ... are the same people who were ardent prosecutors of Protestants'.[52]

The final decline of the absolutist dream

Despite the victory over the Jesuits, for Jansenists the essence of the Church–state problem remained. The absolutist governmental outlook of the Bourbons still required control of the Church, and the *parlements* reduced to obedience. In the struggle against the Jesuits, the *parlements* had at times acted as a quasi-national *parlement*. It was thus unthinkable that the King would not ultimately attempt to reverse the Jansenist victories. In 1770 a royal edict was published that attempted to achieve just that, and deny the right of *parlements* to refuse their consent to royal declarations and edicts.

It is inconceivable that the King did not expect the *Parlement* of Paris to react vigorously to the edict, for, after the victories of the previous decades, its members felt confident of their own powers and their wide support. *Parlement* naturally refused to sign away its hard-won gains and suspended routine judicial business. The chancellor, René de Maupeou, responded by exiling the *Parlement* and hastily replacing it with new compliant recruits. This was such a radical step that it naturally provoked resistance from the other courts of Paris and provincial *parlements*, against which the government also acted. For the government, however, such a revolution was a risky business indeed, increasing alienation from the government and so threatening increased destabilization. Accordingly, the new King Louis XVI restored the old *parlements* in 1774. It was too late, however, to undo the damage done. Under the goad of the so-called Maupeou Revolution, the political or judicial Jansenism of the 1750s and 1760s completed its transition from a politico-religious cause into what could seem, and justifiably be described as, a much more secular one: the Patriot movement. This movement had as its primary goal the defence of the French public against royal despotism and was to play a leading role in the build-up to the French Revolution. The result of the Maupeou Revolution was a great wave of protest, in which there was a war of pamphlets or 'antichancellor writings' between the Patriots and the government. At least 500 works appealed to the nation against the 'despotism' of the government, and began to set the terminological stakes for the eventual outbreak of Revolution in the next decade. Some philosophes did of course intervene in the resistance to the Maupeou Revolution.[53] It remains the case, however, that their voice in the anti-Maupeou camp cannot be described as pivotal; Voltaire, for instance, supported the Maupeou Revolution.

There is abundant evidence that the Patriots were formed from the leadership of the Jansenist struggles of the 1750s and 1760s. Indeed, the 'conspicuous role of Jansenism at all levels of the patriot movement strongly suggests that the movement ... spread by means of the same clandestine channels of communication originally set up for the dissemination of Jansenist ephemeral literature, in particular the weekly *Nouvelles ecclésiastiques*.[54] This was of course a task which the philosophes could never have accomplished, partly on account of their tiny numbers. It was impossible more so because, on such a direct political issue rather than general philosophical goals, their often elite backgrounds prevented any easy consensus. In the final instance, considerable sections of the elite of France naturally saw the Bourbons as the source of legitimate political power and social order. From whichever angle the situation is viewed, it remains the fact that those philosophes who did support the Patriots were mostly bystanders or peripheral supporters of a movement rather than its leaders.

From the overtly political nature of the Patriot movement, at first glance it might seem as if the Jansenist movement was losing itself in politics and that, as France went into the critical decades of the 1770s and 1780s, religion was ceasing to play such a fundamental role in the political life of the country. This is, however, to misunderstand the politico-religious content of the Maupeou Revolution and the desire of the government to attempt to minimize religious controversy by stealth. The Crown's main ally in its struggle with *Parlement* was of course its orthodox, pro-Rome clergy, and it remained so until the Revolution erupted. Indeed, we know that 'the clerical councilors for Maupeou's new *Parlement* of Paris had been recruited by none other than the anti-Jansenist Archbishop of Paris'. An alliance is always a case of compromise, and the orthodox clergy were above all still committed to stamping out or cowing Jansenism within the Church. The Maupeou Revolution was thus also the 'the green light to resume the sacramental harassment of appellants of *Unigenitus*', which the old *parlements* had effectively prohibited.[55] This is partly why a high proportion of the Patriot anti-Maupeou pamphlets were written by Jansenists. The subsequent cases of sacramental and other types of anti-Jansenist harassment also prompted the sharp intervention of the *Nouvelles ecclésiastiques*. The pages of that journal, as McManners has succinctly put it, were 'directed towards popular consciousness'. It was the only newspaper, in fact, in which the masses did not appear as criminals or as credulous non-entities; rather 'the people were the repositories of the truth on which Rome, the Church and the

Monarchy were forever seeking to trample'.[56]

At this point, therefore, as elsewhere in the century, it would be quite misleading to attempt to draw a neat dividing line between the enlightened and Jansenists. In particular, as Kley has put it, the

> necessity of appealing to the broadest possible constituency forced Jansenists further to secularize their sectarian constitutionalism: to reconceptualize, for example, the magistrates' venal offices in terms of the natural right of property, and their representative role in the language of natural law.... In one of his pamphlets [*Le Parlement justifi, par l'impératrice de Russie*], the Jansenist André Blonde even quoted from that boldest of the century's atheistic statements, Baron d'Holbach's *Nature's System*.[57]

We have noted that Rousseau's *Du contrat social* (1762) was little known before 1789. But the process of bringing about a wider awareness of the notion of the General Will as a component of contract theory began in Jansenist literature and polemic long before the Revolution, and before 1762 and the publication of the *Contrat social*. The differences between Rousseauism and Jansenism cannot, of course, be glossed over. It is nevertheless true that, as Roger Barny has emphasized, the Jansenist–Patriot milieu produced the first sizeable and appreciative audience for the *Contrat social*.[58] It is also important to note that some of the pamphlets of the pre-Revolutionary crisis sympathetic to *Parlement*'s appeal for an Estates General in 1787–88 were in fact reprints of Patriot pamphlets which had first appeared in 1771. In his popular *Catéchisme du citoyen* (1775), for example, the Jansenist Guillaume-Joseph Saige 'began with a clarion enunciation of Rousseauian principles'. He argued that sovereign power was to be found only in the General Will; from this position, the logical step was to appeal for an Estates General, as in fact his *Catéchisme* did. These arguments were also found in the learned *Maximes du droit public françois* (1775) of Maultrot and Mey, who also argued for an immediate convocation of an Estates General.[59] So, as Doyle has put it, 'Jansenists were amongst the first to call for genuinely representative institutions, elected assemblies which would spell the end of absolute monarchy'.[60]

That what amounted to a hybrid of Jansenist and Rousseauian constitutionalism (the *Maximes du droit public françois*) appeared was, in some respects, hardly surprising. It is well known that Rousseau himself experienced a Jansenist phase (see his *Confes-*

sions, 1772), although by the 1760s, at least, Rousseau was contemptuous of Jansenists as fanatical subverters of his own vision of Christianity. In his *The General Will Before Rousseau* (1986), Patrick Riley has shown that the concept of the General Will was common in Jansenist literature considerably before the publication of Rousseau's *Contrat social*. Of course a theory of the General Will can be expressed in various terms, and it would be unfounded (and rather naive) to argue that Rousseau's concept of the General Will had been present in the thought of earlier writers coming to the subject from various religious and ideological directions. Nevertheless, as Riley illustrates, concepts of the General Will had some currency long before Rousseau in the thought of several writers including Blaise Pascal (1623–62), Nicholas Malebranche (1638–1715), Pierre Bayle, Bossuet, Fontenelle and Montesquieu. The central point, however, is that Riley's book is a study of the transformation of the idea of the General Will from a religious one (the General Will of God to save all men) into a political one (the General Will of the citizen to place the common good of society over and above himself).

The limitation of Riley's work, however, is that it remains too abstract, too much at the level of the march of theory. If, however, we put Rousseau's 1762 *Du contrat social* in its context – i.e. the practical general will (majority public support for Jansenists against the government) – then the date and the content of Rousseau's work become more explicable. As a concluding remark, therefore, we can say that those who have demonstrated that Rousseau's *Du contrat social* had little currency before the Revolution are in danger of missing the point. For the real question should be: in the great Jansenist-*parlementaire* struggles against the government from the 1750s to the 1780s, how much influence did the concept of their General Will against perceived governmental tyranny have? There can be little doubt that the popular, general appeal to the Estates General as the arbiter of social justice over and above the judgement of the King doomed the concept of absolute rule in France, and was the key in the downfall of the Bourbon regime. Yet, as we have seen, there is a substantial body of evidence to demonstrate that the idea of a General Will expressed through French *parlements* had been a growing concept in the popular movement against clerical and government tyranny since the 1750s. The single most important point with relation to the years prior to the Revolution is that lower clergy, some intellectuals, a section of the elite (*parlements*) and large numbers, if not the majority, of the urban poor formed an active tradition in which the generation and transmission of its ideas was the very same thing as the exercise of its collective social force.

It should hardly need stating that it is impossible to discern the activity of any deist movement in these events – or indeed any evidence indicating that the phenomenon of the Enlightenment, as it has been traditionally conceived, led to the French Revolution. Unfortunately for the modernity hunters, the great Church–state conflicts of eighteenth-century France were fought out in a more or less traditional manner with one Christian faction pitted against another in alliance with particular lay constituencies. But *Parlement*'s conflict with the King had, of course, its limits. After the celebrations occasioned by the death of Louis XV and the consequent downfall of Maupeou had subsided, the potential political significance of the enormously wide Patriot movement was not lost on the *parlements*. The wave of radicalism unleashed by the Maupeou Revolution had sharply reminded the noble membership of the *parlements* that they still had a significant stake in the status quo. With Maupeou now gone, and fearing for their social position, many in the *parlements* felt obliged to think the hitherto unthinkable and ally with the episcopate in order to ensure social order, which naturally entailed an end to much of their more radical outlook. In these circumstances, most Jansenists naturally abandoned their illusions in the *parlementary* leadership, and many welcomed the opportunity of 1789 to bring about a new Church and state.

Notes

1 On toleration in France see, for instance, M. Linton, 'Citizenship and Religious Toleration in France', in O. Grell and R. Porter (eds), *Toleration in Enlightenment Europe* (Cambridge: Cambridge University Press, 2000); C. H. O'Brien, 'Jansenists on Civil Toleration in Mid-18th-Century France', *Theologischen Zeitschrift*, 37 (1981); G. Adams, *The Huguenots and French Opinion 1685–1787. The Enlightenment Debate on Toleration* (Ontario: Wilfred Laurier University Press, 1991).

2 See, for instance, W. Rex, *Essays on Pierre Bayle and Religious Controversy* (The Hague: Martinus Nijhoff, 1965); E. Labrousse, *Pierre Bayle* (Oxford and New York: Oxford University Press, 1983; 1st edn 1963); E. Labrousse, 'Reading Pierre Bayle in Paris', in A. C. Kors and P. J. Korshin (eds), *Anticipations of the Enlightenment in England, France and Germany* (Philadelphia: Philadel-

phia University Press, 1987); K. Sandberg, *At the Crossroads of Faith and Reason. An Essay on Pierre Bayle* (Tucson: University of Arizona Press, 1966); on Bayle and toleration see J. Laursen, 'Baylean Liberalism: Tolerance Requires Nontolerance', in J. Laursen and C. Nederman (eds), *Beyond the Persecuting Society* (Philadephia: University of Pennsylvania Press, 1998).

3 See, for instance, R. Barny, *Prélude idéologique à la Révolution Française: Le Rousseauisme avant 1789* (Paris: Belles Lettres, 1985); C. J. Betts, *Early Deism in France. From the So-Called 'Déistes' of Lyon (1564) to Voltaire's 'Lettres philosophiques' (1734)* (The Hague, Boston and Lancaster: Martinus Nijhoff, 1984); P. R. Campbell, *Power and Politics in Old Régime France, 1720–1745* (London: Routledge, 1996); A. C. Kors, *Atheism in France, 1650–1729. Vol. 1: The Orthodox Sources of Disbelief* (Princeton, N.J.: Princeton University Press, 1990); Kors and Korshin (eds), *Anticipations of the Enlightenment*; M. Linton, 'The Unvirtuous King? Clerical Rhetoric on the French Monarchy, 1760–1774', *History of European Ideas*, 25 (1999); J. McManners, *Church and Society in Eighteenth-Century France* (2 vols, Oxford: Clarendon Press, 1998).

4 One early and almost lone voice in the reassessment of the role of Jansenism in the suppression of the Jesuits was D. Mornet, *Les Origines intellectuelles de la Révolution Française 1715–1787* (6th edn, Paris: Armand Colin, 1967; 1st edn 1933). See also, for instance, O'Brien, 'Jansenists on Civil Toleration'; P. Riley, *The General Will Before Rousseau. The Transformation of the Divine into the Civic* (Princeton, N.J.: Princeton University Press, 1986); J. Shennan, *The Parlement of Paris* (Stroud: Sutton Press, 1998); D. Van Kley, *The Jansenists and the Expulsion of the Jesuits from France 1757–1765* (London: Yale University Press, 1975); D. Van Kley, *The Damiens Affair and the Unraveling of the Ancien Régime* (Princeton, N.J.: Princeton University Press, 1984); D. Van Kley, 'Pierre Nicole, Jansenism, and the Morality of Enlightened Self-Interest', in Kors and Korshin (eds), *Anticipations of the Enlightenment*; D. Van Kley, *The Religious Origins of the French Revolution. From Calvin to the Civil Constitution, 1560–1791* (New Haven and London: Yale University Press, 1996). On Jansenism's roots in the community and its politico-religious opposition to the King and the Roman orthodoxy see D. Garrioch, *The Formation of the Parisian Bourgeoisie 1690–1830* (Cambridge and London: Harvard University Press, 1996), Part One, 'The Jansenist Years'. For those studying Jansenism for the first time, William Doyle's *Jansenism. Catholic Resistance to Authority from the Reformation to the French Revolution* (London: Macmillan, 2000) provides an accessible summary of the field. Some writers, however, have been more grudging in their acceptance of the importance of Jansenist politico-religious struggle. B. Stone, *The Genesis of the French Revolution. A Global-Historical Interpretation* (Cambridge: Cambridge University Press, 1994), pp. 82–3, for instance, whilst acknowledging the work of Dale Van Kley, refers to Jansenism as a 'battle of the past' rather than an 'issue of the future' and subsumes it under the title 'socio-political challenge'.

5 N. Henshall, *The Myth of Absolutism* (London: Longman, 1992).

6 Shennan, *The Parlement of Paris.*

7 On the Huguenots and public opinion see, for example, Adams, *The Huguenots and French Opinion.*

8 On the Edict of Nantes and its Revocation see, for instance, R. M. Golden (ed.),

The Enlightenment and religion

The Huguenot Connection. The Edict of Nantes, its Revocation, and Early Migration to South Carolina (Dordrecht, Boston and Lancaster: Kluwer Academic Publishers, 1988).

9 McManners, *Church and Society in Eighteenth-Century France*, vol. 2, p. 569.
10 Labrousse, *Pierre Bayle*, pp. 7, 9–10.
11 On the Huguenot diaspora see, for instance, G. C. Gibbs, 'The Reception of the Huguenots in England', in O. P. Grell, J. I. Israel and N. Tyacke (eds), *From Persecution to Toleration. The Glorious Revolution and Religion in England* (Oxford: Clarendon, 1991).
12 McManners, *Church and Society in Eighteenth-Century France*, vol. 2, pp. 586, 569.
13 On French Jansenism, in addition to the works of O'Brien, Van Kley and Shennan cited above, see also C.-L. Maire, *De la cause de Dieu à cause de la nation. Les Jansénistes au XVIIIe siècle* (Paris: Galliard, 1998); M. Cottret, *Jansénismes et Lumières. Pour un autre XVIII siècle* (Paris: Albin Michel, 1998); L. Hamon, *Du Jansénisme à la laïcité et les origines de la déchristianisation* (Paris: Editions de la Maison des Sciences de L'Homme, 1987).
14 Conventicles: independent Huguenot congregations.
15 Doyle, *Jansenism*, pp. 30, 39.
16 Van Kley, *The Religious Origins of the French Revolution*, p. 248.
17 McManners, *Church and Society in Eighteenth-Century France*, vol. 2, pp. 364, 377.
18 Doyle, *Jansenism*, pp. 50–1.
19 McManners, *Church and Society in Eighteenth-Century France*, vol. 2, p. 428.
20 On the *Parlement* of Paris and Jansenism see also J. Swann, *Politics and the Parlement of Paris under Louis XV, 1754–1774* (Cambridge: Cambridge University Press, 1995).
21 On the *Nouvelles ecclésiastiques* see, for example, D. A. Coward, 'The Fortunes of a Newspaper: The *Nouvelles Ecclésiastiques*, 1728–180', *British Journal for Eighteenth-Century Studies*, 4 (1981).
22 McManners, *Church and Society in Eighteenth-Century France*, vol. 2, pp. 424, 426.
23 On the development of Jansenist leadership by laymen see, for instance, D. A. Bell, *Lawyers and Citizens. The Making of a Political Elite in Old Regime France* (New York and Oxford: Oxford University Press, 1994).
24 Doyle, *Jansenism*, p. 55.
25 McManners, *Church and Society in Eighteenth-Century France*, vol. 2, p. 433.
26 On public opinion in France, in addition to the works of Baker, Echeverria and Chartier cited in Chapter 2, see also K. Baker, 'Politics and Public Opinion under the Old Regime: Some Reflections', in J. Censer and J. Popkin (eds), *Press and Politics in Pre-Revolutionary France* (Berkeley: University of California Press, 1987), reprinted as 'Public Opinion as Political Invention', in K. Baker, *Inventing the French Revolution. Essays on French Political Culture in the Eighteenth Century* (Cambridge: Cambridge University Press, 1990); and Part III ('Conceptions of the Public Sphere in Eighteenth-Century France') of C. Adams, J. Censer and L. Graham (eds), *Visions and Revisions of Eighteenth-Century France* (Pennsylvania: Pennsylvania State University Press, 1997).

France: the revolt of democratic Christianity

27 Doyle, *Jansenism*, p. 57.
28 McManners, *Church and Society in Eighteenth-Century France*, vol. 2, p. 461.
29 Doyle, *Jansenism*, p. 62.
30 Quoted in McManners, *Church and Society in Eighteenth-Century France*, vol. 2, p. 496.
31 Doyle, *Jansenism*, p. 63.
32 McManners, *Church and Society in Eighteenth-Century France*, vol. 2, pp. 500–1.
33 Ibid., vol. 2, p. 502.
34 Quoted in Shennan, *The Parlement of Paris*, p. 311. For a similar assessment see also Van Kley, *The Damiens Affair*.
35 Doyle, *Jansenism*, pp. 66–7.
36 McManners, *Church and Society in Eighteenth-Century France*, vol. 2, p. 536.
37 J. Van Horn Melton, *The Rise of the Public in Enlightenment Europe* (Cambridge: Cambridge University Press, 2001), p. 274.
38 McManners, *Church and Society in Eighteenth-Century France*, vol. 2, pp. 536, 554.
39 Mornet, *Les Origines intellectuelles de la Révolution Française*, see Part III, 'L'Exploitation de la victoire' and the conclusion.
40 McManners, *Church and Society in Eighteenth-Century France*, vol. 2, p. 620.
41 As early as 1960 D. Bien, in *The Calas Affair* (Princeton, N.J.: Princeton University Press, 1960), argued that the Calas affair was an aberration in an otherwise already relatively tolerant atmosphere.
42 Campbell, *Power and Politics in Old Régime France*, pp. 170–1.
43 Linton, 'Citizenship and Religious Toleration in France', p. 168.
44 McManners, *Church and Society in Eighteenth-Century France*, vol. 2, p. 601.
45 Ibid., vol. 2, pp. 617, 623–4, 672.
46 Abbé Yvon, *Liberté de conscience, resserrée dans bornes légitimes* (London, 1754); J. Ripert de Monclar and Abbé Quesnel, *Mémoire théologique et politique au sujet des mariages clandestins des Protestants de France* (1755–56).
47 O'Brien, 'Jansenists on Civil Toleration', pp. 72–3.
48 Ibid., p. 78.
49 For more on those discussions see McManners, *Church and Society in Eighteenth-Century France*, vol. 2, pp. 616–17.
50 Ibid., vol. 2, p. 619.
51 Ibid., vol. 2, pp. 648–50.
52 Ibid., vol. 2, pp. 651–2; Saint-Vincent quoted on p. 655.
53 Van Kley, *The Religious Origins of the French Revolution*, p. 252.
54 Ibid., p. 272.
55 Ibid., pp. 275–6.
56 McManners, *Church and Society in Eighteenth-Century France*, vol. 2, p. 675.
57 Van Kley, *The Religious Origins of the French Revolution*, p. 268.
58 See Barny, *Prélude idéologique a la Revolution Française*.
59 Van Kley, *The Religious Origins of the French Revolution*, pp. 258, 294.
60 Doyle, *Jansenism*, p. 82.

5

Italy: Roman 'tyranny' and radical Catholic opposition

This final case study provides another different context of the Enlightenment. The experience of Catholic dissidents in the Italian peninsular provides some similarities with the struggles in France, but the very different politico-religious context of the Italian peninsular means that differences tend to outweigh similarities. Differences aside, the point of this chapter is again to illustrate that broad politico-religious struggle – rather than the actions of the philosophes – provided the most significant challenge to the status quo of Enlightenment Europe.

Jansenism and Catholic Enlightenment

The following discussion focuses on those who 'called upon new knowledge, wanted better education, were against superstition, denounced obscurantism, wished to break the Jesuit stranglehold in higher education and contributed to the fall of the Jesuits, were not friendly to schoolmen,[1] [and] shared most of the broad intellectual aims pursued by the men of the Enlightenment': the Jansenists. It is hardly surprising, therefore, that Chadwick has commented, with reference to the Enlightenment and Italian Jansenism, that 'we cannot define where one movement ends and the other begins'.[2] We can thus, hopefully, assume that it is no longer necessary to argue for the validity of the term Catholic Enlightenment.[3] Of course the term Catholic Enlightenment cannot be reduced to Jansenism, and enlightened priests at the heart of the Italian Enlightenment such as Ferdinando Galiani and Antonio Genovesi – who cannot easily be bracketed as Jansenists – prove the point. The fundamental issue implicit in the following discussion, however, is that the so-called deist movement was nowhere more conspicuous by its absence than in the Italian peninsula, where the critique of perceived papal despotism and superstition was left in the the surprisingly effective hands of radical Catholics. The discussion will, therefore, focus little on the absence of deists and concentrate on examining the radical Catholic challenge and its general context.

By some, Jansenists have been regarded as non-representative of the general Catholic reforming trend, but rather as the 'extremist wing' of the Catholic Enlightenment.[4] To portray Jansenists as unrepresentative of the period would be, it seems to me, to render the term Catholic Enlightenment of little use to scholars. If the term is to have any meaning at all within Enlightenment or eighteenth-century studies, it must be to indicate the corpus of reforming and often dissenting intellectual and politico-religious thought which aimed at modernization of the Church and some aspects of society, yet retaining a theological outlook significantly Catholic in orientation. In any case, in the context of France, the only manner in which Jansenism can be rendered extremist is to take a blatantly partisan position: the party line of Rome and the Bourbon dynasty. Rather than extremist, as we have seen, French Jansenism undoubtedly represented the politico-religious outlook of very large numbers of people who understood themselves to be challenging Bourbon extremism and in so doing protecting what they understood to be the traditional freedoms of the people and Gallican Church. The problem has been that, for the philosophes and their modern admirers, French Jansenists have usually been regarded as religious fanatics and therefore conservative, while the Church has considered them to be extreme, beyond the Christian pale.

Similar arguments against the label extremist can be advanced in the Italian context, when during the 1770s and 1780s the ecclesiastical rights of Catholic sovereigns were championed against what was understood as the tyrannic jurisdiction of Rome, which had overthrown the state–Church traditions of the early Church. This movement for radical Church reform (although ultimately derailed) posed potentially the greatest eighteenth-century challenge to Roman orthodoxy, ecclesiastical jurisdiction and curial material interests. Compared to the relative weakness of the Italian Enlightenment, the Catholic challenge to the old regime was vigorous and relatively broadly based. Perhaps even more than the French experience, the challenge from within the Church had a political dimension, one rooted firmly within the peculiar politico-religious conditions of a politically polycentric peninsula. Again, as with the French and English experience, it was not the political or theological ramifications of the Reformation or conflict between the two great European confessions which was central to developments. Rather it was the seemingly narrower and local context of particular Church–state conflict within Italian sovereign states which led to a politicization of religion in a manner which the Reformation and its seventeenth-century aftermath did not generate within the peninsula. Unsurprisingly, the political vocabulary of revolt witnessed in France also emerged in Italian religious thought. It emerged, however, not against the 'tyranny'of authoritarian rulers, but rather against the old regime in the form of what was understood as the antichristian medieval theocracy of the Papal States and the despotic rule of the popes over their European Church empire.

Much of the politico-religious polemic of those decades, as in the French and English experience, was, in the general sense, hardly novel. In this sense the polemic was traditional, but not at all the result of any tradition which finally, as in Gay's view, regained its 'nerve',[5] but rather the result of specific politico-religious conditions. In this context, as usual, the claims for intellectual or spiritual origins are shaky. Miller, for instance, has claimed that Italian Jansenism was decisively influenced by French Jansenism. The only proof of influence adduced, however, is that French and Italian Jansenists had many ideas in common, and that the ideas of Italian Jansenists could be 'traced back' to France. This 'tracing back' certainly owes a great deal to academics who have induced texts to talk to each other, and also to the now waning tradition of attempting to reduce the European Enlightenment to the sum of the French High Enlightenment. Yet there is no evidence to suggest that ideas of the Italian Jansenists were any less the product of local circumstances or that their ideas and struggles were less central in the conflict with the old regime than those of the French Jansenists and their supporters. Nevertheless, it is possible to say, as O'Brien has done, that late Jansenists, such as those in Italy, 'continued to prove receptive to enlightened ideas, such as religious liberty, which were compatible with Jansenist spirituality', using 'arguments similar to those used by Maultrot and Tailhé'.[6]

The idea, then, that Italian Jansenism was decisively influenced by the French experience I will put aside as yet unproven. In any case, searching for origins is less profitable than properly examining this so far under-researched topic. Instead, I will contend that there were very definite local politico-religious reasons as to why reform-minded Italian Jansenists mounted a frontal assault on Roman theocracy and ecclesiastical jurisdiction – especially so in the second half of the century. It is also difficult to ignore the fact that important elements of their politico-religious polemic significantly resembled the seventeenth- and early-eighteenth-century jurisdictionalist (i.e. anti-Rome or anti-curial) tradition.[7]

In any event, it can hardly be denied that the Jansenist politico-religious outlook in France had, in one crucial respect, a great difference from that in Italy. In France many Jansenists wanted to move towards some form of constitutional monarchy. Those less radical in outlook sought, at least, an attenuation of regal intervention within the Church, and thus in effect greater religious freedom which was rightly understood as inimical to traditional Bourbon absolutist goals. In the Italian peninsula, however, the dominant trend was definitively towards absolutism and regal jurisdiction within sovereign Churches as a counterweight to Rome. Thus some partisan modern commentators have lamented that the principal weakness of the Catholic Enlightenment was its tendency to place the Church in a position of dependence upon the state and it 'often seriously jeopardized the independence of the Church as a consequence'.[8] Such a verdict is anachronistic and entirely misses the point, because to bolster the state, even backing absolutist-style rulers' rights within the Church, was then understood as progressive rather than reactionary, a step towards prevailing continental conditions and a step away from the peninsula's medieval past. Given the extreme historical political vicissitudes of Italy, we should not be surprised at this verdict. Treatises in the medieval mirror tradition on the 'good prince' written by great reforming clerics such as Lodovico Muratori only serve to highlight the point.

Anti-curial polemic and its context

Given that many readers will be less familiar with the Italian polemical traditions than with those of France and England, it is worth devoting some time to examining the core elements of the Italian anti-curial polemic and its context prior to the 1760s. At the heart of the radical Catholic critique of the Curia was the accusation that the medieval and contemporary popes had usurped the divine rights of kings. For such critics, popes had meddled in the secular affairs of states and had carved out and vigorously sought to defend and extend a secular domain (the medieval Papal States and substantial landed possessions in other kingdoms). In defiance of the dictum of Jesus Christ – that *Regnum meum non est de hoc mundo* (John 18:36) – they had made themselves priest-kings on the ancient pagan model.[9] The critical significance of that biblical phrase in the Italian peninsula is difficult to overestimate. Indeed, the inclusion of it in the title of the Neapolitan Marcello Eusebio Scotti's *Della Monarchia universale de'papi 'Respondit Jesus: Regnum Meum non est de hoc mundo.' Joan 18. 36* (1789) is indicative of its contemporary politico-religious esteem. In essence, regalist polemic against Roman theocracy and rebuttals of long-standing (and unrealistic) curial claims to suzerainty and dominion over various parts of the peninsula were all components of a drive by Italian sovereigns to justify reclaiming 'lost' jurisdictional rights within their own Churches.

The Papal States were ruled by the Curia in high-medieval fashion, with the ecclesiastical hierarchy also functioning as secular vassals of the Pope: cardinals governing legations (major cities and areas) and the delegations (minor areas) ruled by a prelate. But the fact of temporal rule was simultaneously Rome's ideological strength and its potential Achilles' heel. Theocratic rule was certainly open to attack by means of the biblical evidence of Christ's rejection of an earthly kingdom. But, as its turbulent medieval history demonstrated, without territorial independence the Curia would have had less security and less political influence in the peninsula. In addition, its claim to exclusive sovereign rights in the administration of its wide landed possessions and organizational superstructure across Europe – which provided much of its financial income – would also have been weakened rather than strengthened.

The regalist argument was simple: Christ had never intended that princes should be excluded from government of the Church. Regalist polemicists, even relative moderates such as the influential Modenese reformer, historian and polemicist Lodovico Muratori,[10] claimed that, historically, kings and emperors, with the permission of Rome, had worked together in the administration of the Church. This divinely ordained cooperation had been terminated when the medieval popes – motivated by worldly ambition – had discarded Christ's dictum on the illegitimacy of a temporal kingdom of the Church and had usurped temporal rule for themselves. Muratori, in defence of his Modenese ruler's claims to government within the Modenese Church, had compiled a historical account demonstrating that, until the early ninth century, rulers had possessed the power to intervene in matters of ecclesiastical justice. Thus he could conclude, 'Deny now, if you are able, that the kings, although pious, judged it their own duty to intervene in the correction of the ecclesiastics and in their government', against which the popes did not protest.[11] He consequently felt he had proven the historical case for the princely right to share in the administration of the Church, so justifying his Modenese ruler's case for reclaiming jurisdictional rights lost when the Curia had usurped temporal dominion and separated itself and the Churches of Europe from secular rule.

Jurisdictional conflict of this type became more frequent and more trenchant in the late eighteenth century, for, as the enlightened Pietro Verri recalled at the end of the century, 'it was really an absurdity to see established a jurisdiction independent of the sovereign, with access to the use of force, prisons, tortures and confiscations ... in which the sovereign played no part at all'.[12] For centuries before, however, Italian sovereigns and their supporters had frequently striven to limit the jurisdiction of Rome over their Churches, for the Church had been – and remained – a wealthy and powerful ideological tool. Anti-curial writers of sovereign entities such as Venice, Tuscany and Naples who opposed full Roman jurisdiction over their national Churches and consequently risked the ire of the Roman Inquisition (founded in 1542 to combat Protestantism in Italy) had thus often written and published with somewhat less fear than dissident Catholics resident in the Papal States or other Italian states more closely allied to Rome. In the eighteenth century, the *Encyclopèdie*, for instance, was put on the papal index of prohibited books in 1759, but was never banned in Venice and Italian translations of it were published there. By the mid eighteenth century, however, other sovereign governments had begun to arrogate the responsibility of licensing non-religious books to themselves.

What of the historical evidence for the 'usurpation' of temporal rule? Historians agree that the bare facts of the nexus between the spiritual and temporal authority of the papacy can be traced back at least to the eighth century and the territorial donation made to the Pope by the Frankish King Pepin in AD 756 (and subsequently confirmed by Charlemagne) which laid the foundations for the Papal States. In the ensuing centuries, two elements formed the core of that nexus: the need for spiritual justification for Roman jurisdiction over the Churches of Europe, and the need for independence and security in what was to remain a politically unstable polycentric peninsula. Importantly, the peninsula was often viewed as strategically valuable and thus also fought over by rival extra-peninsular powers. This remained the case until the victory of the Risorgimento and unification in 1861. Historically, the resources of the Papal States had also helped to ensure a degree of political, financial and military security against competing noble Italian dynasties intent on capturing the papacy and its rich financial rewards for themselves. By the eighteenth century, open violence in the struggle for the papal throne was a thing of the past. But, naturally, the economic and political power derived from temporal dominion could still constitute an important factor (although of course very rarely explicitly acknowledged) in maintaining a degree of effective Roman jurisdiction in the Churches of sovereign Italian entities.

The history of the city of Rome itself formed an essential component of its spiritual authority, which was founded upon Petrine doctrine: the spiritual legacy of the chief apostle of Christ, St Peter, claimed as the first Bishop of Rome, and his episcopal successors the popes. The unique temporal and spiritual symbiosis of Petrine doctrine, viewed as divine legitimation and providential historical occasion for the existence of the Papal States, was the core around which all of the replies to the critics of papal temporal dominion were founded. Armed with the Petrine doctrine, any challenge to the temporal dominion of the popes could be viewed as an antichristian challenge to the chief apostle of Christ who, as Cardinal Orsi reminded his readers in his *Della infallibilità e dell' autorità del Romano Pontefice sopra i Concilj Ecumenici* (1741–42), had conferred the keys to heaven upon his Roman episcopal successors.[13] Thus, typically, in his *L'Autorità suprema del romano pontefice* (1789), the curial polemicist Giovanni Marchetti argued that the supremacy of the Pope in the Church and thus the status of Rome in Christianity could be traced back to Jesus himself.[14]

For the heads of sovereign Italian states and their supporters to question outright the temporal dominion of the popes was, therefore, risking an accusation of heresy. Under these circumstances, some prelates could not always be guaranteed to offer unconditional support to their sovereigns in such disputes. More importantly, overtly hostile relations with Rome could destabilize the complex and often fragile nature of political alliances in the peninsula. The Papal States – stretching from just above Pontecorvo south of Rome, sweeping north to cross the Appenines to Ascoli Piceno and up to Ferrara – constituted a geo-political entity of sufficient size that rulers of smallers independent states could not entirely ignore it. Thus, when circumstances were favourable the Curia could still act as at least a temporary focus for alliances, and thus exert influence within the peninsula.

Some of the Italian states such as the Duchies of Mantua, Milan and Parma were, in European terms, statelets, yet still large in relation to the tiny Republics of Lucca and San Marino. In an often hostile European climate, when territory and influence in the peninsula were still sought by competing great powers, the survival of such small sovereign territories depended to some degree upon strategic alliances. As the balance of power between the peninsula's larger neighbours and in Europe as a whole underwent changes, so alliances shifted and changed inside the peninsula. Such changes could result in cooler relations with Rome, or alternatively warmer relations could quickly become the strategic aim of relatively small beleaguered states. But renewed alliance or less tense relations with Rome could also cause Italian sovereigns suddenly to turn a less benign eye on their progressive and reform-minded subjects in order to avoid jeopardizing newly improved relations.

The year 1723 saw the publication of the Neapolitan lawyer Pietro Giannone's pointedly anti-Rome *Istoria civile del Regno di Napoli*. There is no evidence that Giannone was a deist. Neither can he be termed a Jansenist in the technical sense, for his emphasis on Mozaic law was, as regards human nature, quite positive in outlook, contrary to that of most Jansenists. However, there is no doubt that he formed part of the often radical reforming drive evident in early-eighteenth-century Italy which cannot be explained solely in Jansenist terms, and which was regarded as equally heretical by the Curia. He remained, like most radical critics of the Church, within the Christian pale. As elsewhere in Europe even some of those Enlightened Italian thinkers who were ambivalent to the Church still recognized the need for religion to promote an acceptable social order. As Davidson has expressed it, 'from Valletta in the 1690s to Filangieri in the 1780s, Enlightenment writers extended their toleration only to those who accepted both the existence of God and the existence of an afterlife in which the good were rewarded and the evil punished'.[15] The same was true of the enlightened Carlo Antonio Pilati, who wrote in his *Di una riforma* (1767) that any such religion 'will serve the good of the state and the security of the citizens within it'.[16]

That Giannone's jurisdictionalism was uncompromising is evident in his statement that the Church had been and remained in the republic 'and not indeed the republic in the Church'.[17] For Giannone, in addition to the papal usurpation of princely prerogatives and tyrannic rule of the Church, Christians had for centuries been subjected to conscious religious fraud. Popes had corrupted doctrine and cultivated superstition in order to amass power and wealth. They had invented the concept of purgatory in which was to be found a door to heaven for the credulous and inexhaustible riches (via the sale of indulgences) for the papacy. For similar avaricious motives, the popes had also brought back pagan image worship. The substance of the problem was that great wealth and temporal dominion meant popes and bishops 'thought with greater promptness to things temporal, than to those divine and sacred'.[18] Although Giannone's critique was welcomed by many anticurialists and was to be very influential later in the century, the furore of Rome at the publication of his *Istoria civile* and the resultant pressure upon the Neapolitian government obliged him to flee Naples, and he became a target and eventual victim of the Inquisition.

Even if – concomitant with its increasing political weakness – Rome's use of the Inquisition diminished during the century, Giannone's plight was a reminder of the potential risks attached to any direct attack upon Rome. It may be true, as Davidson has argued, that religious persecution in the peninsula was relatively limited.[19] But the fear of the withdrawal of princely protection and consequent abandonment to Rome was sufficient to ensure that some major figures of the Italian Enlightenment preferred not to deal directly with the subject of religion, opting instead to pursue enlightenment on safer ground.[20] Enlightened thinkers such as the Verri brothers or Cesare Beccaria, editors of the journal *Il Caffè*

(1764–66), avoided the subjects of religion and Church reform. *Il Caffè* was almost a mini-version of the famous French *Encyclopèdie* and gained some considerable fame abroad, on account of which the encyclopedists invited its editors to Paris. Yet of well over a hundred articles contained in editions spanning two years, written on a wide variety of topics, none directly attacked the Church, its superstition, its history or indeed papal temporal rule.

Regalism and Jansenism

Most sovereigns, however, continued to have some interest in sponsoring or effectively tolerating attacks on Roman theocracy, for it was the most fertile avenue for justifying their struggle to reclaim lost princely rights and effect reforms within their own Churches. In addition, in a complex and shifting geo-political context, the continuing prosecution by Rome of claims to rights over considerable Church lands in sovereign states,[21] suzerainty over kingdoms such as Parma[22] and Naples,[23] and dominion over Ferrara and Comacchio were of potential concern, even if some or many of them remained only at the level of propaganda.[24]

The continued decline of the papacy in terms of international and intra-peninsular influence in the second half of the eighteenth century, however, meant that attacks on Roman jurisdiction and temporal dominion seemed to some sovereigns and critics to carry less political risk than formerly. Indicative of curial weakness was its failure to assert its ecclesiastical authority even over the small Duchy of Parma, over which it claimed suzerainty. Du Tillot, the Duchy's foremost minister of the mid-century, prohibited mortmain in 1764, on the basis of the negative economic impact of the withdrawal of land from the market. In 1768, in response to this and other later encroachments of Parma on the traditional rights of the Church, Pope Clement XIII issued a Bull (*In coena domini*) declaring all such ecclesiastical legislation since 1764 invalid. It is doubtful whether du Tillot or Clement could have predicted the dramatic international events quickly excited by the publication of the Bull. Under the direction of Bernardo di Tanucci, the leading minister of the Kingdom of Naples, Neapolitan troops occupied the papal territories of Pontecorvo and Benevento (small enclaves south of Rome), and Louis XV occupied those of Avignon. Charles III of Spain and other Bourbon sovereigns also warned the Pope to withdraw the

Bull. In the same year the Jesuits were expelled from France and Tanucci expelled them from Neapolitan soil, an action justified in terms of the divine right of kings.

On behalf of the Dukes of Modena, Muratori disputed Rome's right to dominion over Ferrara[25] and Comacchio[26] (yet took considerable pains to avoid openly heretical formulations). In these disputes historical precedent was of course considered central, but all were ideologically situated in the general historical rebuttal of Roman justifications for temporal rule common to Muratori, Giannone and other polemicists later in the century. Muratori argued that early medieval popes had used the fact of diminishing control over Italy by the Emperor at Constantinople as an excuse to usurp the imperial right to high dominion and effect papal rule over Rome and its environs. But he was careful to assert that the popes and the Roman people still gave obedience to Constantinople until the middle of the eighth century, and popes-elect continued to be subject to confirmation by the Emperor. From this perspective, then, the popes had been merely the governors of Rome on behalf of Constantinople, and, most crucially, the state had intervened as a matter of course in the government of the Church at the highest level. Any claim, therefore, to establishing the origins of legitimate temporal dominion upon this account would of course be untenable. At best, the popes gained high dominion of Rome and its environs by default, and never had a legitimate right to them at all. This account, in terms of grand historical narrative, also had the advantage of placing the final demise of Rome's Byzantine obedience close to the occasion of the Donation of Pepin in 756.

The Exarchate of Ravenna, the north-eastern Italian territory consisting of the lands donated to Rome by King Pepin (which laid the foundation for the Papal States), had – until seized by the Lombards in 751 and then by Pepin – also been territory subject to imperial high dominion. Thus, for the same reason that jurisdictionalist critics considered the Curia's claim to high dominion of Rome to be at best very dubious, the Donation of Pepin was illegitimate: Pepin had donated territory and peoples to Rome 'which were not his'. It did not matter greatly if this latter indictment (made in his *Osservazioni sopra una lettera intitolata Il dominio temporale della Sede Apostolica sopra la Città di Comacchio*, 1708[27]) might have seemed insufficient against those who argued that the donation was that of lands legitimately possessed by right of conquest. Muratori, and most critics of Roman temporal dominion, were anyway convinced that Pepin and his Carolingian successors had always unambiguously retained high dominion over the donated territory. Popes, as vassals of (what were to become from the year 800) the Holy Roman Emperors, only ever held the territory subject to (Holy) imperial will. Thus, in refusing to acknowledge imperial overlordship, the popes had usurped the imperial prerogative. Worse still, 'just as true temporal princes', papal ambition for terrestial empire 'did not neglect any of the solutions of peace or war'.[28]

Intended as part of his general defence of princely rights and as support for the territorial claims of his own Modenese prince, Muratori wrote *Della Fallibilità dei pontefici nel dominio temporale* (1872, posth.). His point was eminently simple. If, as he hoped, his illustration of Roman usurpation of imperial temporal rights had demonstrated that the Curia was not infallible in matters of temporal dominion, Muratori could challenge the extent of papal temporal dominion without challenging the spiritual supremacy of Rome and descending into outright heterodoxy.[29] Such efforts to avoid direct conflict with the papacy were ultimately effective, for Muratori did narrowly escape excommunication. But the conflict was certainly there. Cardinal Orsi, for example, wrote his defence of papal temporal dominion, *Dell'origine del dominio e della sovranità de'Romani Pontifici sopra gli stati a loro temporalmente soggetti* (1742) in good part as a reply to Muratori's account of the origins of the Papal States. Orsi's co-author on the most voluminous eighteenth-century official historical defence of the Curia,[30] Bishop Becchetti, targeted Muratori more than any other writer.

On the question of temporal dominion, there was very little, if any, neutral ground. The issue was too intimately linked to Catholic orthodoxy and therefore potentially destructive of the very basis of Roman supremacy in the Church. As the pro-curial writer Fontanini explained in his defence of Rome's title to Comacchio, the Curia considered that disputes over temporal dominion were engineered only 'in order to present to the Imperial Court and all Europe an odious view of the Curia as a usurper and possessor of the dominions of others'.[31] In other words, to dispute papal temporal claims was understood by the Curia (and often rightly so) as an assault upon the integrity of the Roman Church itself.

Pro-curial accounts of the foundation and progress of temporal dominion were naturally radically different from those of its critics and tended, as jurisdictionalist accounts, to be in agreement amongst themselves on most points. In his *Dell'Origine del dominio e della sovranità temporale de'romani pontifici*, for example, Cardinal Orsi claimed that from Pope Gregory II (715–31) neither the Greek Emperors nor the Holy Roman Emperors had held overlordship over Rome, its territories and the Exarchate of Ravenna. The popes had not usurped territory from the eastern Emperor; rather the people had shaken off the yoke of the eastern Emperor and placed themselves by popular will under the rule of the vicar of Christ, the Bishop of Rome. For Orsi and other pro-curial writers, the Donation of Pepin had indeed been the gift of a freehold. Consequently, in struggling to assert its temporal dominion, Rome had certainly not trodden on the temporal rights of the Holy Roman Emperors.[32] On the contrary, it was rather defending its providential right, for, as Becchetti put it, in the final instance, papal temporal power had come about as the result of Roman bishops being the successors of St Peter: territorial donations and favourable political circumstances in recognition of the divine grace emanating from Rome.[33]

This historiographical conflict between Rome and its critics was no ordinary scholarly debate, for both sides well knew that the stakes were too high for its resolution to rest upon purely academic grounds. The debate could thus unexpectedly turn very nasty indeed when Rome felt the need and possessed the political ability to exert curial discipline inside neighbouring states. Sometimes, with little or no warning, critics of the papacy could find their protection from Rome withdrawn. It was such a shift which, after the publication of his *Istoria civile* in 1723, forced Giannone to flee Naples. Later, in 1736, after being hounded from one northern Italian state to another, Giannone also found his protection withdrawn in Savoyard Piedmont, forming part of the political price for that state's settlement of conflict with the papacy, after which he was finally to die in prison. Similar circumstances also forced the exile of the radical Alberto Radicati, Count of Passerano (1698–1737). In 1725–26 he was supported in his views by Victor Amadeus II (1684–1730), sovereign of his native Piedmont. Subsequently, when Amadeus made a cynical concordat with Rome (1726–27), Radicati had little choice but to flee. So treacherous were these political sands, that a text not formerly considered particularly radical by the papacy might in new political circumstances be considered dangerous.

A typical case in point was the anti-curial historiography of the Suffragan Bishop of Trier, Justinus Febronius (Johann Von Hontheim). Contemporary historians recognized that the critique of the Church in Febronius's *De statu ecclesiae et legitima potestate romani pontificis* (1763) contained nothing new, but represented a more threatening aspect because it came at a time of strained relations between Clement XIII (1758–69) and the states of Europe. In 1764 the book was placed on the papal index of prohibited books. In 1766 Rome issued an edict decreeing a ten-year prison sentence for those who replied to an advertisement of the Venetian printer Giuseppe Bettinelli for subscriptions to a proposed Italian translation of Febronius's work.[34]

The critique of Rome by progressive intellectuals was not limited to questions of religious jurisdiction or the rights of the prince. The economy of the Papal States was in a dire condition, having suffered from the peninsula-wide recession of the seventeenth century[35] and, as the century progressed, from a diminution of foreign income as a result of the attacks on the Church across Catholic Europe. The results of the 1764 famine were particularly tragic in the Papal States. Even in what might be regarded as a purely economic sphere, the economic efficacy of papal rule, the blatant luxury of prelates and the great and inefficiently managed landed possessions of the Church were latent. Why? Because the failure to reform the economy of the Papal States was viewed by some as at least partly symptomatic of their backward quasi-medieval theocratic government.[36] But the principle of Roman theocracy was viewed as non-negotiable by the Curia, and politico-theological history was still seen as its greatest ally.

Eighteenth-century pro-curial historiography was, in content, mostly still reliant on the Counter-Reformation work of Baronius, the *Annales ecclesiastici* (1588–1607). The voluminous historical works of eighteenth-century writers such as Cardinal Orsi, Bishop Becchetti and others were essentially restatements of Baronian orthodoxy.[37] Any notion that unilateral reform of sovereign Churches might, under any circumstances, be acknowledged as legitimate was sternly ruled out by such writers, and the unqualified Petrine right to temporal dominion and supremacy was affirmed.

As Becchetti stated in relation to the Conciliar Movement, the momentous fifteenth-century attempt to subject the Curia to the decisions of general councils of the Church, 'to allow all the faithful to have jurisdiction [in the Church] would be the same as granting democracy, which is to allow error. The faithful have never been known other than with the voice of sheep, of the flock.'[38]

These contending historical views – those of enlightened intellectuals and Catholic anti-curialists versus papal apologists – were fundamental to the ecclesio-political outlooks of their respective protagonists. The result was a historiographical deadlock implicitly expressing contending visions for the future of the Church (even if critics of Rome rarely publicly defined their vision much beyond calls for greater princely jurisdiction). It was a deadlock that remained substantially unaltered, even throughout the great challenge to the papacy during the second half of the eighteenth century, when Italian sovereigns began to undertake unilateral reform of the Church.

The temporal imperative: Roman theology and politics fused

Implicitly confronted with the prospect of diminished control over a vast and wealthy multinational institution, the Curia's determination not to cede any substantial jurisdictional ground, or historico-theological justifications for it, was perhaps to be expected. As Muratori and others opined, ceding historiographical ground on the issue of temporal dominion could not be contemplated without implicitly accepting fallibility on that issue. But, of course, contrary to the (ostensibly) limited polemical aim of Muratori's *Della Fallibilità dei pontefici nel dominio temporale,* as many certainly realized, accepting fallibility on matters of temporal dominion also implicitly raised the question of Rome's venerable justification for it on both the theological and historical level. This dilemma was of course epitomized in the anti-curial use of Christ's dictum *regnum meum non est de hoc mundo.* To most participants of the debate, therefore, it was obvious that the acceptance of curial fallibility in temporal matters would have served to open the gate of jurisdictional demands rather than close it.

Contemporaries, whether pro- or anti-curial, could hardly deny that papal claims to Italian territories would decisively collapse if the papacy was coerced into renouncing temporal dominion, although, as with Muratori's polemic on the fallibility of the Curia on matters of temporal dominion, the existence of tracts advancing curial territorial claims should not be confused with the practical reality of such claims or the intention of the Curia to employ further means to pursue them. We can, however, say with confidence that the polemic had profound implications, for, as we have seen, any admission of 'error' on the question of temporal dominion had potentially serious theological and political implications.

In more immediate political terms, if temporal dominion were renounced, the Roman Church and papacy would then, in practice (if not in theory), be to some degree or another subject to the government of the city of Rome and/or its sovereign. The result, of course, would have been that papal arguments for complete autonomy of the Church from secular authority would have suffered a set-back greater than any since the Middle Ages. Equally as important, the renunciation or loss of the Papal States would have been viewed by their critics as a signal victory in the struggle to return the Church to the purely spiritual realm as advocated in the New Testament. Simultaneously, the loss would also have constituted a large step in the endeavour to reclaim lost princely rights in the Church, leaving papal polemicists with a good deal less effective basis on which to counter claims for greater princely jurisdiction in their Churches.

Another corollary flowing from the loss of temporal dominion would have been a great diminution of the Curia's political clout in the peninsula, which was based partly upon spiritual legitimacy and, as with any other state, partly upon political alliance. Such a situation would undoubtedly – as the Curia certainly realized – have given more confidence to those pressing for autonomous reform of Churches of sovereign states. Reform of sovereign Churches could come in many guises, with spiritual and political but also economic consequences. With a politically much weaker Curia, unilateral reform might be more likely to entail a much increased intervention in the finances and administration of the considerable landed interests of the Church in most Italian states.

Interestingly, on the question of the limitations on curial polemicists, they were also hampered by elements of their own politico-religious doctrine. During the Counter-Reformation, Rome had actively sought to bolster the venerable theory of the divine right of kings. Not surprisingly, then, divine right theory was as healthy as ever in Italy, still widely supported by princes, intellectuals and peoples, and was naturally put to good use in the regalist camp in which many supported strong, often absolutist monarchical rule. Indeed, the form of state power in the Muratorian scheme is royal absolutism, as evidenced in his *Della pubblica felicità oggetto de'buoni principi* (1749). Thus, by divine right, the strong but 'good prince' should not have his prerogatives usurped by the Church, but rather should work hand in hand with the Church to promote a just Christian commonwealth.[39] It is hardly surprising, then, that Muratori, Giannone and most other regalist polemicists sought to demonstrate how, historically, good princes had worked hand in hand with Rome and its prelates in the just government of the Church. As Giannone put it, the problem was that in the medieval period the popes ceased to be vicars of Christ, and instead became princes 'who, like all princes, are attached to the interests of their realms, putting themselves at the head of their armies'.[40]

Being hedged in partly by its own divine right theory, able to exert less political influence in Europe than ever, and feeling unable to modify its politico-theological doctrine without the risk of emboldening its many critics, the Curia's many able propagandists, therefore, such as Cardinal Orsi, Filippo Becchetti, Francesco Zaccaria and Giovanni Marchetti, had very limited room for innovative polemical manoeuvre. There is also evidence to show that, at times, conscious of its decreasing influence and the dangers of conceding polemical ground, the papacy preferred not to take official measures against some anti-curial historical works, lest the measures inflamed an already very difficult situation. One consequence of such passivity was that the Gallican and fiercely anti-curial historiography of Claude Fleury was able to circulate through much of Italy relatively freely.[41] Of course pro-curial replies to Fleury appeared,[42] but sometimes Rome's attempts to combat heterodox writings could also backfire. In order to train clerics to fight new heretical ideas, it was sometimes considered necessary to provide frank and detailed lectures upon the pantheistic and/or rationalist ideas of thinkers such as Baruch Spinoza, Herbert of Cherbury and Thomas Hobbes. Some of these lectures were published – such as those of the learned Abbot Domenico Bencini (who performed a leading role in the college De Propaganda Fide at Rome) in 1720 – and in Turin the growing interest in Spinozan thought in Piedmont was attributed to similar teachings.[43]

Italy: Roman 'tyranny' and radical Catholic opposition

The burgeoning call for the reform of the Church naturally extended to the condemnation of the past and present activities of the Roman Inquisition against heterodoxy. For Giannone, the founding of the medieval Inquisition and its continued existence was proof that the heresy charge had been, and still was, used by the Church to persecute political opponents and perpetuate a corrupt self-serving doctrine. For this and other national-minded intellectuals in the peninsula, it was also a glaring example of a foreign body interfering in the internal affairs of a sovereign state. In sum, declared Giannone, the Inquisition had been founded 'in order to better establish the monarchy of the popes'.[44] Later in the century, Bishop Scipione de'Ricci[45] explained, in his circular to clergy on the forthcoming Jansenist Synod of Pistoia in 1786, that the papacy had for centuries defended superstition and ignorance by denouncing as heretical any attempt to reform the Church by returning to the precepts of the primitive Church (unsurprisingly, the council also condemned the Curia for the usurpation of princely temporal rights).[46]

But despite influential calls for a reform of the European system of justice, including that of Cesare Beccaria (1738–94), who was moved to write the classic Enlightenment text *Dei Delitti e delle pene* (1764) by the inhumanity and arbitrary nature of criminal procedure in Italy and Europe as a whole, the curial defence of the Inquisition remained steadfast. It was an intransigence exemplified in the work of Tommaso Pani. Pani had the misfortune to publish his apology in the very year of the French Revolution, which has left to posterity the worst possible assessment of curial backwardness. In his *Della Punizione degli eretici e del Tribunale della Santa Inquizione* (1789) Pani included chapters on the defence of the death penalty for heresy, on the notion that even the suspicion of heresy could be punished, and on the obligation of secular powers to protect ecclesiastical judges. He warned that without the Inquisition the Catholic faith would be at risk, in turn risking the collapse of the social and political order. Pani was no pro-curial maverick. His views were – if rather bluntly expressed – typical of many eighteenth-century pro-curial thinkers, including Bishop Becchetti.[47]

To have abolished the Roman Inquisition would have been for the Curia to weaken its hand in relation to the intellectual policing of its own state, and to a degree the policing of Roman orthodoxy and its jurisdiction over the Churches of its sovereign neighbours.

The current Tridentine doctrine (derived from the Council of Trent, 1545–63), it can be said, thus remained locked in a stultifying embrace with the imperatives of papal secular dominion and curial jurisdiction. Doctrine and reality do not, of course, always coincide. Beyond rhetoric, Rome could muster little effective opposition to the gradual running down and abolition of the Inquisition Tribunals in several Italian states during the 1760s–1780s. There is no doubt that the decline and eventual end of the Tribunals of Inquisition were indicative of the increasing impotency of Rome in the face of unilateral Church reform. The inability of Rome to concede even quite moderate reform, however, and so provide a much-needed bolster for its practical leadership of the Church without self-jeopardy is vital in understanding the practical weakness of Rome and the growing confidence of anti-curialists in the second half of the eighteenth century.

In the first half of the century, in common with other parts of Europe, there had been a wide call from both pro-curial and anti-curial thinkers for a renewal of faith. That desire for spiritual rebirth is usually described as Jansenist in character. Italian Jansenism was not, however, a unified phenomenon, and its character often varied from one state to another. Jansenism, derived from the thought of Cornelius Jansen (1585–1638), Bishop of Ypres, had originated as an ascetic and theologically pessimistic search for the renewal of Christian piety. But spiritual renewal inevitably meant reconsidering some aspects of doctrine, which of course ran into the rigidity of Counter-Reformation theology. Jansenists thus came to be opponents of the papacy and were duly condemned by Pope Innocent X in 1653.

Although it is true that some pro-curial reforming ecclesiastics did exhibit the theological pessimism characteristic of Jansenism, it was only one facet of a more general reform stance. In the Italian peninsula, especially after the mid-century, Jansenist thought often noticeably lacked or failed to emphasize the doctrinal elements of Jansenism, instead demonstrating a more practical, general reforming zeal. It is thus difficult to define the precise nature of Italian Jansenism, and it is more fruitful to understand anti-curial Italian Jansenism – perhaps exemplified in the thought of Lodovico Muratori and Bishop de'Ricci – as a hybrid of Jansenist, regalist and jurisdictionalist ideas, in which the following common elements can be identified: the desire for a return to Christian origins and the limitation of superstition in the Church, a pastoral adaptation to new times, moral rigour, an acquiescence to the will of sovereigns, and the independence of sovereign Churches from Rome.[48] Important elements of this matrix, however, were also present in the thought of anti-curialists who can hardly be considered as Jansenist, as in that of Pietro Giannone for example, who held a positive view of human nature. To cloud matters more, even ardent pro-curial and essentially conservative thinkers such as the Dominican Cardinal Orsi were also accused of Jansenism.[49] Such accusations serve to compound the practical difficulty of defining Italian Jansenism in relation to Church reform, and raise the relatively little noted question of the political use of the Jansenist label within the various shades of conflict between reform-minded and conservative pro-curial thinkers, and hence the need for caution when applying that label.

One element of thought shared by pro-curial and anti-curial (so-called) Jansenist thinkers was hostility to the Jesuits. For orthodox but liberal and reform-minded Catholics who wanted to break the restraints of Counter-Reformation dogma, the Jesuits were, as Woolf has put it, the 'paladins of papal authority'.[50] Indeed, they were considered by many as propagators of a casuistic defence of Roman doctrine. Prior to the late seventeenth century, the Jesuits had shown considerable capacity to absorb new ideas; but the widespread threat to Roman orthodoxy in the eighteenth century had the effect of narrowing their view of permissible debate. Even many loyal and relatively conservative curial would-be reformers thus had reason to consider the Jesuits a danger to spiritual renewal and even strictly limited Church reform.

In seventeenth-century Italy there were numerous theologians and high ecclesiastics influenced by the reforming tenor of Jansenism. In the first half of the eighteenth century, even in the Curia itself there were those, such as Cardinal Polignac, prepared to encourage Jansenist-inspired reforming tendencies. Polignac was representative of orthodox Catholics who recognized the need for reform of the Church in order to neutralize the most threatening aspects of Enlightenment culture. Reforming prelates such as Archbishop Celestino Galiani (1681–1753) and other thinkers attempted to harness new scientific and philosophical ideas to the service of Catholicism. The confines of that project are, however, evident in the fact that in 1733 Galiani was denounced and felt unable to present his views in print.[51]

Nevertheless, under Pope Benedict XIV (1740–58) two leading ecclesiastics at Rome, Giovanni Bottari and Pietro Foggini, formed a reforming group which included anti-curialists, Jansenists and other reform-minded Catholics who believed in the possibility of internal reform and were united in their hostility to the Jesuits. The group, the Archetto school, which influenced clerics elsewhere in Italy, and was protected in the Curia by some cardinals, attacked the Jesuits by claiming they ascribed a positive role to human free will. But theological polemic increasingly formed only one component of the Jansenist reforming drive, although it could seem more central when Jansenists were under attack – as they were by Jesuits after 1750 – and needed to defend themselves against specific charges of heterodoxy.

Even popes less hostile to reform, such as Benedict, who demonstrated conciliation towards critics of the Church, found themselves caught in a vice of inertia: held between interlocking spiritual and temporal imperatives in an often hostile environment with increasingly little international political leverage at their disposal. It is true that Benedict arrived at some concordats with princes who made some concessions. Nevertheless, he fought to preserve papal temporal dominion and the main elements of Roman spiritual jurisdiction, and to protect the considerable property interests of the Church across Europe. He also remained hostile to anti-Jesuit polemic and renewed the condemnation of Free Masonry.

The relatively conciliatory attitude of Benedict was replaced by that of the more hard-line Clement XIII (1758–69), who was pro-Jesuit. Thus, after the mid-century, the broad movement for Church reform ran into the sands of renewed curial intransigence and repression. The papacy feared that even mild calls for reform might turn into potentially dangerous flashpoints. The prospect of reforming the Church from within thus became very remote. Clement, it seems, recognized more than Benedict that granting reforms entailed great risks. Yet to remain unyielding to the insistent demands for change was to court potentially unilateral action by princes and their supporters and risk a public display of papal weakness – which was subsequently to happen.

Clement's intransigence and the growing European isolation of the Curia prompted a significant change in the strategy of those striving for change. Reform-minded clergy increasingly turned to

Italy: Roman 'tyranny' and radical Catholic opposition

Italian princes as instruments to advance both Church reform and the jurisdictionalist struggle for control over their own Churches. In a number of states, often with the support of anti-curial clergy, acts to limit the power and influence of the Church were passed. Although there is no doubt that sovereign rulers took the reform initiative in the 1760s and 1770s, it would not, however, be correct to say that the shift of reform initiative towards princes began only with Clement XIII. To tie the development of the peninsula's Church–state dynamic so closely to developments internal to the Curia would be to underestimate the growing desire of sovereigns, clergy, administrators and intellectuals for change (the relationship between manifestations of enlightened thinking and the political reality of the peninsula is discussed at the end of this chapter). Before 1758, sovereigns had already taken some action to curb the power of Rome in their Churches, as in Lombardy (1757) and Tuscany (1751–54).

Such unilateral measures aroused in Clement the fear that worse was likely to come and action was needed to avert it. In reality there was little Clement could do, although he could of course attempt to put his own house in order and clamp down hard on those prelates viewed as overly sympathetic to reform. In 1761 he coerced the pro-Jansenist Cardinal Passionei to sign a condemnation of Jansenism. In this environment any remaining overt support for Jansenist ideas amongst pro-curialists naturally began to evaporate. Rome could also cooperate with princes who at times felt the need to limit the extent of radical thought in their own states, such as when, at the request of the Sardinian government, the radical Piedmontese Dalmazzo Francesca Vasca was arrested in Rome in 1768. But the coming storm could not be halted, not even by the election of the energetic Pius VI (1775–99), who vigorously defended the Church from attack and clamped down further on pro-reform clergy in Rome.

Radical Jansenism 1770s–1790s

The height of Jansenist reforming influence was reached in Tuscany under Grand Duke Leopold in the 1780s.[52] Independently of Rome, in alliance with Jansenist clergymen such as Scipione de'Ricci,[53] Leopold wanted to impose reform on the Tuscan Church via provincial and national synods, a movement epitomized by the reforming Synod of Pistoia (1786). But, although Leopold ensured the passage of several acts reforming various aspects of the Tuscan Church, more moderate bishops prevented the full implementation of his planned reforms.

Pius's rigorous defence of orthodoxy and renewed defiance of calls for reform did, however, reap a rich harvest of some considerable importance in the history of intellectual thought. His untimely intransigence pushed reform-minded clerics and others into more extreme denunciations of the history and contemporary reality of papal supremacy and temporal rule. In the late 1770s and 1780s, clerics and ex-clerics produced the most astounding condemnations of papal history – equally as hot as those of the most ardent English Dissenters – which were almost always in harmony with the regalism of princes as an alternative to Rome. Their writings, an important facet of the experience of the European Enlightenment and a reminder that even in the late eighteenth century Catholicism could still adopt radical politico-theological forms, have been, however, little discussed and hardly noted at all outside Italian studies.

Anti-curial Catholics thus not only turned to Italian princes as agents of reform independent of Rome, they also realized it was necessary to openly declaim, with princely support, against the legitimacy of Roman jurisdiction and temporal dominion. To do so they returned resolutely to the anti-curial historiographical traditions of Giannone and Muratori. In this period papal temporal dominion was considered by even the most timid anti-curialists as anathema. Thus even the pious and conciliatory Jansenist professor of philosophy at Genoa, Pier Delle Piane,[54] could note that 'indeed, the popes did not become monarchs and temporal princes via the institutes of Jesus Christ, who said *Regnum meum non est de hoc mundo*'. Corrupted by wealth, the medieval Church had been a strange and monstrous mix of the temporal and the spiritual, in which even the cardinals of the Pope were the equals of kings.[55]

The necessity of a return to a radical critique of Rome was by no one more succinctly advocated than by the Archbishop of Taranto, Giuseppe Capecelatro, who reminded his readers in his *Discorso istorico-politico dell'origine del progresso e della decadenza del potere de' chierici su le signorie temporali* (1788) that whoever wished to deny the legitimacy of the present ecclesiastical system would have to form a new history of past times.[56] Thus he observed that medieval kings, from the example of the ancient kings of Israel, had wished to be crowned by the Pope, as vicar of God and head of the Church, but 'the popes took advantage of this strange fantasy ... in order to believe themselves not only ministers of that pure ceremony, but despots of kingdoms and even of the empire ... This is the true primordial origin of all the famous dominions of Europe which were reputed feoffs of the Roman Church.'[57] Such arguments against temporal dominion were, however, but one part of a much wider accusation of priestcraft, which bore a remarkable similarity to radical Protestant critiques of Catholicism. There is, however, no evidence to suggest that the anti-Rome critique of such thinkers was not home-grown, for it still relied in good part on Muratori and Giannone.

In his trenchantly titled *Della Monarchia universale de'papi*, the radical Neapolitan clergyman Scotti reminded his readers that the governors of the people receive their power from God. The disciples of Christ and their successors, therefore, subordinated themselves to the emperors in all temporal aspects, and even though the emperors were idolaters, the Christians prayed for their prosperity and paid tribute to them.[58] He also described the deeply corrupting effects of the medieval enrichment of Rome, resulting in ambition, usurpation of supremacy and of the divine rights of princes. In order to defend its illegitimate gains, the Curia had become a workshop of falsity and imposture. For gain, Scotti opined, the popes had cultivated a corrupt external religion for the ignorant masses, one reliant upon hypocritical formalism, while it concealed the true Christian doctrine. The considerable forging skills of medieval monks and clerics were thus learnt 'from the new maxims of the Pharisaical Gospel of Rome become carnal', the new Sanhedrin of Christendom. Canon law was born of the avarice and ambition of the 'Universal Judaic Monarchy', created in order to obscure divine scripture and 'to sanction the claim of the papal universal monarchy'. Canon law was, in a word, the 'Talmud' of the popes.[59]

The venom of their analyses should, nevertheless, not be allowed to obscure the fact that Scotti, Capecelatro and others rarely, if ever, wished to abandon Rome as the spiritual, non-executive centre of the Catholic faith. In any case, princes and their supporters were of course aware of the potential dangers of more radical, egalitarian religious reform such as presbyterianism. Sovereigns were naturally concerned to avoid damage to the role of the

Church in the maintenance of an elite-dominated social stability. They were also alert to the possibility of potentially perilous shifts in the complex series of alliances on which rulers of small Italian states often relied for their continued existence. Not surprisingly, sovereigns rarely if ever allowed the spiritual, Petrine legitimacy of Rome to be questioned overtly in the public arena. Thus, the problem for more radical thinkers of the Italian Enlightenment (those who wished to attack Christianity itself) and at times Catholic reformers was that in practice they formed part of a broad alliance of princes, aristocrats, prelates, administrators and intellectuals, the religious and political parameters of which were most often set by sovereigns.

No matter how fiercely anti-curial Catholics attacked the temporal rule of the popes as antichristian, the practical dismantling of the Papal States was not, in political terms, a realistic proposition. Any 'liberation' of Romans from theocratic rule by politically coercive means would have had unpredictable and potentially dangerous consequences in the delicate political conditions of the peninsula.

After the fall of Napoleon and the tumultuous vicissitudes of the establishment, collapse, and re-establishment of French republicanism[60] in the peninsula, the re-establishment of sovereign kingdoms and the theocracy of the Papal States was accompanied by a widely held recognition that radical religious reforming movements were no longer to be encouraged. Quite sensibly, sovereigns did not wish to sponsor attacks on the legitimacy of Roman sovereignty, for in the fragile political conditions of Italy after 1815 – with revolutions occurring in the 1820s and 1830s – the Pope was more prudently seen as a conservative ally. Sovereigns knew very well that, in the hands of those sympathetic to republicanism, the reforming attack against Roman temporal rule might not be accompanied by the traditional regalism. If proof were wanted for the validity of this fear, they had only to read the *Storia del papato* of one Paolo Rivarola.

While under French protection after the entrance of the Republican Army into Lombardy in 1796, Rivarola – probably an ex-priest – translated the *Mystère d'iniquité, c'est-à-dire l'histoire de la papauté* (1611) of the French Huguenot leader Philippe Du Plessis-Mornay.[61] The *Mystère d'iniquité*, a monument to the nature of the Huguenot priestcraft theory, was promoted as official anti-Church propaganda by French and Italian Jacobins.

In Rivarola's pro-republican rendition of the *Mystère d'iniquité*, the *Storia del papato*, the medieval popes were those 'conquerors of the world and ministers of war' who, with an 'unrestrained lust', had claimed the power to create or depose kings. They had claimed direct or indirect dominion over all states of the world, fomenting sackings, massacres and intestine wars of nation against nation. Indeed, popes and other princely despots 'had always used the mantle of religion and the veil of imposture to cover their treacherous designs'. The principal occasion for the apostasy of Rome was not just papal iniquity, but the 'treachery, the imbecility and worthlessness' of kings who, 'prostrate at the feet of the popes', granted the popes temporal dominion. Almost immediately, as the papal despots 'deified' their plunder, there arose, 'favoured by ignorance and superstition', the 'monstrous colossus of the papacy'.[62]

It can be argued, therefore, that the continued existence of the link between Roman orthodoxy and temporal rule into the nineteenth century owed a great deal to the eventual defeat of French and native anticlerical republicanism, and the fear of restoration sovereigns that any reforming movement might prove detrimental to the security of their own newly restored regimes. Only when the polycentric nature of the peninsula was itself 'reformed' by the Risorgimento (despite the best efforts of extra-peninsula power to maintain papal independence), and competing princely interests were subordinated to the Italian national state, was it politically possible to dismantle papal temporal power decisively. Even then, however, the Curia stubbornly refused to accept that a European theocracy was no longer a tenable political concept and would not recognize the loss of their temporal power. It was not until 1929 that the question of the Pope's relation to the Italian state was settled by the Lateran Treaty of 1929, which set up an independent Vatican City state.

Given the traditional preeminence accorded to a relatively narrow band of elite thinkers in Enlightenment studies, it should be no surprise that Franco Venturi – perhaps the greatest of Italian historians of the Enlightenment – has rarely discussed Jansenism. It is difficult, however, to comprehend how the often complex fundamentals of the eighteenth-century Italian peninsula can be understood if the question of Church and state is not thoroughly addressed. And it is, of course, not possible to discuss state and

Church in eighteenth-century Italy without addressing oneself to the question of Jansenism. It has always seemed absurd to me that Italian Jansenism has traditionally been divided into two camps: political and theological. As we have seen, the political realities of the peninsula meant that any desire for reform meant a challenge to Rome, and a challenge to Rome inherently invoked the intensely political question of the relationship of Church to state. We must never forget that all eighteenth-century rulers acknowledged the importance of religion in maintaining an acceptable social order, and so it was unthinkable that a sovereign would declare disinterest in the question. Thus Peter Leopold of Tuscany – acknowledged as a leading enlightened ruler of the peninsula – abolished the Inquisition in Tuscany in 1782, but the edict of abolition explicitly referred to the prince's duty of maintaining religion. In that document he enjoined his bishops to monitor the beliefs of the faithful and 'whenever the circumstances of a case require it, we must proceed with severity; and when the use of the secular arm is needed, we shall consider it our duty to intervene'.[63] The same transfer of responsibility for prosecuting dissent had occurred in Parma (1769) and Lombardy (1775), and although it is true that Joseph II's Patent of Toleration (1781) allowed some non-Catholic Christian worship, he still insisted on the prosecution of deists. As Joachim Whaley has commented, 'there is a clear distinction between most notions of toleration and religious indifference'.[64]

We can say, then, that in an era of confessional states, the issue of Church and state was at the heart of Enlightenment thinking, but nowhere more deeply central and embedded than in the Italian peninsula. In this sense, then, we can perhaps argue that the Italian Enlightenment was more consistently political in nature – although not explicitly in its manifestation – than other 'national' Enlightenments. What, then, was the relationship between the development of Enlightenment thinking on religion and the political realities of the peninsula?

Two facts stand out above all others: the centrality of Rome to religious change and the evident decline in the international and peninsular influence of Rome. Rome was now perceived by Italian sovereigns as less capable of rallying extra-peninsular support to its defence, and so it is unthinkable that – regardless of whether the Enlightenment ever arrived or not – sovereigns would not seize the opportunity of redefining state–Church boundaries, which had for long been keenly resented, in their favour. After all, this had been accomplished by Protestants and by the Gallican Church. To attempt to disaggregate Enlightenment and state and Church is thus little more than to play games with history, or as Voltaire put it, to play tricks on the dead. But even glancing for a moment at the issue from this counterfactual vista is to remind ourselves what an absurdity it would be not to place Jansenism firmly on the map of the Enlightenment. But to raise this topic is also to raise that of Enlightened despotism and its relationship to intellectual change.

This is not the place for continuing the old debate on the nature of enlightened despotism. We can say, however, that Joseph II's Patent of Toleration which did not extend to deism and the abolition of the Inquisition were decisions taken with the health of the Church and thus of the state firmly in mind. So, the imperatives of sovereigns and those of reformers could coincide on very important issues, which is just one more example of how misleading it can be to attempt to build a Chinese wall between the enlightened and non-enlightened. In this period it was at times those very state imperatives that could provide the appropriate political conditions for the expression of reforming/enlightened thought. We know, for instance, that in some cases the intellectual calls for the abolition of the Inquisition Tribunal were published only after the process of legislation against them had already begun. To emphasize the need to comprehend the diversity of Enlightenment political and social contexts and thus of the nature of the Enlightenment itself, it should be remembered that Venice was the home for many outspoken writers, yet its Tribunal of Inquisition was only abolished in 1797 after the Republic's defeat by Napoleon.

To argue that the philosophes of Europe often reflected emerging reality, rather than initiating it, is not to diminish the stature of the phenomenon we call the Enlightenment. Thus, without a blush, we can admit that, as Owen Chadwick has put it, 'the courts and the legal profession were ending torture before he [Cesare Beccaria] wrote a word'.[65] To speak out, courageously, for justice and by the impact of your pen hasten the end of a despicable medieval practice is typical of the spirit of many in that century, reflecting the fact that wide layers of society had become more aware of the gap between social potential and its often sad, brutal and backward reality. Neither is it to belittle the Enlightenment to talk of a Catholic or Protestant Enlightenment. On the contrary, to do so is to illustrate the

The Enlightenment and religion

width, breadth and scope of the intellectual ferment in eighteenth-century Europe.

Notes

1 'Schoolmen': orthodox Catholic theologians.
2 O. Chadwick, 'The Italian Enlightenment', in R. Porter and M. Teich (eds), *The Enlightenment in National Context* (Cambridge: Cambridge University Press, 1981), p. 103.
3 On the Catholic Enlightenment see, for instance, the discussion in S. J. Miller, *Portugal and Rome c. 1748–1830. An Aspect of the Catholic Enlightenment* (Rome: Università Gregoriana Editrice, 1978), ch. 1. On the general reforming trend in early-eighteenth-century Italy see V. Ferrone, *The Intellectual Roots of the Italian Enlightenment. Newtonian Science, Religion and Politics in the Early Eighteenth Century* (New York: Humanities Press, 1995; 1st edn 1982).
4 Miller, *Portugal and Rome*, pp. 2–3.
5 See P. Gay, *The Enlightenment. An Interpretation. Vol. 2: The Science of Freedom* (London: Wildwood House, 1973; 1st edn 1969), ch. 1 'The Recovery of Nerve'.
6 C. H. O'Brien, 'Jansenists on Civil Toleration in Mid-18th-Century France', *Theologischen Zeitschrift*, 37 (1981), p. 93.
7 On the seventeenth century see my *Idol Temples and Crafty Priests. The Origins of Enlightenment Anticlericalism* (London: Macmillan, 1999).
8 Miller, *Portugal and Rome*, pp. 2–4.
9 For an analysis of eighteenth-century anti-curial historiography see my *Idol Temples and Crafty Priests*.
10 Some of the leading Italian and Austrian Jansenist reformers looked upon Muratori and his *Della Regolata Divozione dei Cristiani* (Venice, 1747) as a guide to the reform of the Church.
11 L. Muratori, *Dissertazioni sopra le antichità italiane* (3 vols, Milan, 1751), vol. 3, *Dissertazione 70*, pp. 460, 468. The *Dissertazioni* are the posthumous translation of the *Antiquitates italicae medii* (6 vols, Milan, 1738–42) by the nephew of Muratori, Gian-Francesco Soli Muratori.
12 P. Verri, 'Memoria cronologica dei cambiamenti pubblici dello stato di Milano 1750–1791', in *Lettere inediti di Pietro e Alessandro Verri*, ed C. Casati (Milan, 1879), vol. IV, pp. 360–1, quoted in N. Davidson, 'Toleration in Enlightenment Italy', in O. Grell and R. Porter (eds), *Toleration in Enlightenment Europe* (Cambridge: Cambridge University Press, 2000), p. 236.
13 Cardinal Orsi, *Della infallibilità e dell'autorità del Romano Pontefice sopra i concilj ecumenici* (2 vols, Roma, 1741–42), vol. 1, sigs. 5ᵛ–6ʳ.
14 Giovanni Marchetti (Archbishop of Ancyra), *L'Autorità suprema del romano pontefice* (Rome, 1789), 'Al Lettore', pp. 5–6.
15 Davidson, 'Toleration in Enlightenment Italy', p. 237.
16 C. A. Pilati, *Di una riforma* (1767), quoted in Davidson, 'Toleration in Enlightenment Italy', p. 237.
17 Pietro Giannone, *Istoria civile del Regno di Napoli* (Naples, 1770; 1st edn 1723), vol. 1, p. 62.

196

18 Ibid., vol. 1, p. 461; vol. 2, pp. 315, 398; vol. 3, p. 339. For Giannone's views on papal corruption see the analysis of his *Istoria civile* and *Triregno* in my *Idol Temples and Crafty Priests.*

19 Davidson, 'Toleration in Enlightenment Italy', p. 234.

20 Of the very few enlightened who struck in print (anonymously) against the Church in this period was Amidei Cosimo (*d.* 1784), in his *La Chiesa e la repubblica dentro i loro limiti* (sine loco, but Florence, 1768).

21 See, for example, the curial publications: *Sommario de'documenti che giustificano il supremo ... dominio della Santa Sede sopra de'feudi ecclesiastici in Piemonte* (Rome, 1727); and the *Dimostrazione della sovranità temporale della Sede Apostolica ne i feudi ecclesiastici del Piemonte* (Rome?, 1725?).

22 See, for example, the papal official document *Ragioni della Sede Apostolica sopra il ducato di Parma e Piacenza esposte a sovrani e principi cattolic d'Europa* (Rome, 1741).

23 On Rome's claim see, for example, Cardinal S. Borgia's *Difesa del dominio temporale della Sede Apostolica nelle Due Sicilie. In risposta alle scritture publicate in contrario* (Rome, 1791).

24 The status of Rome's claim to suzerainty over the Kingdom of Naples is perhaps best captured in the title of Tommaso Turbolo, *Libera ed independente sovranità de' Rè delle due Sicilie ... vindicata contro l'assurde ... pretensioni della Corte di Roma* (1788). For an anti-curial assessment of the areas of Italy claimed by the Pope see the anonymous *Il dominio spirituale e temporale del papa* (London, but Italy, 1783); the curial reply to this text was Francesco Antonio Zaccaria, *Denunza solenne fatta alla Chiesa e ai Principi Cattolici di un anticristiano* (Assisi, 1783).

25 See Muratori, *Ragioni della Serenissima Casa d'Este sopra Ferrara confermate e difese in risposta al dominio temporale della Sede Apostolica* (Modena, 1714).

26 On Muratori and Comacchio see below. On the curial defence against Modenese territorial claims see, for instance, G. Fontanini's *Il Dominio temporale della Sede Apostolica sopra la Città di Comacchio. Si aggiunge la Difesa del medesimo dominio ... in risposta alle tre ultime scritture pubblicate in contrario* [i.e. Muratori's writings] (Rome, 1709); and his *Difesa seconda del dominio temporale della Sede Apostolica sopra la Città di Comacchio* (Rome, 1711).

27 Lodovico Muratori, *Osservazioni sopra una lettera intitolata Il dominio temporale della Sede Apostolica sopra la Città di Comacchio* (sine loco, but Modena, 1708), pp. 5–7.

28 Lodovico Muratori, *Annali d'Italia* (12 vols, Milan, 1744–49), vol. 4, pp. 164–5, 293, 396.

29 L. Muratori, *Della Fallibilità dei pontefici nel dominio temporale*, ed. C. Foucard (posthumous, Modena, 1872).

30 Three works constitute the history of the Church commenced by Orsi and continued by Becchetti: Giuseppe Agostino Orsi, *Della Istoria ecclesiastica* (21 vols, Rome, 1746–62); Filippo Angelico Becchetti, *Della Istoria ecclesiastica dell'eminentissimo Cardinale Giuseppe Orsi* (13 vols, Rome, 1770–81); Becchetti, *Istoria degli ultimi quattro secoli della Chiesa* (10 vols, Rome, 1788–96).

31 Fontanini, *Il dominio temporale ... sopra la Città di Comacchio*, p. 389.

32 For a summary of this type of defence see also Fontanini, *Il dominio temporale ... sopra la Città di Comacchio*, p. 59; for a later but similar defence see Alfonso Muzzarelli, *Dominio temporale del papa* (1789); and his *Della Civile giurisdizione ed influenza sul governo temporale esercitata dai Romani Pontifici* (posthumous, Rome, 1816).

33 Cardinal Orsi and Bishop Becchetti, *Storia ecclesiastica* (52 vols, Rome, 1835–62), tome 100, p. 6. The *Storia ecclesiastica* was the first complete edition of the Orsi–Becchetti history of the Church, which remains mostly as it was published, in *fascicoli*, which I have termed tomes.

34 Francesco Zaccaria wrote against Febronius in his *Anti-Febbronio ... o sia apologia polemico-storico del primato del papa* (Pesaro, 1767; 2nd edn 1770); and (under the pseudonym Theodorus à Palude) in his *Antifebronius vindicatus seu suprema romani pontificis potestas adversus Justinum Febronium* (Francofurti and Lipsiae, 1772).

35 On the seventeenth-century crisis and eighteenth-century recovery see D. Sella, *Italy in the Seventeenth Century* (London: Longman, 1997); and D. Carpanetto's still useful discussion 'Trade and Manufacture. The Historiographical Problem of the Crisis of the Seventeenth Century', in D. Carpanetto and G. Ricuperati, *Italy in the Age of Reason 1685–1789* (Harlow: Longman, 1987).

36 For a useful summary of the economic condition of the Papal States and the fate of reform proposals see Carpanetto and Ricuperati, *Italy in the Age of Reason*; and F. Venturi, *Italy and the Enlightenment* (London: Longman, 1972).

37 The *Storia critico-cronologica de' romani pontifici* (Naples, 1765–68) of Giuseppe Piatti, and the *Vitae pontificum Romanorum ex antiquis monumentis* (Parma, 1739) of Antonio Sandini, for instance, differed little from the analysis of Baronius, Becchetti and Orsi.

38 Becchetti, *Istoria degli ultimi quattro secoli della Chiesa*, vol. 1, p. 17; for essentially similar arguments see also Orsi, *Della infallibilità e dell'autorità del Romano Pontefice*; and Marchetti, *L'Autorità suprema del romano pontefice*.

39 Lodovico Muratori, *Della Pubblica felicità oggetto de'buoni principi* (Lucca, but Venice, 1749), preface, p. 2. For more on the duties of the good prince see Muratori's 'Rudimenti di Filosofia morale per il Principe Ereditario di Modena', in *Scritti inediti di L. A. Muratori* (Modena, 1872), pp. 219–20.

40 Giannone, *Istoria civile*, vol. 2, pp. 190–1.

41 Fleury's most influential work was the *L'Histoire ecclèsiastique* (1691–1720), translated into Italian by Gaspare Gozzi (Venice, 1739, with several subsequent editions). On the lack of consistent official opposition to the publication of Fleury's work in Italy see Alfonso Prandi, 'La Storia ecclesiastica di P. Giuseppe Orsi e la sua Genesi', *Rivista di storia della Chiesa in Italia*, 34 (1980), pp. 435–8.

42 Cardinal Orsi professed to have written against Fleury in his *Della storia ecclesiastica* (1746–62) but his targetting of Muratori is just as frequent; for another reply to Fleury see Giovanni Marchetti's *Saggio critica sopra la storia ecclesiastica di Fleury* (Rome, 1780; 2nd edn 1782–83).

43 For a discussion of the thought of Abbot Bencini see Ferrone, *The Intellectual Roots of the Italian Enlightenment*, pp. 146–9.

44 Giannone, *Istoria civile*, vol. 3, pp. 322, 333.

45 On Ricci see, for instance, *Gli amici e i tempi di Scipione dei Ricci: saggio sul giansenismo Italiano* (Florence, 1920), and the chapter on Ricci in C. A. Bolton, *Church Reform in Eighteenth-Century Italy (The Synod of Pistoia, 1786)* (The Hague: Martinus Nijhoff, 1969).

46 *Atti e decreti del concilio diocesano di Pistoja* (2nd edn, Florence, 1788), pp. 5, 80–1. See also Bolton, *Church Reform in Eighteenth-Century Italy*. For a similar critique of the Inquisition see also the anonymous *Istoria del pontificate romane e sue relazioni con le potenze della Cristianità* (Geneva, 1785), pp. 82–3.

47 For another uncompromising justification of the Inquisition see Orsi and Becchetti, *Storia ecclesiastica*, tome 161, pp. 115–17.

48 On the nature of Jansenism in the Italian pensinsula and the difficulty of definition see, for instance, A. Jemolo's still useful *Il Giansenismo in Italia prima della rivoluzione* (Bari: Laterza, 1928); E. Codignola's *Illuministi, giansenisti, e giacobini nell'Italia del settecento* (Florence: La Nuova Italia, 1947); and P. Zovatto's *Introduzione al giansenismo Italiano* (Trieste: University of Trieste, 1970). For an overview of the debate on Jansenism as a political phenomenon leading to the Risorgimento and to Italian unification under liberal and democratic principles see the Introduction to Miller's *Portugal and Rome*.

49 Orsi was attacked by his adversaries as Jansenist because of his writings (*Dissertazione dogmatica e morale* [Rome, 1727] and his *Dimostrazione teologica* [Milan, 1729]) in defence of the moral and theological tradition of the Church. On the Jansenism charge and Orsi see, for instance, Jemolo, *Il Giansenismo in Italia*, pp. 162–200.

50 S. Woolf, *History of Italy 1700–1860* (London: Routledge, 1991; 1st edn 1979), p. 75.

51 Perhaps the most useful discussion of the early-eighteenth-century reform movement inside the Church is Ferrone, *The Intellectual Roots*.

52 For a useful summary of the Tuscan Catholic Enlightenment see S. J. Miller, 'The Limits of Political Jansenism in Tuscany: Scipione de'Ricci to Peter Leopold, 1780–1791', *Catholic Historical Review*, 80: 4 (1994).

53 One of the most important texts indicative of this period is Scipione de'Ricci (ed.), *Raccolta di opuscoli interessanti la religione* (Pistoia, 1783).

54 There are no firm biographical details available on Delle Piane, but see Carmelo Caristia, *Riflessi politici del giansenismo italiano* (Naples: Morano Editore, 1965), pp. 178–80, 321–2, for some speculative comments.

55 Pier Niccolò Delle Piane, *Storia cronologica de' papi da S. Pietro all'odierno pontificato di Pio VII cavata da' migliori autori con annotazioni* (Genoa, 1802; 1st edn 1798), pp. 5, 133.

56 Giuseppe Capecelatro, *Discorso istorico-politico dell'origine del progresso e della decadenza del potere de'chierici su le signorie temporali* (Filadelfia, but Naples, 1788), preface, p. 8.

57 Ibid., pp. 34–6.

58 Scotti, *Della Monarchia universale de'papi*, pp. 11–12, 16–17.

59 Ibid., pp. 21–2, 61–2, 65, 67, 133. The curial reply to Scotti came in the form of Francesco Antonio Zaccaria's *Il Discorso di un anonimo, della monarchia universale de'Papi, Napoli 1789* (Rome, 1791).

60 On specifically Italian republicanism see, for instance, Renzo De Felice, *Il*

The Enlightenment and religion

Triennio giacobino in Italia 1796–1799 (Rome: Bonacci, 1990); and Furio Diaz and A. Saitta, *La questione del'giacobinismo italiano* (Rome: Istituto storico italiano, 1988).

61 Little biographical detail is available on Rivarola, but for a reference to him see Renato Soriga, *L'Idea nazionale italiana dal sec. XVIII alla unificazione* (Modena: Collezione storico del Risorgimento Italiano, vol. 28, 1941), pp. 116, 120–31; and Caristia, *Riflessi politici del giansenismo italiano*, p. 165. Rivarola translated Mornay's work possibly in collaboration with one Giuseppe Toietti, about whom biographical information is not available.

62 Paolo Rivarola, *Storia del papato di Filippo de Mornay, Cittadino Francese. Tradotta, ed accresciuta con alcune Note al testo, e col supplemento al fine* (4 vols, Pavia, 1796–1802), vol. 2, pp. 150–1, 161–2; vol. 3, pp. 2, 75–6, 161–2.

63 Quoted in Davidson, 'Toleration in Enlightenment Italy', p. 242.

64 J. Whaley, 'Religious Toleration in the Holy Roman Empire', in Grell and Porter (eds), *Toleration in Enlightenment Europe*, p. 184.

65 Chadwick, 'The Italian Enlightenment', p. 99.

6

The 'public sphere' and the hidden life of ideas

The hidden life of ideas

The Enlightenment has been seen as the intellectual honey pot from which the origins of the modern world were to be sought. As Dorinda Outram has noted in her *The Enlightenment* (1995), philosophers and political commentators have interpreted the Enlightenment in 'the hope of defining the meaning and future of the modern world. The Enlightenment is probably unique ... in its attracting such interest and in the extent to which such philosophical interpretations have influenced the thinking of professional historians.'[1] For decades, the connection between the Enlightenment and modernity has been viewed as unproblematic. In his review of European Enlightenment studies *Per una storia illuministica* (1973), for example, Furio Diaz uncritically noted that the years *c.* 1955–70 had been ones in which hope for economic, political and cultural reform and improvement had been dominant. It was 'natural', therefore, that historians searched in history for 'times and processes' which reflected their own objectives of progress – and they found them in the philosophes.[2]

As the discussions in this book have illustrated, attempting to understand, define or justify the present through an examination of the past is an activity fraught with danger. Boucher has gone as far as stating that '[t]o impose present historical modes of enquiry upon past texts is, by definition, an anachronism',[3] and it is difficult to deny the essence of his assessment. Given that we write historical accounts primarily by subjecting historical texts to our own intellectual analysis, objective historical accounts are more of an ideal than a possibility. Historical accounts are, therefore, by definition, interpretations: to write history we must interpret texts. So, in the practice of historiography, rather than throw our hands up in horror at a long-recognized dilemma, we have little choice but to live with the problem of anachronism and try to remain aware of its dangers. One of the most important elements in the attempt to reduce the anachronistic in historical analysis is of course to set the subject of historical study as firmly as possible in its own historical context. Unfortunately, in terms of intellectual history, this simple injunction is at times a very tall order indeed. As regards historical texts, on the most general level, the output of past thinkers reflects certain elements of the nature and current phase of their own society. The rank or milieu to which authors belong or gravitate towards, and the broader struggles, challenges and changes occurring around them, are often less detectable in the historical record than we might wish. Of course, texts also reflect moments and phases of the writer's own more personal experiences, education and beliefs, yet those moments and phases too often remain insufficiently known to posterity.

Thus, even when historians feel they have 'well-documented' studies of individual thinkers, the full reconstruction of the interaction of the historical subject with his/her society and immediate surroundings remains an ideal rather than a practical proposition. So, in pursuing the context of a historical figure, a realization of the frequent practical limitations of research is necessary. Most importantly, for this present discussion, past writers rarely inform us of or acknowledge all of the influences acting upon them. After all, why should they have done so, when the demands of their present task – rather than intellectual confessions for the sake of posterity – were of course paramount. In any case, writers often take current common-or-garden attitudes, principles or trends as given, while others are considered as of no importance or deemed irrelevant and thus never appear in their writings. What was obvious to contemporary writers and readers, therefore, may not seem obvious at all to future generations. As Henry Guerlac has noted, 'written history can only be highly selective', partly because of the sheer mass of data available, but also because of the choice exercised by contemporaries in recording events. Thus we can know only what 'the participants in events or those who came soon after ... determined that we should know. They placed in the intentional record ... those men and events which appeared to them as exceptional, striking and wholly outside the ordinary dull routine of private existence.'[4]

The 'public sphere' and the hidden life of ideas

As we have seen, perhaps the most 'self-evident' and therefore tempting moment when searching for the influences which acted upon a writer is identifying a concept or argument in his or her work which had apparently been articulated by a previous thinker. The first point to make is that, on the subject of the Enlightenment, we ought to be very surprised indeed if pre-Enlightenment thinkers had not touched upon many issues dear to the enlightened. Why? Because many of the aspirations, political dilemmas, perceived social evils and controversies of the eighteenth century were still similar to those of previous centuries. So, in eighteenth-century works, ideas that at first sight may seem like 'borrowings' from the past may well have had their origin in the eighteenth century, but – and this is the crucial point – might still be justified via the citation of past authorities. For a philosophe to cite, for instance, Machiavelli in a discussion on political philosophy may or may not indicate the influence of Machiavelli. Polemicists of most ages and on diverse subjects have brought illustrious past thinkers to their aid, irrespective of whether their thought commenced with or was significantly influenced by that past thinker or not. The tradition of seeing the philosophes as greatly influenced by a reading of the classics is a case in point. The 'influence' of the classics is certainly not definable as influence in the simple causal sense or is at least not provable. However, searching in the classics for *justification* of their views and hopes for the future was a sensible tactic for enlightened propagandists. Associating themselves with the classics helped bolster their views against their potential detractors, simply because classical writers were still held in high intellectual and aesthetic regard, and were usually considered more politically 'neutral' than recent or contemporary writers. Thus what was normal literary/academic practice and political prudence becomes, in the hands of historians, defined as definite influence. The same can be said of the supposed influence of Renaissance writers. As Boucher, for example, has commented, 'to say that Machiavelli, Hobbes and Rousseau all saw a role for a civic religion in order to secure adherence to a common morality and maintain obedience to the laws, is not to say that they all meant the same thing. What it does mean is that they all believe that a dual obligation within a realm or state is inimical to good order.'[5]

Another problem with interpreting historical texts is posed by the tactics sometimes used by eighteenth-century writers to disguise authorial identity, primary intentions or influences in order to avoid the undue attention of the censor. But, of course, such tactics not only pose a problem for modern historians, they constituted a circumstance which early modern readers habitually had to negotiate. In principle, then, 'mistaken' or alternative analyses of texts may enter the historical record relatively soon after the publication of the text in question and may lay undetected for generations. This is partly because modern historians sometimes consider eighteenth-century assessments of texts automatically to have more historical credibility than later interpretations. Thus, Enlightenment writers, wittingly or unwittingly, could consider a Christian text critical of certain proofs of Christianity – such as the Bayle's *Dictionnaire historique et critique* – as therefore antichristian, written from a radical Christian perspective only in order to avoid censure. This was a bold fiction of the philosophes, but one which has been repeated by a series of writers into the mid twentieth century. We know that all the evidence – and there is a lot of it – firmly indicates that Bayle remained a Calvinist. The view of him as a sceptic or philosophe has persisted (amongst some even into the present) because it also neatly coincided with the desire to see the Enlightenment as the duel between reason and faith, and thus the first key steps to modernity. Bayle was a Calvinist, yet at the same time we know that he advocated a more thoroughgoing religious toleration than many philosophes. This fact alone should cause historians to wonder about the role and nature of broader intellectual tendencies – in this case Protestant – which flowed into and helped form the Enlightenment.

The 'public sphere' and the top-down model of intellectual change

The recognition of public opinion as a crucial force within the development of the Enlightenment has been hampered by two factors: the influence of the concept of public opinion as drawn from the writings of philosophes themselves, and the dominance of the traditional top-down approach to intellectual change.

Chartier, for instance, has noted that the French philosophes themselves distinguished between the opinion of the uninformed, capricious and noisy multitude and that of 'enlightened' public opinion.[6] It is very important for our understanding of the Enlightenment that we realize that protagonists of the Enlightenment often thought in this manner. It does not, however, oblige historians to use the reasoning of the philosophes as a predicate to their own research on the question of public opinion in religious change. The distinction of the philosophes between the rude masses and the enlightened again implicitly raises the question of whether historians can locate any fruitful dividing line between the enlightened and non-enlightened. As we have seen, finding such a dividing line is very problematic indeed, simply because we now know that the Enlightenment was a much broader affair than research into the various little elite coteries of philosophes across Europe has traditionally suggested. Sifting through the works of the philosophes for definitions of the people or public opinion will not, therefore, necessarily inform us about the *reality* of the relationship between popular or public opinion and religious change. I wish to argue that, in practice, the search for a clear distinction between popular or public opinion is a misleading avenue of research.

Even though Baker has indicated that the *concept* of public opinion as a political force in France was first raised in about 1750 in discussion on the controversy over the refusal of the sacraments to Jansenists,[7] the formulation of that idea does not mean that public opinion as a political force had just arrived. As we have seen, the politico-religious events in late-seventeenth- and eighteenth-century England (for instance the Sacheverell affair) and the furore surrounding the oppression of Jansenists in France in the decades before 1750 are ample proof of the earlier existence of public opinion as a political force. It can just as convincingly be argued, therefore, that the imputed birth of the concept of public opinion indicated that in a pressing politico-religious situation there was need to express a familiar socio-political power in new terms. It has been argued that the arrival of public opinion in the 1750s as a political force engendered a 'new political culture, recognised as a novelty by contemporaries'.[8] It is certainly the case that the Jansenist controversy was inextricably political and brought about a new broad political circumstance in so far as the King and his government were often on the defensive and quite unable to solve the problem of widespread and stubborn resistance to their politico-religious aims. The force that brought about that change of Bourbon governmental fortunes, however, was the traditional one of politico-religious struggle. It is true that printed matter was utilized to promote resistance to the King's aims, but this too was nothing qualitatively new in itself. In any case, the most influential and enduring publication in that struggle was the *Nouvelles ecclésiastiques*, hardly the embodiment of a new socio-political force, but clear in its understanding of public opinion as tribunal. As the editors of the *Nouvelles ecclésiastiques* wrote in January 1732, '[t]he public is a judge that they [King and government] have been unable to corrupt'.[9]

As we have seen, in the struggle against *Unigenitus*, the political balance between ruler and ruled had been perceptibly shifting since 1715. The situation in the 1750s could be described by contemporaries as a novelty because that decade marked the high point of that struggle in which the King's authority had been defied, often with relative impunity. That defiance, often led by the *Parlement* of Paris, was grounded on the knowledge that broad support for defiance existed amongst the masses. Thus any attempt to separate supposedly lowbrow popular opinion from 'educated' public opinion in this context would be to misunderstand the very nature of resistance to the King's will. Such an attempt would also be to underestimate the 'sociological complexity' of eighteenth-century urban culture.[10] Evidence for the emergence of the new force of public opinion in the late Enlightenment, therefore, is not entirely consonant with historical circumstances. As I have illustrated in the final section of Chapter 2, it is much more convincing to argue that public opinion as a political force was nothing new to Europe, but that the nature and appearance of public opinion changed according to context. As one commentator has put it, 'common sense suggests that there has always been some kind of collective opinion, as well as an array of different forms of public "interface" between the state and the people it governs'.[11] As Campbell has argued, if public opinion as an unofficial 'tribunal' did not exist prior to mid-eighteenth-century France, then how can we explain the function of provincial *parlements*, or taxation edicts appealing to notions of 'the public'.[12]

There were those, of course, who had an interest in talking-up the birth of public opinion as a new social force. As we know, the philosophes and other interested parties chose to write on what was new in the eighteenth century and tended to exaggerate their role in events or developments if they were deemed to realize or encourage enlightenment. More importantly, however, we know that most philosophes viewed the process of enlightenment in class terms. As

Voltaire put it, the 'rabble ... are not worthy of being enlightened'.[13] Given that this view was common, can we really expect the philosophes to be frank about the important role of the lower orders in the formation and expression of public opinion? As we have seen, however, the evidence demonstrates quite clearly that, in the struggle against the oppression of the Jansenists, the most crucial factor in turning the balance of opinion against the King was the unity of the lower orders and elements of the higher (especially in the form of the members of the *Parlement* of Paris).

The writings of the philosophes, therefore, cannot be relied on as a guide to the nature of public opinion in the eighteenth century. In this sense, important facets of the bottom-up process of intellectual change have been repeatedly ignored or suppressed. Historians in search of the roots of modernity have also contributed to muddying the waters. On the subject of public opinion, they too have wished to find in the writings of the philosophes evidence for palpably modern or proto-modern developments and have ignored telling evidence that there was no 'birth' of public opinion as such, but rather a relatively slow evolution of its traditional form, dependent on time, place and to a degree on the circulation of printed matter. Habermas's *The Structural Transformation of the Public Sphere* (1989) has been very influential in arguing for the emergence of a 'public sphere' in late Enlightenment France. According to Habermas, this 'public sphere' is to be identified with only one social grouping, the bourgeoisie, and in a set of institutions including salons, academies and Masonic lodges. For Habermas the Enlightenment public sphere was also a fundamentally secular phenomenon, and he attributed little or no importance to religion and politico-religious struggle. As one writer has commented, Habermas has been so influential because his analysis seemed to offer a potential solution to the problem of the relationship between the Enlightenment and the French Revolution,[14] and his description of the intellectual life of late-eighteenth-century France is to some degree now accepted by many historians. As we have already noted, however, there is also a growing consensus that the Enlightenment was a broader phenomenon than has been traditionally understood – as illustrated so well in Munck's *The Enlightenment* – and cannot be said to have been a phenomenon composed only of the wealthy elite. Rather the Enlightenment shaded sideways and downwards from the bourgeoisie into the lower orders.

The idea, then, of a new public sphere inhabited only by the bourgeois frequenters of the salons and such like is problematic. Acceptance of Habermas's view would serve to mask the reality of a more dynamic and interactive flow of ideas, in which the various orders had a reciprocal intellectual relationship, even if well-to-do contemporaries did not wish to acknowledge it.

It is incontestable that the public sphere grew in the eighteenth century, but it grew as public opinion – aided but not caused by an expansion of print culture and rising literacy levels[15] – began to assert itself against the intolerant religious policies of confessional states, particularly in early-eighteenth-century France and late-seventeenth-century England. In the Italian peninsula the political situation was quite different and the nature of politico-religious struggle did not result in the same degree of widening of the public sphere as in England and France. In the Italian statelets the threat of Roman religious intervention tended to bind those critical of the Roman Curia to their immediate sovereign as protector of their 'national religious liberties'. These sovereigns thus endured significantly less of a public politico-religious challenge than did the monarchies of England and France, with the result that the peninsula's public sphere remained relatively restricted until the arrival of the French revolutionary army in 1796.[16]

We have seen how the 1670s and 1680s saw a widening and deepening of the public sphere in England as a crisis-ridden monarchy was unable to repress the broad surge of public outrage at its perceived Catholic-absolutist aims. After the ejection of Catholic James II, the new King was obliged to concede the Toleration Act and he and his government proved increasingly unable to restrain the press. Large numbers of the publications of this widening public sphere were politico-religious in content, and their authors were not deists or philosophes, but Dissenters and other discontents within and without the Anglican Church. Decades later, first-hand observance of this public sphere was of course the origin of the praise of English freedom in Voltaire's *Letters Concerning the English Nation* (1733).[17] In 1680s France, by contrast, the monarchy felt strong enough to openly pursue its confessional and absolutist desires by violently suppressing the Huguenots. The Bourbon project of eradicating Jansenism, however, was to prove a very costly disaster, serving only to deepen broad public outrage against perceived absolutist excesses, generate unexpected allies and, in the process, considerably widen the public sphere after 1715. The dynamo of that widening public sphere of opinion was, as we have seen, a cross-class alliance of *advocats,* low-level clerics, and broad literate and semi-literate echelons of Paris and other cities. The post-1715 public sphere in France, like its earlier manifestation in England, was brought into being by politico-religious struggle.[18] In both countries that sphere quickly broadened, stretching beyond the nascent bourgeoisie and its salons to those who read newspapers, frequented coffee houses and became interested in current religious, social and political issues. Most importantly, it was a climate in which 'social and religious traditions seemed readily to have co-existed with newer forms of rationality and enlightened pragmatism',[19] so rendering the search for a dividing line between the enlightened and non-enlightened very difficult.

Nevertheless, most texts on the Enlightenment implicitly or explicitly portray the intellectual elite as cutting the path of intellectual progress, illuminating the route for the intellectually inert or docile lower orders. Given the educational advantages of the eighteenth-century elite (and those few from the lower orders who effectively joined their ranks), the top-down approach to intellectual change might seem simple common sense. The dominance of the elite in the historical record, however, has been widely construed as evidence of the *only* significant locus of intellectual change. This, as we have seen, is in good part because many historians have been concerned – consciously or unconsciously – to demonstrate that our present can be traced back to the writings of the philosophes, rather than to more fundamental events and trends amongst a much broader stratum of the populace. As Darnton has put it in his study of 'Grub Street hacks', 'perhaps the Enlightenment was a more down-to-earth affair than the rarefied climate of opinion described by textbook writers, and we should question the overly highbrow, overly metaphysical view of intellectual life in the eighteenth century'.[20]

In principle, the issue of how far enlightened thinkers were constrained or aided in their intellectual endeavours by the prejudices, predilections and conceptual awareness of the broad masses can hardly be considered irrelevant to historians of intellectual change. If we should doubt the potential importance of the attitudes of the lower orders in the early modern period, then we should remind ourselves that the fear of a return to the chaos of the Civil War period haunted the elite in England for decades. Indeed, a similar statement can be made about the French elite and the fear of a return to the events of the French Revolution. As the preceding chapters have illustrated, the influence of the broad population on political and intellectual trends is indubitable as long as historians do not, *a priori*, rule it out from their research endeavours. So, regardless of the best efforts of the likes of Voltaire to keep the Enlightenment an elite phenomenon, there were social, political and religious changes occurring which laid fundamental challenges to the old regime. Voltaire and other philosophes were part of those changes, part of the process, while at the same time also a reflection of it.

Given the gamut of evidence available, we can confidently designate late-seventeenth- and eighteenth-century European society as one experiencing intellectual crisis or at least ferment. This notion of intellectual crisis was the type of approach taken by one of the seminal texts in Enlightenment studies, Paul Hazard's *The Crisis of European Consciousness* (1935). The politico-religious struggles in France and England above all demonstrate that the increasingly broad and more complex intellectual world of that time could no longer easily be contained in the political, economic, religious and social corset of the confessional state. It is very difficult, therefore, to view the debates between Huguenots, Catholics, Anglicans and English Dissenters in post-1685 France, post-Civil War England and later in the Italian peninsula as simply an activity of the elite unconnected with and uninfluenced by the opinions, hopes and fears of society's lower echelons. Few historians doubt that these conflicts were important, even central, in the development and expression of large sections of public opinion. Historians are, however, far less convinced, often dismissive, on the question of the relationship of those struggles to the development and nature of the Enlightenment. The task, then, is to identify the nature of the interaction between mass opinion and the output of the elite writers of the period. It is very difficult, for example, to see how we can understand changes in the polemic of English Dissenters in post-Restoration England and its adoption by more radical thinkers without examining the state–Church arrangement and the institutional disadvantaging of the careers of well-educated Dissenters. Similarly, antipathy to the Bourbon dynasty cannot be understood in any rounded sense without attempting to take into consideration, for instance, the 'desacralization' of the French monarchy by its own clerics who in the second half of the century published telling moral evaluations of kings.[21]

Similar considerations must be brought to bear when considering the public sphere, for, as we have seen, it is not as 'transparent' as some historians have imagined. Surveys of the eighteenth-century press such as Censer's *The French Press in the Age of Enlightenment* (1994), while undoubtedly well researched, tend to miss the point. Censer certainly illustrates the growth of the public forum and the variety of its forms, yet unfortunately his research fits only too well the traditional drive to map the origins of modernity at the expense of more piercing research questions. It remains the case that the growth in the numbers of publications and in the size and nature of audiences for them provides us with only a very limited window upon events and intellectual change. The press is not a phenomenon which can be understood – in any historically meaningful sense of the word – on its own terms. The importance of the press for intellectual history lies in its relationship to general or particular attitudes, trends and changes. What periodicals printed is easy to determine, yet what was thought about their contents is much more important and is very difficult indeed to assess. Given, however, Censer's concentration on the press as a growing phenomenon, rather than as a means of intellectual interaction and even galvanizer to action, it is perhaps unsurprising that he devotes just a few lines to the *Nouvelles ecclésiastiques*. We know, of course, that the evidence points to the *Nouvelles ecclésiastiques* having a prominent role in fomenting and supporting major resistance to royal authority amongst the masses as well as the elite. Yet, frustratingly – and without reference to the *Nouvelles ecclésiastiques* itself – Censer also feels constrained to refer to the *parlements'* struggle with the monarchy: 'From the *parlements* ... emerged a critique of absolutism and both the suggestion and practice of a local government designed to provide for the individual.... [T]he Jansenists, with a long-term hostility to repression, developed a thorough-going critique of hierarchy.'[22]

It is by now an academic commonplace that the written word is open to misinterpretation or a variety of interpretations. That warnings about this fundamental difficulty are still needed should therefore be understood as a measure of how the significance of this elementary problem has nevertheless been underestimated. What is less frequently discussed or indeed recognized is the importance of the general problem of audience: as much attention must be given to the nature of the audience as the text itself if we are to understand its reception and impact. Even where this consideration has been raised, it has rarely been in the context of Enlightenment studies. Nevertheless, in 1985 Boucher, for instance, reminded us that texts 'will appear differently in different company, and the essence of the problem of interpretation ... is identifying the appropriate company in terms of which the text should be comprehended'. A text may appear to be fully articulated by an author, or authors, and although 'the sequence of words remains the same, its capacity for evoking different meanings is incalculable'.[23] The question of audience, then, remains crucial in our endeavours to understand eighteenth-century intellectual life. The direction of the discussion on Bayle encountered in this book so far has been that of the poor Calvinist Bayle falling foul of the wrong audience. Or did he? Should we be so presumptuous, indeed arrogant, as to allow the assumption that, because he was so infamously 'misread' by a few elite radical thinkers, he was generally 'misread'? Did his Christian thought have no impact on the vast majority of his readership who were of course not sceptics or deists, but Christians (and principally Protestants)? From this point of view, much work on the place of Bayle in the dynamic of eighteenth-century intellectual development remains to be completed.

Boucher's use of the term 'incalculable' may well be theoretically appropriate when discussing the inherent capacity of texts for multiple readings. In practice, however, the nature of the misinterpretations of any text will to an extent be circumscribed by the nature of the period in which the text is read, that is to say the context of its reception. In the late seventeenth and eighteenth centuries, religious oppression and dissent were still very much live issues and radical Christian critiques of religion and the Church were still hot property. As we have seen, in that circumstance we should expect to find some interested 'parties' declaring – in order to frighten off increasing disaffection – such radical Christian critiques as antichristian, that is to say deistic or atheistic. Many anti-Church or anti-religious thinkers also welcomed certain elements of embittered religious polemic between or within Churches as proof of priestcraft and the bankruptcy of contemporary theology. Yet the issue of narrative cannot be restricted to texts broadly within the humanities field, for narrative possesses the same inherent qualities regardless of the field or discipline of endeavour. Thus, even with scientific writings, the potential for a 'misreading' of a text was considerable, for science in this period – especially prior to 1750 – was also understood by many as one of various means of confirming or denying the presence and nature of divinity in the cosmos. Thus, for some, Newtonian science was a proof of the exquisitely complex divine ordering of nature, yet for others it was proof that God had only a remote or non-existent relationship to his creation.

If Voltaire and others wilfully misread Bayle (and it seems undeniable that some did), we could say it was a travesty. But on another level, utilizing aspects of a discussion for ends never envisaged by the author was part of the polemical spirit of that age (and remains so even now). From this perspective, such 'misreadings' and borrowings form an important part of the Enlightenment itself. Such borrowings and distortions give us a partial insight into an otherwise obscure component of the process of intellectual change and influence in Enlightenment Europe, serving to remind us that intellectual change is rarely a simple linear process. Recognition of this crucial yet often elusive aspect of the life of texts should prompt historians to attach much greater importance to understanding the various audiences for a work. It should also prompt us to consider carefully how elements of long-established political or religious traditions and polemics have been appropriated for ends not originally envisaged by their authors. One such example is the work of the eminent Enlightenment historian Edward Gibbon.

In his *Decline and Fall of the Roman Empire* (1776–81), considered to be one of the Enlightenment's seminal historical texts, Gibbon's immersion in Protestant anti-Catholic culture is, nevertheless, evident. In his account of the medieval Church, he borrowed very heavily from Protestant historiography, although historians have traditionally not wanted to recognize it. Peter Gay, for instance, claimed that the contribution of Christianity to Gibbon's historiography was 'modest and subterranean' and that he was 'usually unaware of it'.[24] Aside from the obviously impossible task of determining if Gibbon was actually 'unaware of it', the influence of Protestant historiography in Gibbon's account of the medieval Church was certainly not modest. Indeed, his account of the medieval Church is so similar to the traditional Protestant view that his analysis – aside from his famous style – could be ascribed to any one of a number of preceding Protestant writers. Gibbon drew upon pervasive anti-Catholic historical caricatures deeply imbued in the psyche of most English Protestants, so much so that his caricature of the medieval Church was drawn upon by English Protestants, even moderate Anglican clerics.[25] Was Gibbon aware of the extent of that influence? It is most likely that his estimation of the medieval Church seemed to him a self-evident historical truth which he duly articulated. This is, however, not at all the same as denying or ruling out general influence. The sketch of Church history with which Gibbon and the majority of the rest of the population of England were familiar was that of Catholic medieval priestcraft 'exposed' in thousands of different publications since the Reformation.[26] So, the influence of the sea of broad attitudes in which Enlightenment thinkers thought and wrote can at times be at least illustrated with some degree of common-sense certainty. There is, therefore, even in this celebrated case, every reason to significantly qualify any notion of an exclusively top-down model of intellectual change.

We know that the development and popular dissemination of sophisticated anticlerical theories directed against Roman Catholicism and the Anglican Church were a pervasive feature of seventeenth- and eighteenth-century dissenting polemic. Even if it is a process difficult to measure, there is little doubt that this polemic fed, in various ways, into the thought of more radical Christians and sceptics. Elements of this broad process of influence are now recognized by some few historians; yet the search for 'pivotal' texts which set Europe intellectually ablaze and supposedly produced Enlightenment anticlericalism is still a feature of Enlightenment studies.[27] The paucity of such texts and lack of evidence for their influence has, however, never seemed to present any deterrent to such endeavours, which brings us back to the issue of readership. The fears generated by the appearance or reports of atheistic or deistic texts in early modern Europe may well at times have been out of proportion to their number for very good reasons. As we have seen, we may include amongst those reasons the scare-mongering tactics of apologists, the enjoyment of scandal and the titillation of the forbidden, but also the undoubted and vexing existence of anticlericalism and religious heterodoxy within oral culture. As Hunter has warned, with respect to late-seventeenth-century England:

it is important that we do not retrospectively overestimate the significance of opinions which have come down to us in printed form, since there was clearly a more anonymous, oral dimension to heterodoxy which caused great concern at the time and which can be easily undervalued. In fact, this fashionable, common-sensical scepticism stands a better claim to being the true alternative to the new science as the high road to modernity than Jacob's putative tradition of subversive radicalism.[28]

Anachronism and toleration

The search for radical triggers of intellectual change is closely linked to the question of the role of the individual on the historical plane. The core of the causal model by which studies on Enlightenment Europe operate has usually been one in which the individual writer/ thinker or at least very small groups of like-minded individuals perform the primary, if not exclusive role in intellectual change. This model of intellectual change may seem a self-evident one to many, perhaps especially to those who have been reared on the 'great man theory' of historical change, that is to say the deeds and thoughts of powerful, fortuitous or especially gifted individuals. Clearly, in the history of Europe, the role of many individuals appears to have been central to intellectual change. One need only note such names as Machiavelli, Luther, Calvin, Hobbes, Newton, Locke, Descartes, Rousseau and others. How would the history of ideas have developed without the input of those particular individuals? On the subject of the Reformation, for instance, we could say that an expanding and changing Europe was ripe for religious change, and that if not Luther, Calvin and King Henry VIII, then some other individuals would have performed a similar role in breaking the hegemony of Rome. Such speculative history is of very limited use to historians, but it can undoubtedly serve to focus and restimulate debate on persistently difficult questions. What can we say, then, about the role of the individual with regard to the longer-term impact of seventeenth-century religious, political and social stresses?

This may seem an impossibly grand question, but it is in fact connected to a discussion which has threaded its way throughout this book. The issue of whether the Enlightenment should be seen as a development external to Christianity is pivotal to the question of the role of the individual in historical development. The belief that the ideas of elite individuals such as the philosophes should be seen as a development external to Christianity has predisposed researchers towards an exclusively top-down approach to intellectual change: for only the elite and a very few others put such radical ideas indelibly into the historical record. But few, if any, have sought to enquire – aside from its strong common-sense overtones – what 'external influence' might mean. Individuals in all societies undergo socialization at an early age, and this cultural conditioning continues into adulthood. Consequently, we experience life within sometimes implicit and sometimes explicit systems of ideas or ideological frameworks. In eighteenth-century Europe, this framework was almost exclusively Christian in origin and orientation. Christian ethics underpinned most of the laws, mores and cultural practices of day-to-day life. The nature of the various organs of cultural transmission – including, for example, the family, the Church, education and the state – meant that the social force of cultural transmission was very difficult indeed to escape completely. But it was not, of course, a closed, hermetically sealed system, in which change never took place, otherwise one could not account for intellectual change on the macro or micro level. Nevertheless, the influence of Christianity was very difficult, if not impossible, to avoid, even by those few who professed to have left Christianity behind them and entered upon their own personal avenue of life.

It is not surprising, then, despite often exhibiting the most trenchant anticlericalism, that many radicals and deists continued to subscribe to some sort of Christianity or religion exemplified by elements found in the Old or New Testament. Very, very few indeed of the enlightened professed to having no god at all – as Porter has commented, there were few atheists amongst the philosophes.[29] Unfortunately, this wide range of religious thought, and its marked degrees of adherence to Christianity or Christian concepts, has still not been adequately acknowledged by many historians who persist in viewing the Enlightenment simplistically as a box containing radical things of interest to them and their readers. Yet, the term deist itself, precisely because of the complexity of the religious scene, is of almost no use at all in explaining religious thought: some so-called deists believed in the revelation of Jesus, some in the precepts of the New Testament, others only in the Creation, most in the social necessity of a public Church (even if they themselves did not believe in the efficacy of prayer) and so on.

The very same cultural inertia which prevented the rise of any mass deist movement also ensured that the enlightened were often not the solid campaigners for the unsullied 'modern' principle of toleration as they have been traditionally described. It is time to cease the attempt to impose the modern concept of toleration on the Enlightenment, if only because it means that otherwise the Enlightenment will never live up to expectations. How, for instance, can the modern concept of toleration be reconciled with that of slavery, which was supported or at least not condemned by most philosophes? Voltaire, like many others,[30] was never a champion of unrestricted religious freedom, and it seems – parallel with his views on the Huguenots – he approved of the English bar on Dissenters from public office.[31] Indeed, as Marisa Linton has noted, not all of the philosophes supported the restoration of the public right of the Huguenots to exist even as an 'acknowledged community', although they promoted themselves as champions of toleration.[32] Indeed, Voltaire showed almost no interest at all in the situation of his Protestant fellow countrymen until 1762 and the Calas case. The reason, as Adams explains, was that he was unable to forgive the Huguenots for the Camisard Revolt against the Sun King, seeing it as indicative of the politically subversive and fanatical record of French Calvinism.[33] As a consequence, Voltaire had supported the measures which had been taken by the French state against the Huguenots[34] and was, perhaps unsurprisingly, accused of resorting to cheap anti-Huguenot sensationalism in order 'simply to increase sales' of his writings.[35] Indeed, if we approach the Enlightenment with an expectation of finding selfless radical intellectuals fighting for the liberty of all, we will never properly understand what we have termed the Enlightenment.

Without a greater understanding of the complex interaction of politics, religion, social class and the multi-dimensionality of the historical record and its limitations, too many students of the Enlightenment will remain perplexed even at the writings of its heroes. It is still a challenge, for instance, for us to understand how Voltaire's *Traité sur la tolérance* could defend the injustice perpetrated against Calas, but still argue that the Huguenots were inherently republican, thus tending to justify the French government's continuing denial of their most basic rights. Facing criticism on this point, 'Voltaire replied that he had never said "that the Huguenots are in principle enemies of kings" but, he added, he was convinced that there was a good deal of truth in this view'.[36] So much for Voltaire's thoroughgoing toleration! Similarly, Rousseau stubbornly refused to become involved in defending the Huguenots. Although he put the case for Huguenot freedom of conscience, only in one work (*Lettre à Christophe de Beaumont*, 1763) did he explicitly put the case for Huguenot relief. As Adams has put it, '[l]ike most of his contemporaries ... he was not a religious pluralist', but rather thought atheism and sceptics should be fought by citizens bringing 'their *public professions* of belief into harmony with the established cult of the society in which they lived' (my italics).[37]

In the early 1760s the tide of fortune did, quasi-officially, turn for the Huguenots. From those years Versailles effectively changed its Protestant policy, physical repression of the Huguenots all but stopped and, increasingly, key figures in the administration expressed sympathy for the Huguenots.[38] As we have seen, however, this was not a victory for the philosophes. Rather it was a victory for an already *de facto* toleration, and the realization that religious division – as graphically demonstrated by the startling victories of political Jansenism – could immensely damage the monarchy. Clearly this is not the Enlightenment traditionally presented to readers, and presents us with a rather more complex situation than has usually been acknowledged.

Efforts to broaden Enlightenment studies out from the few canonical texts which have traditionally formed its core are still limited. Although a few scholars have reminded us that some of the enlightened saw the Enlightenment 'as a process, not a completed project',[39] this has not generally translated into a closer examination of the process of becoming enlightened. Thomas Munck's *The Enlightenment* (2000) is one of the few recent studies that attempt to do just that. Munck examines various strata of eighteenth-century society, and sees the Enlightenment as a process of 'becoming' in which the precise dividing lines between the enlightened and the supposedly 'non-enlightened' are very often unclear. The problem, however, is that studies such as Munck's are still insufficient in number and range. As a consequence, the elements of context provided in the above discussions on England, France and Italy have rarely been recounted or contrasted with an understanding of the canonical thinkers of the Enlightenment. This has been at the cost of distortions within Enlightenment studies and the perpetuation of myths about the origins of modernity.

Notes

1 D. Outram, *The Enlightenment* (Cambridge: Cambridge University Press, 1995), p. 8.
2 Furio Diaz, *Per una storia illuministica* (Naples: Garzanti, 1973), p. 9.
3 D. Boucher, *Texts in Context. Revisionist Methods for Studying the History of Ideas* (Lancaster and Dodrecht: Nijhoff, 1985), p. 271.
4 H. Guerlac, 'Some Historical Assumptions of the History of Science', in A. Crombie (ed.), *Scientific Change ... from Antiquity to the Present* (London: Heinemann, 1963), pp. 797–8.
5 Boucher, *Texts in Context*, pp. 234–5.
6 R. Chartier, *The Cultural Origins of the French Revolution* (Durham, N.C.: Duke University Press, 1991), pp. 27–30.
7 See K. Baker, 'Politics and Public Opinion under the Old Regime: Some Reflections', in J. Censer and J. Popkin (eds), *Press and Politics in Pre-Revolutionary France* (Berkeley: University of California Press, 1987).
8 Chartier, *The Cultural Origins*, p. 30; see also pp. 31–4.
9 Quoted in P. R. Campbell, *Power and Politics in Old Régime France, 1720–1745* (London: Routledge, 1996), p. 303.
10 T. Munck, *The Enlightenment. A Comparative Social History 1721–1794* (London: Arnold, 2000), p. 23; see also pp. 22–6 for a useful discussion of some of the problems inherent in attempting to trace clear delineations between popular and elite culture.
11 Ibid., p. 15.
12 Campbell, *Power and Politics in Old Regime France*, p. 303.
13 Quoted in D. Daily, *Enlightenment Deism. The Foremost Threat to Christianity* (Pennsylvania: Dorrance, 1999), p. 44.
14 C. Adams, J. Censer and L. Graham (eds), *Visions and Revisions of Eighteenth-Century France* (Pennsylvania: Pennsylvania State University Press, 1997), Introduction, p. 6.
15 On the Enlightenment literacy and education see, for instance, Munck, *The Enlightenment*, ch. 3 'Broadening the Horizon: Ways and Means'; on print culture see especially chs 4 and 5.
16 On the restricted nature of the public sphere in the Italian peninsula see, for instance, M. Isabella, 'Italy, 1760–1815', in H. Barker and A. Burrows (eds), *Press, Politics and the Public Sphere in Europe and North America, 1760–1820* (Cambridge: Cambridge University Press, 2002).
17 Published in French as part of his *Lettres philosophiques* in 1734.
18 On Jansenism and the public sphere see, for instance, J. Van Horn Melton, *The Rise of the Public in Enlightenment Europe* (Cambridge: Cambridge University Press, 2001), ch. 2.
19 Munck, *The Enlightenment*, pp. vii, 30. For discussion on various aspects of English dissent and Enlightenment see, for example, K. Haakonssen (ed.), *Enlightenment and Religion. Rational Dissent in Eighteenth-Century Britain*

The Enlightenment and religion

(Cambridge: Cambridge University Press, 1996); and M. Fitzpatrick, 'Heretical Religion and Radical Political Ideas in Late Eighteenth-Century England', in E. Hellmuth (ed.), *The Transformation of Political Culture. England and Germany in the Late Eighteenth Century* (Oxford: German Historical Institute, 1990).

20 R. Darnton, *The Literary Underground of the Old Regime* (Cambridge, Mass. and London: Harvard University Press, 1982), p. 2.

21 See M. Linton, 'The Unvirtuous King? Clerical Rhetoric on the French Monarchy, 1760–1774', *History of European Ideas*, 25 (1999). The notion of the 'desachralization' of the monarchy, as put forward by J. W. Merrick (*The Desachralization of the French Monarchy in the Eighteenth Century*, Baton Rouge, La.: Louisiana State University Press, 1992) and D. Van Kley (*The Damiens Affair and the Unraveling of the Ancien Régime*, Princeton, N.J.: Princeton University Press, 1984), however, does not seem to me to be convincing without placing it securely within a process of disenchantment that began much earlier in the eighteenth century within the struggles discussed above in Chapter 4.

22 J. Censer, *The French Press in the Age of Enlightenment* (London: Routledge, 1994), p. 116.

23 Boucher, *Texts in Context*, p. 1.

24 P. Gay, *The Enlightenment. An Interpretation. Vol. 1: The Rise of Modern Paganism* (London: Norton, 1995; 1st edn 1966), p. 326.

25 See, for instance, G. Gregory's *A History of the Christian Church from the Earliest Periods to the Present Time* (London, 1790).

26 On the distortions of history propagated by Protestant scholars and polemicists see my 'Where was your Church before Luther? Claims for the Antiquity of Protestantism Examined', *Church History: Studies in Christianity and Culture*, 68: 1 (1999).

27 For a summary of the attempts to chart the influence of the libertine tradition on the formation of the Enlightenment see I. Wade, *The Intellectual Origins of the French Enlightenment* (Princeton, N.J.: Princeton University Press, 1971), pp. 28–57.

28 M. Hunter, *Science and the Shape of Orthodoxy. Intellectual Change in Late Seventeenth-Century Britain* (Woodbridge: Boydell and Brewer, 1995), p. 9. Here he is commenting upon the work of Margaret Jacob, who has promoted the idea of a radical, subversive English Enlightenment; see for instance her *The Radical Enlightenment. Pantheists, Freemasons and Republicans* (London: Allen and Unwin, 1981).

29 R. Porter, *Enlightenment Britain and the Creation of the Modern World* (London: Penguin, 2000), p. 9.

30 On the limitations of toleration in the Italian peninsula, France and England see N. Davidson, 'Toleration in Enlightenment Italy', M. Linton, 'Citizenship and Religious Toleration in France', and J. Israel, 'Spinoza, Locke and the Enlightenment Battle for Toleration', all in O. Grell and R. Porter (eds), *Toleration in Enlightenment Europe* (Cambridge: Cambridge University Press, 2000).

31 Fitzpatrick, 'Toleration and the Enlightenment Movement', p. 41.

32 Linton, 'Citizenship and Religious Toleration in France', pp. 165, 168.

33 G. Adams, *The Huguenots and French Opinion 1685–1787. The Enlighten-*

ment Debate on Toleration (Ontario: Wilfred Laurier University Press, 1991), pp. 49, 119, 143.

34 See for instance Voltaire's *Le Siècle de Louis* (London, 1752).
35 Adams, *The Huguenots and French Opinion*, p. 122.
36 Voltaire, quoted in ibid., p. 218.
37 Ibid., pp. 147, 156–60.
38 Ibid., p. 201.
39 Outram, *The Enlightenment*, p. 2.

APPENDIX

Indicative bibliography of Protestant thought on natural religion

Historians have too often given the impression that those who wrote positively on the subject of natural religion (or the religion of nature) were enemies of the Church. Yet, as this Appendix indicates, the topic of natural religion was one of the most common within Christian literature of this period, and was not a topic reserved only for hostile replies to enemies of Christianity. Of the many English Protestant works relating to the positive importance of natural religion to Christianity, I here list just a few examples indicative of the tenor and variety of support or acceptance of natural religion alongside revealed religion.

Anon., *A Collection of Hymns for public worship: on the general principles of natural and revealed religion* (Salisbury, 1778).

Anon., *Protestant System; containing discourses on the principal doctrines of Natural and Revealed Religion* (London, 1758).

Anon. (Harleian Miscellany), *Natural and Revealed Religion explaining each other, etc.* (1744).

Blackwell, T. (Principal of the Marischal College), *Schema sacrum, or, a Sacred scheme of natural and revealed religion, etc.* (Edinburgh, 1710).

Bourn, S., *The Christian Catechism. Wherein the principal truths of natural religion, and the truth and divine authority of the Christian religion, are asserted and proved, etc.* (Birmingham, 1744).

Burnett, G. (Vicar of Coggeshall), *A Defence of Natural and Revealed Religion: being an abridgment of the sermons preached at the lecture founded by the Honble. Robert Boyle, Esq.* [and others] (London, 1737); another edition by S. Letsome and J. Nicholl (eds) in 1739.

Burnett, T. (Rector of West Kington, Wilts.), *The Demonstration of True Religion, in a Chain of consequences from certain and undeniable*

Appendix

principles; wherein the necessity and certainty of natural and reveal'd religion, with the nature and reason of both, are proved and explain'd: and in particular, the authority of the Christian revelation is establish'd ... in sixteen sermons (London, 1726).

Cheyne, G., *Philosophical Principles of Religion: natural and revealed: in two parts* (London, 1715).

Clarke, S. (Rector of St James's), *A Discourse concerning the Unchangeable Obligations of Natural Religion, and the Truth and Certainty of the Christian Revelation. Being eight sermons preach'd ... in the year 1705* (London, 1706).

Emes, T., *The Atheist turn'd Deist, and the Deist turn'd Christian, or, the union and reasonableness of the natural, and the true Christian religion* (London, 1698).

Foster, J. (Doctor of Divinity), *A Vindication of some Truths of Natural and Revealed Religion ... To which is added, A Dialogue between a Calvinist, a Socinian, an Arminian, a Baxterian, and a Deist, etc.* (London, 1746).

Heathcote, R., *The Use of Reason asserted in Matters of Religion, or, Natural Religion the Foundation of Revealed, in answer to a sermon preached before the University of Oxford* (London, 1756).

Hunt, J., *The sources of corrupting both natural and revealed religion exemplified in the Romish Doctrine of Penance and Pilgrimages. A Sermon [on Mark vi. 12] preached ... Feb. 27, 1734–5* (London, 1735).

Johnston, G., Rev., *The Eternal Obligation of Natural Religion, etc.* (1732).

Nye, S., *A Discourse concerning Natural and Revealed Religion, evidencing the truth and certainty of both, etc.* (London, 1696).

Pelletreau (Minister of the French church of St Patrick), *An abridgement of sacred history, from the creation of the world to the establishment of Christianity. Together with a catechetical explanation of the principles of natural and revealed religion* (Dublin, 1760).

P. L. T., *A Preservative against Atheism and Infidelity; proving the fundamental principles of natural religion, and the necessity and certainty of reveal'd religion* (London, 1706).

Shaw, F., *A Summary of the Bible: or, the Principal heads of natural, and revealed religion* (London, 1730).

Squire, S. (Bishop of St David's), *Indifference for Religion inexcusable; or a serious, impartial and practical review of the certainty, importance, and harmony of religion both natural and revealed* (London, 1758).

Sykes, A., *The principles and connexion of natural and revealed religion distinctly considered* (London, 1740).

Thomas, J., *Christianity the perfection of all Religion, natural and revealed* (London, 1728).

Appendix

Tuntstall, J. (Vicar of Rochdale), *Academica; Part the first, containing several discourses on the certainty, distinction, and connection of Natural and Revealed Religion* (London, 1759).

Wilkins, J. (Bishop of Chester), *Of the Principles and Duties of Natural Religion: two books. By ... John, late Lord Bishop of Chester. To which is added, a Sermon preached at his funerals, by William Lloyd, etc.* (London, 1678).

Selected bibliography

Seventeenth- and eighteenth-century works

Ainsworth, H., *An Arrow against Idolatry. Taken out of the Quiver of the Lord of Hosts* (1611).

Anon., *Il dominio spirituale e temporale del papa o siano ricerche sul vicario di Gesù Cristo e il principe di Roma* (London, but Italy, 1783).

Anon., *Istoria del pontificate romane e sue relazioni con le potenze della Cristianità* (Geneva, 1785).

Becchetti, F. A., *Della Istoria ecclesiastica dell'eminentissimo Cardinale Giuseppe Orsi* (13 vols, Rome, 1770–81).

Becchetti, F. A., *Istoria degli ultimi quattro secoli della Chiesa* (10 vols, Rome, 1788–96).

Blount, C., *The First Two Books of Philostratus, concerning the life of Apollonius Tyaneus* (London, 1680).

Borgia, S., Cardinal, *Difesa del dominio temporale della Sede Apostolica nelle Due Sicilie. In risposta alle scritture publicate in contrario* (Rome, 1791).

Capecelatro, G., *Discorso istorico-politico dell'origine del progresso e della decadenza del potere de'chierici su le signorie temporali* (Filadelfia, but Naples, 1788).

Convocation of Canterbury, *A Representation of the present state of Religion, with regard to the ... growth of infidelity, Heresy, and Profaneness* (London, 1711).

Cosimo, A., *La Chiesa e la repubblica dentro i loro limiti* (sine loco, but Florence, 1768).

D. E., *The Prodigious Appearance of Deism* (London, 1710).

Dennis, J., *Priestcraft distinguished from Christianity* (London, 1715).

Dennis, J., *The Danger of Priestcraft to Religion and Government, with some Politick Reasons for Toleration* (London, 1702).

Fontanini, G., *Difesa seconda del dominio temporale della Sede Apostolica sopra la Città di Comacchio* (Rome, 1711).

225

Selected bibliography

Fontanini, G., *Il Dominio temporale della Sede Apostolica sopra la Città di Comacchio. Si aggiunge la Difesa del medesimo dominio ... in risposta alle tre ultime scritture pubblicate in contrario* [i.e. Muratori's writings], (Rome, 1709).

Giannone, P., *Istoria civile del Regno di Napoli* (Naples, 1770; 1st edn 1723).

Gregory, G., *A History of the Christian Church from the Earliest Periods to the Present Time* (London, 1790).

Halyburton, T., *Natural Religion insufficient; and Reveal'd necessary to man's happiness* (Edinburgh, 1714).

Howard, R., *The History of Religion. As it has been manag'd by Priestcraft* (London, 1709).

Le Paige, L. A. (1712–1802), *Lettres historiques sur les fonctions essentielles du Parlement; sur les droits des pairs, et sur les loix fondamentales du royaume* (Amsterdam, 1754).

Locke, J., *A Letter Concerning Toleration* (London, 1689).

Marchetti, G. (Archbishop of Ancyra), *L'Autorità suprema del romano pontefice* (Rome, 1789).

Muratori, L. A., *Annali d'Italia* (12 vols, Milan, 1744–49).

Muratori, L. A., *Della Fallibilità dei pontefici nel dominio temporale*, ed. C. Foucard (posthumous, Modena, 1872).

Muratori, L. A., *Della Pubblica felicità oggetto de'buoni principi* (Lucca, but Venice, 1749).

Muratori, L. A., *Dissertazioni sopra le antichità italiane* (3 vols, Milan, 1751).

Muratori, L. A., *Osservazioni sopra una lettera intitolata Il dominio temporale della Sede Apostolica sopra la Città di Comacchio* (sine loco, but Modena, 1708).

Muratori, L. A., *Ragioni della Serenissima Casa d'Este sopra Ferrara confermate e difese in risposta al dominio temporale della Sede Apostolica* (Modena, 1714).

Muratori, L. A., 'Rudimenti di Filosofia morale per il Principe Ereditario di Modena', in *Scritti inediti di L. A. Muratori* (Modena, 1872).

Muzzarelli, A., *Della Civile giurisdizione ed influenza sul governo temporale esercitata dai Romani Pontifici* (posthumous, Rome, 1816).

Muzzarelli, A., *Dominio temporale del papa* (1789).

Orsi, G. A., Cardinal, *Della infallibilità e dell'autorità del Romano Pontefice sopra i concilj ecumenici* (2 vols, Roma, 1741–42).

Orsi, G. A., Cardinal, *Della Istoria ecclesiastica* (21 vols, Roma, 1746–62).

Orsi, G. A., Cardinal and Bishop Becchetti, *Storia ecclesiastica* (52 vols, Rome, 1835–62).

Piane, P. N. delle, *Storia cronologica de' papi da S. Pietro all'odierno*

Selected bibliography

pontificato di Pio VII cavata da' migliori autori con annotazioni (Genoa, 1802; 1st edn 1798).

Pistoia, Diocese of, *Atti e decreti del concilio diocesano di Pistoja dell' anno 1786* (2nd edn, Florence, 1788).

Prideaux, Humphrey, *A Letter to the Deists* (London, 1696).

Prideaux, Humphrey, *Life of Mahomet* (1697).

Priestley, J., *A General History of the Christian Church from the Fall of the Western Empire to the Present Time* (4 vols, Northumberland, USA, 1802–3).

Priestley, J., *The Doctrine of Philosophical Necessity Illustrated* (London, 1777).

Ricci, S. de (ed.), *Raccolta di opuscoli interessanti la religione* (Pistoia, 1783).

Rivarola, P. *Storia del papato di Filippo de Mornay, Cittadino Francese. Tradotta, ed accresciuta con alcune Note al testo, e col supplemento al fine* (4 vols, Pavia, 1796–1802).

Roman Curial publications:

Sommario de'documenti che giustificano il supremo ... dominio della Santa Sede sopra de'feudi ecclesiastici in Piemonte (Rome, 1727).

Dimostrazione della sovranità temporale della Sede Apostolica ne i feudi ecclesiastici del Piemonte (Rome?, 1725?).

Ragioni della Sede Apostolica sopra il ducato di Parma e Piacenza esposte a sovrani e principi cattolicic d'Europa (Rome, 1741).

Stephens, W., *An Account of the Growth of Deism in England* (London, 1696).

Tindal, M., *Christianity as Old as the Creation* (London, 1730).

Tindal, M., *The Rights of the Christian Church* (4th edn, London, 1708).

Toland, J., *A Critical History of the Celtic Religion and Learning* (London, 1740).

Toland, J., *An Apology for Mr Toland* (1697).

Toland, J., *Christianity not Mysterious* (London, 1696).

Toland, J., *Letters to Serena* (London, 1704).

Toland, J., *Tetradymus. Containing ... Clidophorus; or, of the Exoteric and Esoteric Philosophy ... of the Antients* (London, 1720).

Toland, J., *Vindicius liberius: or M. Toland's Defence of Himself, against the Lower House of Convocation* (London, 1702).

Trenchard, J., *The Natural History of Superstition* (London, 1709).

Turbolo, T., *Libera ed independente sovranità de' Rè delle due Sicilie ... vindicata contro l'assurde ... pretensioni della Corte di Roma* (1788).

Voltaire, F. M. A. de, *Le Siècle de Louis* (London, 1752).

Zaccaria, F., *Anti-Febbronio ... o sia apologia polemico-storico del primato del papa* (Pesaro, 1767; 2nd edn 1770).

Zaccaria, F., *Antifebronius vindicatus seu suprema romani pontificis*

Selected bibliography

potestas adversus Justinum Febronium (Francofurti and Lipsiae, 1772).

Zaccaria, F. A., *Denunza solenne fatta alla Chiesa e ai Principi Cattolici di un anticristiano* (Assisi, 1783).

Zaccaria, F. A., *Il Discorso di un anonimo, della monarchia universale de'Papi, Napoli 1789* (Rome, 1791).

Secondary sources

Adams, C., Censer, J. and Graham, L. (eds), *Visions and Revisions of Eighteenth-Century France* (Pennsylvania: Pennsylvania State University Press, 1997).

Adams, G., *The Huguenots and French Opinion 1685–1787. The Enlightenment Debate on Toleration* (Ontario: Wilfred Laurier University Press, 1991).

Ashcraft, R., 'Latitudinarianism and Toleration: Historical Myth versus Political History', in *Philosophy, Science, and Religion in England 1640–1700* (Cambridge: Cambridge University Press, 1992).

Aston, N., 'Anglican Responses to Anticlericalism: Nonconformity and the Ideological Origins of Radical Disaffection', in N. Aston and M. Cragoe (eds), *Anticlericalism in Britain c. 1500–1914* (Stroud: Sutton Publishing, 2001).

Aston, N. and Cragoe, M. (eds), *Anticlericalism in Britain c. 1500–1914* (Stroud: Sutton Publishing, 2001).

Baker, K., 'Politics and Public Opinion under the Old Regime: Some Reflections', in J. Censer and J. Popkin (eds), *Press and Politics in Pre-Revolutionary France* (Berkeley: University of California Press, 1987).

Baker. K., 'Public Opinion as Political Invention', in *Inventing the French Revolution. Essays on French Political Culture in the Eighteenth Century* (Cambridge: Cambridge University Press, 1990).

Baker, K. (ed.), *The French Revolution and the Creation of Modern Political Culture. Vol. 1: Political Culture of the Old Regime* (Oxford: Pergamon, 1987).

Barny, R., *Prélude idéologique à la Révolution Française: Le Rousseauisme avant 1789* (Paris: Belles Lettres, 1985).

Barnett, S. J., *Idol Temples and Crafty Priests. The Origins of Enlightenment Anticlericalism* (London: Macmillan, 1999).

Barnett, S. J. (ed.), *Isaac Newton's Observations on the Prophecies of Daniel and the Apocalypse of St John* (Lampeter: Edwin Mellen Press, 1999).

Barnett, S. J., 'Where was your Church before Luther? Claims for the Antiquity of Protestantism Examined', *Church History: Studies in Christianity and Culture*, 68: 1 (1999).

Selected bibliography

Bell, D. A., *Lawyers and Citizens. The Making of a Political Elite in Old Regime France* (New York and Oxford: Oxford University Press, 1994).

Bennett, G., 'Conflict in the Church', in G. Holmes (ed.), *Britain after the Glorious Revoloution 1689–1714* (London: Macmillan, 1982; 1st edn 1969).

Berman, D., *A History of Atheism in Britain* (New York: Croom Helm, 1988).

Betts, C. J., *Early Deism in France. From the So-Called 'Déistes' of Lyon (1564) to Voltaire's 'Lettres philosophiques' (1734)* (The Hague, Boston and Lancaster: Martinus Nijhoff, 1984).

Bien, D., *The Calas Affair* (Princeton, N.J.: Princeton University Press, 1960).

Black, J. and Porter, R. (eds), *Dictionary of Eighteenth-Century History* (London: Penguin, 1996).

Bolton, C. A., *Church Reform in Eighteenth-Century Italy (The Synod of Pistoia, 1786)* (The Hague: Martinus Nijhoff, 1969).

Bossy, J., *Christianity in the West 1400–1700* (Oxford and New York: Oxford University Press, 1985).

Boucher, D., *Texts in Context. Revisionist Methods for Studying the History of Ideas* (Lancaster and Dodrecht: Nijhoff, 1985).

Bradley, J., 'The Religious Origins of Radical Politics in England, Scotland and Ireland, 1662–1800', in J. Bradley and D. Van Kley (eds), *Religion and Politics in Enlightenment Europe* (Notre Dame, Ind.: Notre Dame University Press, 2001).

Bradley, J. and Van Kley, D. (eds), *Religion and Politics in Enlightenment Europe* (Notre Dame, Ind.: Notre Dame University Press, 2001).

Briggs, R., *Early Modern France 1560–1715* (Oxford and New York: Oxford University Press, 1998; 1st edn 1977).

Byrne, J., *Glory, Jest and Riddle. Religious Thought in the Enlightenment* (London: SCM Press, 1996).

Campbell, P. R., *Power and Politics in Old Régime France, 1720–1745* (London: Routledge, 1996).

Caristia, C., *Riflessi politici del giansenismo italiano* (Naples: Morano Editore, 1965).

Carpanetto, D. and Ricuperati, G., *Italy in the Age of Reason 1685–1789* (Harlow: Longman, 1987).

Cassirer, E., *The Philosophy of the Enlightenment* (Boston: Beacon Press, 1962; 1st edn in German 1932).

Censer, J., *The French Press in the Age of Enlightenment* (London: Routledge, 1994).

Censer, J. and Popkin, J. (eds), *Press and Politics in Pre-Revolutionary France* (Berkeley: University of California Press, 1987).

Selected bibliography

Chadwick, O., 'The Italian Enlightenment', in R. Porter and M. Teich (eds), *The Enlightenment in National Context* (Cambridge: Cambridge University Press, 1981).

Champion, J., 'Europe's Enlightenment and National Historiographies: Rethinking Religion and Revolution (1649–1789)', *European Review of History*, 0 (1993).

Champion, J., *The Pillars of Priestcraft Shaken* (Cambridge: Cambridge University Press, 1992).

Champion, J., '"To Govern is to Make Subjects Believe": Anticlericalism, Politics and Power, *c.* 1680–1717', in *Anticlericalism in Britain c. 1500–1914* (Stroud: Sutton Publishing, 2000).

Chartier, R., *The Cultural Origins of the French Revolution* (Durham, N.C.: Duke University Press, 1991).

Clark, J. C. D., *English Society 1688–1832. Ideology, Social Structure and Political Practice during the Ancien Régime* (Cambridge: Cambridge University Press, 1985).

Codignola, E., *Illuministi, giansenisti, e giacobini nell'Italia del settecento* (Florence: La Nuova Italia, 1947).

Collinson, P., *The Birthpangs of Protestant England. Religions and Cultural Change in the Sixteenth and Seventeenth Centuries* (Basingstoke: Macmillan, 1998).

Cottret, M., *Jansénismes et Lumières. Pour un autre XVIII siècle* (Paris: Albin Michel, 1998)

Coward, D. A., 'The Fortunes of a Newspaper: The *Nouvelles Ecclésiastiques*, 1728–180', *British Journal for Eighteenth-Century Studies*, 4 (1981).

Cragg, G. R., *Reason and Authority in the Eighteenth Century* (Cambridge: Cambridge University Press, 1964).

Cragg, G. R., *The Church and the Age of Reason 1648–1789* (London: Penguin, 1962).

Daily, D., *Enlightenment Deism. The Foremost Threat to Christianity* (Pennsylvania: Dorrance, 1999).

Darnton, R., *The Literary Underground of the Old Regime* (Cambridge, Mass. and London: Harvard University Press, 1982).

Davidson, N., 'Toleration in Enlightenment Italy', in O. Grell and R. Porter (eds), *Toleration in Enlightenment Europe* (Cambridge: Cambridge University Press, 2000).

Diaz, F., *Per Una storia illuministica* (Naples: Garzanti, 1973).

Diaz, F. and Saitta, A., *La questione del'giacobinismo italiano* (Rome: Istituto storico italiano, 1988).

Doyle, W., *Jansenism. Catholic Resistance to Authority from the Reformation to the French Revolution* (London: Macmillan, 2000).

Dykstal, T., *The Luxury of Skepticism. Politics, Philosophy and Dialogue*

Selected bibliography

in the English Public Sphere 1660–1740 (Charlottesville: University Press of Virginia, 2001).

Echeverria, D., *The Maupeou Revolution. A Study in the History of Libertarianism. France, 1770–1774* (Baton Rouge: Louisiana State University Press, 1985).

Evans, R. R., *Pantheisticon. The Career of John Toland* (New York: P. Lang, 1991).

Fara, P., '"Master of Practical Magnetics": The Construction of an Eighteenth-Century Natural Philosopher', *Enlightenment and Dissent*, 15 (1995).

Felice, R. de, *Il Triennio giacobino in Italia 1796–1799* (Rome: Bonacci, 1990).

Ferrone, V., *The Intellectual Roots of the Italian Enlightenment. Newtonian Science, Religion and Politics in the Early Eighteenth Century* (New York: Humanities Press, 1995; 1st edn 1982).

Fitzpatrick, M., 'Heretical Religion and Radical Political Ideas in Late Eighteenth-Century England', in E. Hellmuth (ed.), *The Transformation of Political Culture. England and Germany in the Late Eighteenth Century* (Oxford: German Historical Institute, 1990).

Fitzpatrick, M., 'Toleration and the Enlightenment Movement', in O. Grell and R. Porter (eds), *Toleration in Enlightenment Europe* (Cambridge: Cambridge University Press, 2000).

Fitzpatrick, M., 'Toleration and Truth', *Enlightenment and Dissent*, 1 (1982).

Funkenstein, A., *Scientific Imagination from the Middle Ages to the Seventeenth Century* (Princeton, N.J.: Princeton University Press, 1986).

Garrioch, D., *The Formation of the Parisian Bourgeoisie 1690–1830* (Cambridge and London: Harvard University Press, 1996).

Gay, P., *The Enlightenment. An Interpretation. Vol. 1: The Rise of Modern Paganism* (London: Norton, 1995; 1st edn 1966).

Gay, P., *The Enlightenment. An Interpretation. Vol. 2: The Science of Freedom* (London: Wildwood House, 1973; 1st edn 1969).

Gibbs, G. C., 'The Reception of the Huguenots in England', in O. P. Grell, J. I. Israel and N. Tyacke (eds), *From Persecution to Toleration. The Glorious Revolution and Religion in England* (Oxford: Clarendon, 1991).

Golden, R. M. (ed.), *The Huguenot Connection. The Edict of Nantes, its Revocation, and Early Migration to South Carolina* (Dordrecht, Boston and Lancaster: Kluwer Academic Publishers, 1988).

Goldie. M., 'Priestcraft and the Birth of Whiggism', in N. Phillipson and Q. Skinner (eds), *Political Discourse in Early Modern Britain* (Cambridge: Cambridge University Press, 1993).

Selected bibliography

Goldie, M., 'The Theory of Religious Intolerance in Restoration England', in O. P. Grell, J. I. Israel and N. Tyacke (eds), *From Persecution to Toleration. The Glorious Revolution and Religion in England* (Oxford: Clarendon, 1991).

Grell, O. and Porter, R. (eds), *Toleration in Enlightenment Europe* (Cambridge: Cambridge University Press, 2000).

Grell, O. P., Israel, J. I., and Tyacke, N., *From Persecution to Toleration. The Glorious Revolution and Religion in England* (Oxford: Clarendon, 1991).

Guerlac, H., 'Some Historical Assumptions of the History of Science', in A. Crombie (ed.), *Scientific Change. Historical Studies in the Intellectual, Social and Technical Conditions for Scientific Discovery and Technical Invention from Antiquity to the Present* (London: Heinemann, 1963).

Gunnell, J., 'The Myth of the Tradition', in P. King (ed.), *The History of Ideas* (New Jersey: Croom Helm, 1983) (originally published in the *American Political Science Review*, 78: 1, 1978).

Haakonssen, K., 'Enlightened Dissent: An Introduction', in *Enlightenment and Religion. Rational Dissent in Eighteenth-Century Britain* (Cambridge: Cambridge University Press, 1996).

Haakonssen, K. (ed.), *Enlightenment and Religion. Rational Dissent in Eighteenth-Century Britain* (Cambridge: Cambridge University Press, 1996).

Habermas, J., *The Structural Transformation of the Public Sphere. An Enquiry into a Category of Bourgeois Society,* trans. Thomas Burger (Cambridge, Mass.: MIT Press, 1989; 1st edn in German 1962).

Hamon, L., *Du Jansénisme à la laïcité et les origines de la déchristianisation* (Paris: Editions de la Maison des Sciences de L'Homme, 1987).

Hankins, T., *Science and the Enlightenment* (Cambridge: Cambridge University Press, 1995).

Harrison, P., *'Religion' and the Religions in the English Enlightenment* (Avon: Cambridge University Press, 1990).

Haydon, C., *Anti-Catholicism in Eighteenth-Century England, c.1714–1780* (Manchester: Manchester University Press, 1993).

Henshall, N., *The Myth of Absolutism* (London: Longman, 1992).

Herrick, J. A., *The Radical Rhetoric of the English Deists. The Discourse of Skepticism, 1680–1750* (Columbia: University of South Carolina Press, 1997).

Holmes, G., *The Trial of Doctor Sacheverell* (London: Methuen, 1973).

Hunter, M., *Science and the Shape of Orthodoxy. Intellectual Change in Late Seventeenth-Century Britain* (Woodbridge: Boydell and Brewer, 1995).

Selected bibliography

Hunter, M., 'The Problem of Atheism in Early Modern England', *Transactions of the Royal Historical Society*, 35 (1985).

Isabella, M., 'Italy, 1760–1815', in H. Barker and S. Burrows (eds), *Press, Politics and the Public Sphere in Europe and North America, 1760–1820* (Cambridge: Cambridge University Press, 2002).

Israel, J., *Radical Enlightenment. Philosophy and the Making of Modernity 1650–1750* (Oxford: Oxford University Press, 2001).

Israel, J., 'Spinoza, Locke and the Enlightenment Battle for Toleration', in O. Grell and R. Porter (eds), *Toleration in Enlightenment Europe* (Cambridge: Cambridge University Press, 2000).

Jacob, M. (ed.), *The Enlightenment. A Brief History with Documents* (Boston, Mass.: St Martin's/Bedford, 2001).

Jacob, M., *The Radical Enlightenment. Pantheists, Freemasons and Republicans* (London: George Allen and Unwin, 1981).

Jemolo, A., *Il Giansenismo in Italia prima della rivoluzione* (Bari: Laterza, 1928).

Knights, M., *Politics and Opinion in Crisis, 1678–81* (Cambridge: Cambridge University Press, 1994).

Kors, A. C., *Atheism in France, 1650–1729. Vol. 1: The Orthodox Sources of Disbelief* (Princeton, N.J.: Princeton University Press, 1990).

Kors, A. C., '"A First Being, of Whom We Have No Proof": The Preamble of Atheism in Early-Modern France', in A. C. Kors and P. J. Korshin (eds), *Anticipations of the Enlightenment in England, France and Germany* (Philadelphia: Philadelphia University Press, 1987).

Kors, A. C. and Korshin, P. J. (eds), *Anticipations of the Enlightenment in England, France and Germany* (Philadelphia: Philadelphia University Press, 1987).

Labrousse, E., *Pierre Bayle* (Oxford and New York: Oxford University Press, 1983; 1st edn 1963).

Labrousse, E., 'Reading Pierre Bayle in Paris', in A. C. Kors and P. J. Korshin (eds), *Anticipations of the Enlightenment in England, France and Germany* (Philadelphia: Philadelphia University Press, 1987).

Laursen, J., 'Baylean Liberalism: Tolerance Requires Nontolerance', in J. Laursen and C. Nederman (eds), *Beyond the Persecuting Society* (Philadephia: University of Pennsylvania Press, 1998).

Lee, S. (ed.), *Dictionary of National Biography*, vol. 57 (1899).

Linton, M., 'Citizenship and Religious Toleration in France', in O. Grell and R. Porter (eds), *Toleration in Enlightenment Europe* (Cambridge: Cambridge University Press, 2000).

Linton, M., 'The Unvirtuous King? Clerical Rhetoric on the French Monarchy, 1760–1774', *History of European Ideas*, 25 (1999).

Maire, C.-L., *De la cause de Dieu à cause de la nation, Les Jansénistes au XVIIIe siècle* (Paris: Galliard, 1998).

Selected bibliography

McGuinness, P., 'Christianity not Mysterious and the Enlightenment', in P. McGuinness, A. Harrison and R. Kearney (eds), *John Toland's Christianity not Mysterious. Texts, Associated Works and Critical Essays* (Dublin: Lilliput Press, 1997).

McManners, J., *Church and Society in Eighteenth-Century France* (2 vols, Oxford: Clarendon Press, 1998).

Merrick J. W., *The Desachralization of the French Monarchy in the Eighteenth Century* (Baton Rouge: Louisiana State University Press, 1992).

Miller, S. J., *Portugal and Rome c. 1748–1830. An Aspect of the Catholic Enlightenment* (Rome: Università Gregoriana Editrice, 1978; also published in *Miscellanea Historiae Pontificiae*, vol. 44, Rome, 1978).

Miller, S. J., 'The Limits of Political Jansenism in Tuscany: Scipione de'Ricci to Peter Leopold, 1780–1791', *Catholic Historical Review*, 80: 4 (1994).

Milton, A., *Catholic and Reformed. The Roman and Protestant Churches in English Protestant Thought* (Cambridge: Cambridge University Press, 1995).

Mornet, D., *Les Origines intellectuelles de la Révolution Française 1715–1787* (6th edn, Paris: Armand Colin, 1967; 1st edn 1933).

Mossner, E., *Bishop Butler and the Age of Reason* (Bristol: Thoemmes Books, 1990; 1st edn 1936).

Munck, T., *The Enlightenment. A Comparative Social History 1721–1794* (London: Arnold, 2000).

Nicholls, D., *God and Government in an Age of Reason* (London and New York: Routledge, 1995).

Oakeshott, M., *On History and Other Essays* (2nd edn, Oxford: Blackwell, 1985).

O'Brien, C. H., 'Jansenists on Civil Toleration in Mid-18th-Century France', *Theologischen Zeitschrift*, 37 (1981).

Outram, D., *The Enlightenment* (Cambridge: Cambridge University Press, 1995).

Pailin, D., 'British Views on Religion and Religions in the Age of William and Mary', *Method and Theory in the Study of Religion*, 6: 4 (1994).

Pailin, D., 'Herbert of Cherbury. A Much Neglected and Misunderstood Thinker', in P. Creighton and E. Axel (eds), *God, Values and Empiricism. Issues in Philosophical Theology* (Macon, Ga.: Mercer University Press, 1989).

Pailin, D., 'The Confused and Confusing Story of Natural Religion', *Religion*, 24 (1994).

Pocock, J. G. A., 'Post-Puritan England and the Problem of the Enlightenment', in P. Zagorin (ed.), *Culture and Politics from Puritanism to the Enlightenment* (Berkeley: University of California Press, 1980).

Pocock, J. G. A., *The Ancient Constitution and the Feudal Law. A Study of*

Selected bibliography

English Historical Thought in the Seventeenth Century (Cambridge: Cambridge University Press, 1957).

Popkin, R. H., 'The Deist Challenge', in O. P. Grell, J. I. Israel and N. Tyacke (eds), *From Persecution to Toleration. The Glorious Revolution and Religion in England* (Oxford: Clarendon, 1991).

Popkin, R. H., *The History of Scepticism from Erasmus to Spinoza* (Berkeley: University of California Press, 1979; 1st edn 1960).

Popkin, R. H. and Vanderjagt, A., *Scepticism and Irreligion in the Seventeenth and Eighteenth Centuries* (Leiden and New York: E. J. Brill, 1993).

Porter, R., *Enlightenment Britain and the Creation of the Modern World* (London: Penguin, 2000).

Porter, R., *The Enlightenment* (Basingstoke: Macmillan, 1990).

Prandi, A., 'La Storia ecclesiastica di P. Giuseppe Orsi e la sua Genesi', *Rivista di storia della Chiesa in Italia*, 34 (1980).

Price, J. V. (ed.), *The History of British Deism* (8 vols, London: Routledge, 1995).

Redwood, J., *Reason, Ridicule and Religion. The Age of Enlightenment in England 1660–1750* (London: Thames and Hudson, 1976).

Rex, W., *Essays on Pierre Bayle and Religious Controversy* (The Hague: Martinus Nijhoff, 1965).

Riley, P., *The General Will Before Rousseau. The Transformation of the Divine into the Civic* (Princeton, N.J.: Princeton University Press, 1986).

Rivers, I., *Reason, Grace and Sentiment. Vol. 2: Shaftesbury to Hume* (Cambridge: Cambridge University Press, 2000).

Roche, D., *France in the Enlightenment* (Cambridge, Mass.: Harvard University Press 1998; 1st edn 1993).

Rodolico, N., *Gli amici e i tempi di Scipione dei Ricci: saggio sul giansenismo Italiano* (Florence, 1920).

Rudé, G., *Europe in the Eighteenth Century. Aristocracy and the Bourgeois Challenge* (London: Weidenfeld and Nicolson, 1972).

Sandberg, K., *At the Crossroads of Faith and Reason. An Essay on Pierre Bayle* (Tucson: University of Arizona Press, 1966).

Schaffer, S., 'The Political Theology of Seventeenth-Century Natural Science', *Ideas and Production*, 1 (1983).

Scott, J., 'England's Troubles: Exhuming the Popish Plot', in T. Harris, P. Seaward and M. Goldie (eds), *Politics of Religion in Restoration England* (Oxford: Blackwell, 1990).

Sella, D., *Italy in the Seventeenth Century* (London: Longman, 1997).

Shapin, S. and Schaffer, S., *Leviathon and the Air-Pump. Hobbes, Boyle, and the Experimental Life* (Princeton, N.J.: Princeton University

Press, 1985), especially chs 7–8.

Shennan, J., *The Parlement of Paris* (Stroud: Sutton Press. 1998).

Siebert, F. S., *Freedom of the Press in England 1476–1776* (Urbana: University of Illinois Press, 1952).

Skinner, Q., 'Meaning and Understanding in the History of Ideas', *History and Theory*, 8 (1969).

Soriga, R., *L'Idea nazionale italiana dal sec. XVIII alla unificazione* (Modena: Collezione storico del Risorgimento Italiano, vol. 28, 1941).

Stone, B., *The Genesis of the French Revolution. A Global-Historical Interpretation* (Cambridge: Cambridge University Press, 1994).

Sullivan, R., *John Toland and the Deist Controversy* (Cambridge, Mass.: Harvard University Press, 1982).

Swann, J., *Politics and the Parlement of Paris under Louis XV, 1754–1774* (Cambridge: Cambridge University Press, 1995).

Sykes, N., *Edmund Gibson, Bishop of London 1669–1748. A Study in Politics and Religion in the Eighteenth Century* (London: Oxford University Press, 1926).

Thomson, O., *Mass Persuasion in History* (Edinburgh: Paul Harris, 1977).

Tyacke, N., *Aspects of English Protestantism c.1530–1700* (Manchester and New York: Manchester University Press, 2001).

Van Horn Melton, J., *The Rise of the Public in Enlightenment Europe* (Cambridge: Cambridge University Press, 2001).

Van Kley, D., 'Pierre Nicole, Jansenism, and the Morality of Enlightened Self-Interest', in A. C. Kors and P. J. Korshin (eds), *Anticipations of the Enlightenment in England, France and Germany* (Philadelphia: Philadelphia University Press, 1987).

Van Kley, D., *The Damiens Affair and the Unraveling of the Ancien Régime* (Princeton, N.J.: Princeton University Press, 1984).

Van Kley, D., *The Jansenists and the Expulsion of the Jesuits from France 1757–1765* (London: Yale University Press, 1975).

Van Kley, D., *The Religious Origins of the French Revolution. From Calvin to the Civil Constitution, 1560–1791* (New Haven and London: Yale University Press, 1996).

Venturi, F., *Italy and the Enlightenment* (London: Longman, 1972).

Venturi, F., *Settecento Riformatore. Vol. 2: La Chiesa e la Repubblica dento i loro limiti* (Turin: Einaudi, 1976).

Verri, P., 'Memoria cronologica dei cambiamenti pubblici dello stato di Milano 1750–1791', in *Lettere inediti di Pietro e Alessandro Verri*, ed. C. Casati (Milan, 1879).

Wade, I., *The Intellectual Origins of the French Enlightenment* (Princeton, N.J.: Princeton University Press, 1971).

Wade, I., *The Structure and Form of the French Enlightenment. Vol. 1:*

Selected bibliography

Esprit Philosophique (Princeton, N.J.: Princeton University Press, 1977).

Walsh, J. and Taylor, S., 'The Church and Anglicanism in the "Long" Eighteenth Century', in C. Haydon, J. Walsh and S. Taylor (eds), *The Church of England c.1689–c.1833* (Cambridge: Cambridge University Press, 1993).

Ward, A., Prothero, G. and Leathers, S. (eds), *Cambridge Modern History. VI: The Eighteenth Century* (Cambridge: Cambridge University Press, 1934; 1st edn 1909).

Ward, W., *Christianity under the Ancien Régime 1648–1789* (Cambridge: Cambridge University Press, 1999).

Whaley, J., 'Religious Toleration in the Holy Roman Empire', in O. Grell and R. Porter (eds), *Toleration in Enlightenment Europe* (Cambridge: Cambridge University Press, 2000).

Woolf, S., *History of Italy 1700–1860* (London: Routledge, 1991; 1st edn 1979).

Wootton, D., 'The Republican Tradition: From Commonwealth to Common Sense', in *Republicanism, Liberty, and Commercial Society, 1649–1776* (Stanford, Calif.: Stanford University Press, 1994).

Young, B., *Religion and Enlightenment in Eighteenth-Century England. Theological Debate from Locke to Burke* (Oxford: Clarendon Press, 1998).

Zaret, D., *Origins of Democratic Culture. Printing, Petitions and the Public Sphere in Early Modern England* (Princeton, N.J.: Princeton University Press, 2000).

Zovatto, P., *Introduzione al giansenismo Italiano* (Trieste: University of Trieste, 1970).

Index

Please note that 'n.' after a page reference indicates the number of a note on that page.

Index

Lightning Source UK Ltd.
Milton Keynes UK
UKOW06f0235140616

276263UK00001B/66/P